Persecution of the Liberal Party by the Díaz Regime.
By Alberto Beltrán.

THE DESERT REVOLUTION

Baja California,

1911

The
Desert
Revolution

BAJA CALIFORNIA, 1911

Lowell L. Blaisdell

The University of Wisconsin Press · Madison, 1962

Published by
The University of Wisconsin Press
430 Sterling Court, Madison 6, Wisconsin

Printed in the United States of America by
George Banta Company, Inc.
Menasha, Wisconsin

Library of Congress Catalog Card Number 62-9258

ACKNOWLEDGMENTS

The writer would like to make the following acknowledgments. The first is to his wife, Dr. Doris A. Blaisdell, who helped, hour after weary hour, not only in typing, proofreading, and offering suggestions, but also enormously in making style revisions, offering fresh ideas, gathering materials from many of the periodical sources, obtaining interviews, and making the index. Dr. Francisco Dueñas Montes of Mexicali, Baja California, Mexico, provided great assistance. A lifelong student of the Flores Magón revolution, he helped in first extending the author's interest in the subject, enabling him to obtain a number of rare sources, and offering many excellent suggestions. Also very helpful were Dr. Stanley R. Ross of the University of Nebraska, with suggestions and the loan of books; Dr. Charles C. Cumberland of Michigan State University; Dr. John P. Harrison, now of the Rockefeller Foundation, New York City, and formerly of the National Archives, who directed the author to materials concerning the Liberal movement; Dr. Edwin Carpenter of the Huntington Library, San Marino, California, and formerly at the Library of the University of California at Los Angees; and Dr. Daniel Cosío Villegas of *Historia Mexicana*, who offered encouragement and assisted the writer in gaining access to the Mexican Archives of National Defense. To Mrs. Woodrow Wilson the author is grateful for permission to examine the Woodrow Wilson Papers in the Library of Congress.

The author also wishes to thank the Cartographic Laboratory at the University of Wisconsin for preparing the maps; the Taller de Gráfica Popular of Mexico City for permission to reproduce Alberto Beltrán's "Persecution of the Liberal Party" from *450 Anos de lucha;* the Union Title Insurance Company of San Diego, California, for the use of photographs from its Historical Collection; the History Department at Texas Technological College, Lubbock, Texas, for providing the funds for typing; Mrs. Bob Parker for concentrated work in doing the typing; Dr. Merton Dillon of Texas Technological College for reading several of the chapters; and Mrs. Sara McLarty and Mrs. Edna Gott of Lubbock, Texas, for aiding with the proofreading.

LOWELL L. BLAISDELL

Lubbock, Texas
May, 1961

CONTENTS

ILLUSTRATIONS

INTRODUCTION

Several threads run through this study. The greater part deals with a somewhat neglected facet of the Mexican Revolution of 1910–1911: while the major drive of the revolutionists, led by Francisco I. Madero, was sweeping the long-entrenched Díaz dictatorship out of office, the anarchist Ricardo Flores Magón, striving for the same objective and a more fundamental transformation of society as well, spearheaded a movement of his own that won temporary success only in Baja California. During its short life the Flores Magón revolution displayed a number of characteristics that aroused wonder and even suspicion. In the nineteenth century Baja California had been an area sometimes coveted by the United States. Adventurous Americans, notably the notorious William Walker, had attempted filibusters to take the territory away from Mexico. In 1911, the most conspicuous of the peculiarities of the Flores Magón movement seemed to be an obvious filibustering tendency. The main object of this study is to examine the revolution in Baja California, observe how an aura of filibustering became associated with it, and demonstrate that, for the most part, the impression of separatism is erroneous.

Several subsidiary issues derive from the first theme. Some

attention has been focused on the diplomatic relations between the United States and Mexico over the events in Baja
California, the impact of the American neutrality laws on
Flores Magón and his Liberal Party, the nature of the plans
of this anarchist group, momentarily on the verge of implementation of its ideas, the hard-fought little battles of the
frontier revolution, and the colorful personages and factions
that this movement churned up.

A second major thread running through this narrative is
the prominent part played by Ricardo Flores Magón on the
Mexican political scene. His career extended over a vitally
important quarter-century of Mexico's history. His remains
rest in the Rotunda of Illustrious Men in Mexico City. Not
only in 1911, but especially before that date and to some degree afterwards, he exerted a considerable influence on
Mexico's politics. Most Mexicans think of him as one of the
great Precursors of their modern revolution: the man who
prepared the way for the great men of the 1910 to 1920
period. The beginning of this account is an assessment of his
work as a Precursor. When the revolution of 1910 to 1911
broke out, Flores Magón and the Liberals sought, largely
without success, to spread their ideas throughout Mexico.
Heretofore comparatively little attention has been paid the
Magonistas for their part in this endeavor. Therefore, an effort has been made to describe the instances in which they
made a distinctive impression, the reasons for their lack of
general success, the intense dislike that Flores Magón felt for
Madero, and his analysis of the inadequacy of his rival's goals
and movement. A lifelong revolutionist, Flores Magón after
1911 continued, unavailingly, to pursue the same objectives.
The last part of this study is a summary and analysis of his
activities on the revolutionary scene during the remaining
decade of his life.

Thirdly, this writing endeavors to show that Flores Magón
was more than a revolutionist confined to the Mexican
stage. He viewed himself in a broader context. He had many
contacts with American radicals and those from other countries. He conceived of his movement as a phase of a world-

wide revolution: Anarchism had no country. So radical were his ideas that, despite his signal lack of practical success, he bears comparison with such nineteenth-century revolutionists as Bakunin and Marx, or, in this century, Lenin and, more recently, Castro. Since in our time professional revolutionaries have aroused keen interest, Flores Magón deserves more study than he has received. This anarchist of half a century ago stirred up in the United States and elsewhere, for a brief period, intense feelings, as well as a number of problems analogous to those raised more tellingly, because more successfully, by Castro today.

In recent years, a number of American scholars have made contributions to the study of the Mexican Revolution and the crucial years from 1910 to 1920. Most of the present study falls within the scope of Mexican history. As such, it should be regarded as an addition or supplement to Charles C. Cumberland's *Mexican Revolution: Genesis under Madero* (1952), Howard F. Cline's *The United States and Mexico* (1953), Stanley R. Ross's *Francisco I. Madero: Apostle of Mexican Democracy* (1955), and Robert Quirk's *The Mexican Revolution, 1914–1915: The Convention of Aguascalientes* (1960).

THE DESERT REVOLUTION

Baja California,

1911

CHAPTER I

A Revolutionist

On Thursday, August 4, 1910, a small reception took place at the Los Angeles railway station. Some three hundred laborers cheered as three passengers alighted. The arrivals, Ricardo Flores Magón, Antonio Villarreal, and Librado Rivera, were Mexican exiles just released from an American prison.[1] The welcoming ceremony constituted the prologue to an exciting political drama, whose central character, Ricardo Flores Magón, was the leader of the trio. Less than a year later he was to be back in jail, having precipitated a revolution that kindled furious strife in Mexican and American California. A half-century later, the revolutionary episode still arouses controversy in Mexico.

Flores Magón's Baja California revolt occurred simultaneously with a larger movement that swept Mexico: Francisco Madero's democratic upheaval that toppled Porfirio Díaz, dictator-president for more than thirty years. Insofar as the revolution in Baja California was directed against Díaz, it was part of the larger upheaval, though it was under different leadership and confined by circumstances to an isolated locale. However, Flores Magón and Madero aimed at radically different ultimate objectives, and the difference in aim distinctly colored their respective revolutionary means. Finally, peculiar local conditions prevailing in Baja California endowed the Magonista movement with a flavor entirely its own.

Ricardo Flores Magón was born in the ruggedly picturesque mountains of Oaxaca in southern Mexico in the year 1873. By striking coincidence his birthday fell on the anniversary of Mexican independence, September 16. His father was an Indian, and his mother a Mestizo. The senior Flores Magón, who was a veteran of the Mexican War and of the struggle against Maximilian, as well as an ardent supporter of Juárez, acquainted his son with the problems arising out of Mexico's victimization by foreign nations. At the same time, the boy had a chance for close-range observation of communal living as practiced by the Indians of Oaxaca. In order that they might obtain the best education available, Ricardo and his older and younger brothers, Jesús and Enrique, attended school in Mexico City.[2] At an early age, Ricardo, in a Rousseau-like reaction, was struck by the glaring contrast between the unspoiled natural beauty of Oaxaca and the artificialities of the complex human society in the capital. These early experiences helped to develop in him a sensitive and combative spirit.[3]

Subsequently, as a law student in the scholarly and relatively free atmosphere of the capital's university, young Flores Magón first embraced the twin passions of his life: political agitation and journalism. In 1892, Porfirio Díaz's second successive reëlection, following a constitutional amendment permitting indefinite consecutive reëlections, set off the first demonstration of major importance against the latter-day Díaz. Students and workers led a small-scale manifestation through the streets of Mexico City, and Flores Magón played a prominent part as an idealistic student agitator. A year later, he assisted in the publication of a short-lived periodical, *El Demócrata*. For his role in the student action, he went to jail briefly, for the first of many times. For helping to publish the journal, he had to go into hiding for the first of many times.[4]

Following the events of 1892 and 1893, Flores Magón's life

for several years remains virtually a closed book. Apparently, he had to abandon political activity because, after the death of his father, he and his brothers, while continuing their legal training, had to support their mother, who was in very poor health and circumstances.

When, in August, 1900, an engineer, Camilo Arriaga, launched an oppositionist political force, the Liberal Party, Flores Magón could remain silent no longer and joined the new party. Almost simultaneously, he founded the weekly journal *La Regeneración,* whose title was intended to suggest the dawn of a new era in Mexico. Between 1901 and 1903 the young rebel, in addition to his work on *La Regeneración,* edited or contributed to periodicals such as *La República Mexicana, El Hijo del Ahuizote,* and *Excélsior.* In all of these, he attacked Porfirismo vigorously. More and more, his name, or his pseudonyms, became conspicuously associated with opposition to the government.[5]

Persecution and imprisonment were the wages of dissent. In 1903, after several earlier assaults and arrests, Flores Magón was confined in a dank, rat- and spider-infested dungeon in Mexico City's Belén prison. Upon attaining freedom, early in 1904 the editor fled to the United States, hopeful that the chagrin of exile would be mitigated by free access to the public print with which to attack Díaz. In the months that followed, he was joined by a number of young friends and disciples, among them his brother, Enrique, Antonio Villarreal, Librado Rivera, the brothers Juan and Manuel Sarabia, Lázaro Gutiérrez de Lara, Praxedis Guerrero, and Antonio de Pío Araujo.[6]

In the United States, though repeatedly forced to move from place to place, the Liberals nevertheless reorganized. Their experience in Mexico had indicated that opposition within the framework of the law was not only dangerous but also futile against a dictator who disregarded the legal restrictions on his power. The Liberals determined to resort to a more direct course of action. Consequently, in September, 1905, command was established in an "Organizing Junta of the Liberal Party," with Ricardo Flores Magón as president, and several of his associates in the other executive posts.[7] Preparations were undertaken for a two-pronged attack: first, to try to undermine the old president through the power of the written word, and, second, to forge the Liberal Party into the engine of his destruction.

In their first objective, Flores Magón and his companions succeeded well. With many adherents living close to the border, it became possible to build up a courier service to distribute copies of *La Regeneración* throughout the country. Among the working classes, to whom the weekly was especially intended to appeal, the undercurrent of opposition to Díaz was slowly growing.[8]

Aside from the wide distribution of the journal, the propaganda campaign took a significant step forward when, on July 1, 1906, the Junta issued an over-all political and economic program, whose chief author was Juan Sarabia, aided by Ricardo Flores Magón. In the form of a manifesto it was circulated in Mexico by the same manner as *La Regeneración*, and with like effects. The statement advocated a number of reforms: a one-term presidency, assurance of all basic civil liberties, the breaking of the Catholic church's strangle hold, vast improvement in educational facilities, Mexican citizenship as a prerequisite for property ownership, land for the landless and land reform for the impoverished peasantry and Indians at the expense of rich landlords who did not make full use of their holdings, confiscation of the illegally acquired riches of Díaz and his leading supporters, abolition of child labor, and a guaranteed minimum wage, as well as other improvements in the laborers' lot. The proclamation also referred critically to capitalism as a system of exploitation, and, without direct appeal to violence, urged the Mexican people to rid themselves of their oppressors. Though the statement contained suggestions of socialism, there was no advocacy of the *principle* of land expropriation or socialization of property. It amounted to a program of progressive social reform; its contents were aptly summarized in the new party slogan, "Reform, Liberty, and Justice."[9]

This Liberal manifesto, the first inclusive anti-Díaz declaration, is an important document in the prehistory of the Mexican Revolution. Madero's program, drawn up later, fell considerably short of the 1906 statement in comprehensiveness and depth of understanding of Mexico's social and economic problems. When the Constitution of 1917 was drawn up, for instance, Article 123, concerning minimum-wage rights for workers, was derived from, among other places, the Liberal pronouncement.[10]

The Junta's second aim, to overthrow the government by armed resistance, proved very difficult of attainment, despite Herculean efforts. Beginning in 1904, party units were slowly built up in Mexico. By 1908, there were some forty to sixty small groups scattered throughout the country. At specified times, upon instruction from the Junta, they were to attempt armed revolt. In 1906 and 1908, a series of uprisings took place, by plan or by accident. As raids across the American border promised the participants at least some hope of a haven in the event of failure, it was not surprising that the risings at the frontier hamlets of Jiménez, Coahuila, in 1906 and Las Vacas, Coahuila, and Las Palomas, Chihuahua, in 1908, originated on American soil. Other brief revolts erupted at Acayucán, Vera Cruz, in 1906 and Viesca, Coahuila, in 1908. A major attempt at Juárez in 1906 misfired because of government detection of plans, and the Viesca revolt broke out without specific instructions from the Junta.[11]

For several reasons, these raids and uprisings accomplished little. Lack of funds and equipment, the efficacy of government spying, and the tenuous nature of the lines of communication between armed groups and their leadership, separated from each other by an international boundary, made even limited success difficult. Moreover, the Liberal Junta's organizational ability stood in inverse proportion to its ideological fervor. Thus, as in similar previous instances in European countries, these raids and uprisings amounted to mere pinpricks that helped alert the populace to the dire need for change but did not seriously undermine the government.

The attacks had been planned to secure the second objective of the dual program, but, in effect, tactical gains were scored in reaching the first objective, anti-Díaz propaganda.

The Junta also fomented strikes as a means to weaken the government's power. Thanks partly to the influence of *La Regeneración,* these efforts were more damaging to the government's prestige than were the raids and uprisings. In 1906, the American-owned copper mines of Cananea, Sonora, were struck. The Mexican regime used repressive measures that brought death and injury to numerous workers; and its burden of guilt was increased by the appearance of a group of superfluous American strikebreakers who crossed the line from Arizona. Again, a series of work stoppages in textile centers in eastern Mexico in 1906 and 1907 culminated in the Río Blanco, Vera Cruz, strike, which was ruthlessly crushed at the cost of increased unpopularity for the dictatorship.[12]

The efforts of the Junta against Díaz would probably have met with more success, notwithstanding their signal organizational ineptitude, had they not been relentlessly exposed to a systematic campaign of harassment instigated by the Mexican dictator, which prevented them from executing plans of any degree of complexity. In San Antonio, in 1904, an assassin made an attempt on Flores Magón' s life, but failed. In St. Louis, later in the same year, the United States Post Office revoked *La Regeneración's* second-class mailing privilege, and some of the Junta were temporarily jailed on a libel charge for publishing the statement that a certain Mexican state government official was a "miserable eunuch." In 1906 and 1907, after a flight to Toronto and Montreal, Flores Magón hid in San Francisco, Sacramento, and then Los Angeles. As the result of the uprisings of 1906, the Mexican government posted a twenty-thousand-dollar reward for his capture. American officials co-operated in the search. In 1907, as a minimal precaution, *La Regeneración* was dropped in favor of a short-lived substitute, *Revolución.* While walking in the streets of Los Angeles in August, 1907, Flores Magón, Villarreal, and Rivera were arrested, and subsequently roughed up, by the local police, during the course of an attempt at abduction engineered by spies in the employ of the Mexican government. Earlier in the same year, Manuel Sarabia had been temporarily shanghaied from Douglas, Arizona, to Hermosillo, Sonora, and a year earlier there had been an attempt to rush Rivera by train from St. Louis to Mexico.[13] After being detained in jail for twenty months on minor counts in 1907 and 1908, Flores Magón and his colleagues were charged with violation of the neutrality laws. Although the Liberals were obviously guilty, the evidence on which the Justice Department obtained its conviction was shaky.[14] For Flores Magón, a prison sentence of eighteen months followed. His discharge in August, 1910, marked the completion of exactly three uninterrupted years in prison.[15] By that date, he had been held at one time or another in St. Louis, Los Angeles, and Yuma and Florence, Arizona.

The severity of the Liberals' harassment was primarily caused by the American officials' failure to resist the efforts of the Mexican government at close surveillance over prominent exiles. At various times, the Post Office Department, the Immigration Bureau of the Department of Commerce and Labor, the Department of Justice, the Department of State, and various state and territorial authorities seem to have adopted an overly latitudinarian view of the scope of their functions in an attempt to accede to Mexico's desires. While the Magonistas' border raids gradually provided the Justice Department with some evidence for the neutrality laws prosecution of 1908, that agency gratuitously aided the dictator by permitting private detectives in his pay to hound the leaders, allowing arbitrary arrests, and finding ways of putting the burden of legal proof on the Liberal Party. Eventually the glaring contrast between the United States' libertarian traditions and the treatment meted out to the Mexican proscripts came to the attention of conscientious congressmen. While the Liberal leaders were serving their sentence, their American friends were able to recount the events of the previous five years at hearings before the House of Representatives Rules Committee, June 10 to 14, 1910.[16]

By the time Ricardo Flores Magón was first convicted of violation of the neutrality laws, he had earned considerable fame in his own country. For the decade during which the path of opposition was most dangerous, he had been in the forefront of the struggle against the aging dictator. While the middle- and upper-class opponents of Díaz, reluctant to use force, shied away from the Liberals, the Junta president and his associates became identified with the unspoken desires of the working classes, the largest element in the population. Had this stratum been less deficient in political articulation and sophistication, the Liberals' influence would have loomed even larger. Furthermore, in the absence, prior to 1910, of any generally-agreed-upon program and any recognized champion of opposition to Díaz, Flores Magón, by means of his pioneer work and his eloquence, had become the ideological chief— as distinguished from guerrilla leader—of the still largely silent struggle against the dictatorship. It is on the basis of these achievements that he is remembered as one of the greatest predecessors, if not the premier Precursor, of the Mexican Revolution.[17]

Ricardo Flores Magón's character and political philosophy took final shape during the eventful years following 1900. Although among conventional people some distinction between personality and political beliefs is common, in Flores Magón's case the distinction was entirely absent: his creed was his character, and his character his creed. After the turn of the century, unswerving radicalism and rebellion best describe both the man and his ideas.

The precise nature of the forces that determined Flores Magón's extreme radicalism can only be surmised, partly because material relating to his life prior to 1900 is scarce and also because repeated imprisonment and the threat thereof made him exceedingly reticent about his background. It seems safe to conclude that the long years of confinement, harassment, and exile embittered him against existing society and caused him to seek its overthrow. His sterility may or may not have been of psychological significance.[18] Aside from the influence of Indian communal life, as early as 1903, it is known, he gained access, through Camilo Arriaga, who had an extensive library, to the writings of such European revolutionaries as Kropotkin, Bakunin, Malatesta, and Marx.[19] Their works he devoured.

Perplexity, admiration, or hatred were the usual responses to this man. Because he was so difficult to know or to comprehend, he puzzled many. In prison, neither jailers nor fellow inmates could figure him out. At liberty, caution commanded a furtive, semi-anonymous existence, always close to a hiding place. Only his intimate disciples thoroughly understood him. His high-minded idealism, savage determination, and unswerving pursuit of his goals aroused great enthusiasm among some of his associates. On the other hand, most strangers, and even, at times, his intimates, found him overbearing, unscrupulous, and obstinately uncompromising.

By 1906, Flores Magón had irrevocably committed himself to anarchism. Increasingly, this interest of Flores Magón's caused friction within the Junta. He had desired, for example, to make the manifesto of 1906 more radical, but Juan Sarabia and Arriaga dissuaded him from so doing. As it was, he wrote those portions that were most critical of the status quo and appealed most eloquently for a change. For several reasons it was not widely known at the time that Flores Magón was an anarchist. He concealed his true beliefs from the public and from some of the Junta; those members of the Junta who knew found it politic to keep the information to themselves. And as people became absorbed in the practical side of the struggle against Díaz, Flores Magón's political ideas tended to pass relatively unnoticed.[20]

In their philosophy and political aims the majority of anarchists were the heirs of Michael Bakunin, the famous Russian revolutionary[21] who was the sometime friend and enemy of Karl Marx. Marx also influenced the anarchists, although only insofar as they agreed with his critical analysis of capitalism and his prediction of its doom. Marx and Bakunin had disagreed violently over the large role that Marx implicitly assigned to the state, as represented by the leaders of a successful revolution, in laying the foundation of a new order. Bakunin's descendants shared their master's loathing for anything suggestive of control over people and, hence, government.

The anarchists, then, regarded contemporary economic and political institutions as the embodiment of an all-pervasive bourgeois hypocrisy. Working people should seek to achieve class unity in order to topple capitalism by force. In a new society, land and property would be held and worked communally. Organized government would be dispensed with so that true human freedom in the most complete sense of the word might be realized. Such were the tenets of Flores Magón's political faith. To the standard contention that a program such as this was hopelessly utopian, he argued in reply that history showed that mankind advances not by degrees but by leaps, and the time had come to make such a leap.[22]

By its very nature, anarchism is difficult, if not impossible, of realization. In the era when it enjoyed a certain popularity, its followers found the ancient dilemma of ends-versus-means a peculiarly troublesome one. Should they seek their goal of complete statelessness and unstained freedom through methods equally stainless? This procedure, in a world in which corruption offered short-term advantages, would leave them perpetually at the toe mark, their aim not only unrealized, but not even approached. Or should they try to work toward their idealistic objective by adopting the dubious devices that they roundly condemned in the despised existing society? To achieve their goal thus would be impossible, since a pure end, logically, was unattainable by impure means. Of course, in practice, the anarchists, like other humans, evaded the dilemma, either by using high-minded methods in hopes that, somehow, humanity would follow their example, or by resorting to questionable means in hopes that, after all, temporary success would advance them on the road to their ultimate goal.

Flores Magón preferred the second of these methods. In putting it to use, his characteristic extremism carried him to extraordinary lengths as he was seeking to advance his revolutionary cause in Mexico. In 1908, for instance, in an atmosphere of impending revolutionary action, he wrote from jail:

All is reduced to a mere question of tactics. If from the start we had called ourselves anarchists, only a few would have listened to us. Without calling ourselves anarchists, we have inflamed minds . . . against the possessing class. . . . No liberal party in the world has the anti-capitalist tendencies of we [sic] who are about to begin a revolution in Mexico, and we would not have been able to achieve this had we merely called ourselves socialists instead of anarchists. Thus everything is a question of tactics.

We must give lands to the people during the course of the revolution; thus they will not be deceived. We must also give them possession of the factories, mines, etc. In order not to have everybody against us, we should continue the same tactics that we have already used with so much success: we will continue to call ourselves liberals during the course of the revolution, and will in reality continue propagating anarchy and executing anarchistic acts. We must take away from the landed gentry and give to the people.

. . . .

There will be some landowners, observing what is happening to others, who will not reject negotiations, and thus there will be no immediate pretext to attack them or to take away their property. In this case, which doubtless will happen frequently, the laborers can be encouraged to demand "impossibilities," with the result that the bosses will be obliged to shut down. . . . Thus . . . the workmen will have consummated expropriation, and the anarchist character of the Junta will remain veiled. . . . Only the anarchists will know that we are anarchists, and we will advise them not to call themselves such in order not to frighten imbeciles . . . who are accustomed to hear the anarchists spoken of unfavorably. Rather than imbeciles, they are merely ignorant. We should not be unjust.

. . . .

The workmen on the ranches will be given a portion of the land on which they have been working, reserving what is not thus utilized for the remaining poor. . . . People will see the excellence of work done in common compared with the work done individually and thus will desire to work the land communally, while the Junta then will not face the hateful job of giving a piece of land to everyone who asks for it.

At the beginning we will not molest foreign landowners, waiting until people have material to defend and arms to make
themselves respected. When they have something to defend . . . ,
all will be willing to take up the rifle.

It is very possible that our revolution will break the European
equilibrium, and that people there will decide to do what we
have done. If we carry out what I propose, the European powers
may fall upon us, but . . . I am sure that our brothers on the
other side of the ocean will not let us perish.[23]

Like other advocates of violent anarchism, Flores Magón
was blind to the obvious fact that methods such as these were
incompatible with his elevated ideals, and were absolutely
certain to frustrate the attainment of those ideals. The tactics
he urged were somewhat similar to those of the notorious
Nechaev, Bakunin's onetime disciple, whose celebrated
Revolutionary Cathechism advocated deceit, murder, and
betrayal, as long as the revolutionary cause was served.[24] Subsequently the resemblance will become more striking still.[25]

While Flores Magón and his friends lingered in American
prisons as a result of their conviction of violating the neutrality laws, important events were unrolling in Mexico. In 1908,
Díaz, in an interview with an American reporter, James
Creelman, announced that he would relinquish the presidency
at the expiration of his current term in 1910, and declared
himself prepared to countenance the formation of an officially sanctioned "loyal" opposition. Though the old dictator
promptly reversed himself and decided to stand for office
after all, an opposition did make a cautious appearance.
One oppositional element was led by General Bernardo
Reyes. It failed to attract significant support because it spoke
for hardly anyone but a few wealthy, disgruntled families
who happened to be among the "outs," and because Reyes
himself had been for a long time a close associate of Díaz.
The second element was led by Francisco I. Madero, who,
though a member of a wealthy and prominent Coahuila
landowning family, had a much wider appeal because he
stood out as a vigorous spokesman for democracy as a principle. Madero began to attract attention in 1908 by writing

The Presidential Succession in 1910, a *livre de circonstance*. Then, in 1910, as head of the Anti-Reëlectionist Party, he ran for president against the incumbent. When this election turned out as all previous Díaz elections had, the challenger was forced to flee to the United States. From there, while his own country seethed with unrest, he issued the Plan of San Luis Potosí: Mexico must have political democracy; revolution had become the only way to achieve it; and Madero himself would assume the title of "Provisional President," pending the satisfactory outcome of the struggle about to unfold.[26]

When the Liberal trio, after three years in jail on one charge or another, were released in August, 1910, the situation in Mexico was more fluid than it had been for many years. After their arrival in Los Angeles, Flores Magón, Villarreal, and Rivera, as well as other Liberals who soon joined them, threw themselves into renewed political activity with feverish energy. Preparations were made for the re-establishment of *La Regeneración* and the reactivation of armed attacks on Mexico. Remembering with indignation the events of 1907 to 1908, some elements of Los Angeles labor, including Socialists, syndicalists, and Mexicans, were prompted to give the Junta their moral, and sometimes material, support. An energetic subscription drive undertaken by the moderate Socialists was largely responsible for a four-hundred-dollar contribution which put the Junta on its financial feet.[27] Headquarters were opened in a second-floor office at 519½ East Fourth Street, other appeals for funds were broadcast, and on September 3, 1910, the first issue of *La Regeneración*, now in the third phase of its history, appeared. As a revolutionary writer and propagandist, Flores Magón had the genius of a Marat or a Thomas Paine. His first flaming editorial indicates that his skill had not eroded during his long years of incarceration:

We come to tell the Mexican people that the day of their liberation is near. Before our eyes is the splendid dawn of a new day; the noise of the liberating tempest . . . echoes in our ears; that rumbling is the revolutionary spirit; the entire Nation is a volcano on the verge of spouting forth the fire within its entrails.

. . . The apostle is going from ear to ear announcing when and where the cataclysm will begin, and the rifles await impatiently the moment when they will be removed from their hiding places to shine brilliantly under the sun of the combatants. Mexicans, to war![28]

Flores Magón's anarchist orientation began to emerge in the weekly's subsequent issues.[29] On November 19, literally on the eve of the Mexican Revolution, the editor used the agrarian-anarchist rallying cry, "Land and Liberty," the exact slogan of the Russian *narodniki* of the 1860's and 1870's, which he, and later Emiliano Zapata, made famous in Mexico. Regarding active fighting, the *Regeneración* of November 26 assured its readers that the "Liberal Junta are working eagerly in the preparation of a formidable movement against despotism and capitalist exploitation," and on December 3 the paper repeated that Liberal forces would soon take the field.

However, events in Mexico hampered considerably the Junta's preparation for direct revolutionary action. Even with the opportunity presented by the fluid situation, the Liberals found that the public response to their appeals was not encouraging. Madero, through his energetic, courageous, and futile candidacy in the recent "election," and his determination to return and lead a revolution on Mexican soil, continued to attract the public's fancy. Flores Magón, who had been fighting Díaz for years before Madero began to stand out as a well-known public figure, now found himself overshadowed. In another day, back in 1905 and 1906, Madero, now a rival, had even contributed his personal and financial support to the Liberal movement, then in its San Antonio–St. Louis period, though he had soon thereafter dropped the Liberals as too radical.[30] Then, during the long years when Flores Magón was consigned to prison, reaping no more than oblivion for his efforts, Madero captured the popular imagination. To the older revolutionary, this was galling indeed.

The two revolutionists were as different as Lamartine and Blanqui. Whereas Flores Magón was fanatical, suspicious, ruthless toward his enemies, and occasionally embittered,

Madero was gentle, moderate, patently sincere, and forgiving. As a thinker Flores Magón was by far superior: he unfailingly penetrated to the heart of a problem, exposing lies, cant, and hypocrisy. Madero's ideas, on the other hand, though democratic, were pedestrian, his perceptions rather limited, and his thought processes sometimes muddied by the spiritism to which he was attracted. Flores Magón was purely an intellectual. The hardships of persecution and imprisonment had not the slightest effect on the integrity of his ideas, but they did make him exceedingly cautious of his person, frequently inhibiting him in his movement. By contrast, the diminutive Madero surprised the world by emerging as a man of action endowed with great physical courage, as even his murderer, the heartless Victoriano Huerta, attested. Flores Magón had the greater mind; Madero was the greater man.

The Anti-Reëlectionist movement began action on November 20, 1910. For several reasons it gained momentum only very slowly, despite Madero's popularity. On the inception date, the leader failed in an attempt to establish himself on Mexican soil in Coahuila. There was an insufficiency of funds and organization. Though the great majority of local leaders eventually accepted Madero's guidance, albeit reluctantly and intermittently, the problem of primacy was especially troublesome as long as he was forced to remain in the United States. As a result, for three months the Maderistas barely sustained themselves, making an impression only in Chihuahua, where guerrilla forces did fairly well.[31]

The Liberals drew little advantage from the Anti-Reëlectionists' difficulties. They had even greater troubles of their own. For one thing, they suffered from the congenital affliction of small-scale radical movements: factionalism. An almost unrelieved wrangle had developed over the issue of anarchism. The Junta members who were anarchists, chiefly Ricardo Flores Magón, his brother Enrique, and Librado Rivera, had for some time been concealing both immediate plans and ultimate aims from the others, who were led by Villarreal.[32] As the hour of decisive action arrived, mutual confidence and understanding were undermined. Since the

Junta were then anxiously seeking assistance from as many liberal, reformist, or radical groups as possible, in Mexico, the United States, or anywhere else, the consequences of the dispute extended beyond the family circle. Moderate American Socialists, for example, at times contributed various kinds of important aid, on the ingenuous assumption that the Mexican Liberals, as their name seemed to imply, stood for a brand of reformism only slightly different from their own. The trouble was that the Socialists dealt usually with Gutiérrez de Lara, who was only an associate, not a full-fledged, member of the Liberal Party, and with Villarreal, both of whom held views which differed from the Junta president's and resembled the American Socialists' own. The Madero boom aggravated the internecine struggle, because the non-anarchist faction among the Liberals, along with various American well-wishers, were favorable to the possibility of a Magonista-Maderista union of forces.

In December the conflict came into public view. *La Regeneración* usually ran an English page for the benefit of interested and helpful Anglo-Americans. Throughout the fall its editor was Alfred G. Sanftleben, an American Socialist of German origin.[33] An article in which he remarked that the Liberals and Maderistas were working well together was corrected the following week by Flores Magón, who declared that the Liberals would not fuse with middle-class reactionaries. A week thereafter Sanftleben resigned, announcing that he could not "understand the economics and policies, and the utterances versus the tactics of the Liberal Party."[34] More acute symptoms of dissidence were to appear later.

Internal strife notwithstanding, the Liberals swung into action. In November and December, the tactic with regard to the Maderistas was decided upon, forms and instructions concerning military procedures were sent out, advance agents were dispatched to key areas, recruiting efforts were accelerated, and a few units took up field positions.

In regard to the Maderistas, the Magonistas at long last drifted into a *modus operandi* in lieu of a policy: it ranged from grudging military co-operation to outright enmity. A circular of November 16 informed Liberals that the Madero Revolution was imminent, advised them to take up arms simultaneously, and warned them not to make common cause, but to establish contact only for the purpose of winning back various comrades who had mistakenly joined the moderates.[35] Similarly, in *La Regeneración,* the puzzled reader was likely to find the Maderistas praised in one column and disparaged in the next.[36]

The administrative preparations for revolution consisted of an enrollment blank to record recruits and a list of directions entitled "General Instructions to the Revolutionaries." The former was stamped by the Junta and signed by Ricardo Flores Magón and Villarreal. It declared the recruit was "enrolled in the junta's registry," urged him to sustain the "emancipating principles of the Program of July 1, 1906," and concluded with the somewhat anachronistic slogan, "Reform, Liberty, and Justice." The "General Instructions" contained a number of interesting directions: military groups were enjoined to proclaim the Liberal program of *1906;* obtain funds from government offices or private individuals, after issuance of revolutionary vouchers; send funds to the Junta; leave neutral foreigners unmolested; be especially careful not to perpetrate harmful, arbitrary, or criminal acts under the guise of revolution; and treat the Maderistas correctly but coolly. One provision promised the soldiers a salary of a dollar a day and the officers a higher wage than Díaz paid his troops. Another unusual clause recommended election of officers whenever feasible.[37] Anarchists often advanced this proposal to democratize a necessarily undemocratic institution, but since ancient times the experiment has enjoyed a degree of success only within guerrilla forces.

As the Maderistas took up arms, the Magonistas did likewise. Toward the close of the year, Flores Magón wrote one of his agents in the field that, as soon as organizational problems had been solved, a starting date would be set for the Liberal uprising throughout Mexico. Pending this, the agent should utilize the Maderista movement to carry on guerrilla action.[38]

As it happened, an official starting date was never announced, for the Liberals' organizational troubles proved to be far greater than the Anti-Reëlectionists'. The imprisonment of the leaders had inevitably had a disintegrating effect on the local units. Nor did it help to have the Junta groping for exact military information at its headquarters almost two thousand miles northwest of the center of Mexico. Nevertheless, by late 1910 and early 1911, Liberals were fighting in four of the five states contiguous to the American border: Sonora, Chihuahua, Coahuila, and Tamaulipas; in three of the next tier of four states: Sinaloa, Durango, and San Luis Potosí; in central Mexico, in Jalisco, Tlaxcala, and Vera Cruz; and, in the south, in Tabasco and Yucatán.[39] In all cases, the units were small, as they had been in 1906 and 1908.

The outstanding performance of the early days took place in Chihuahua in December. Praxedis Guerrero, talented both as a libertarian writer and as a guerrilla fighter, left Junta headquarters in order to fight in the field.[40] Starting with thirty men, he captured a train on the western branch of the Mexican Central Railroad south of Juárez, and began to raid southward. After burning bridges and gathering recruits, he succeeded in taking the town of Casas Grandes. Then, at the village of Janos, on December 30, 1910, Guerrero was killed while fighting the Díaz Federals.[41] His death was a serious loss to the Liberals, who, as later events showed, were not well stocked with reliable leaders.

Meantime, the Junta's chief efforts were concentrated on opening a campaign in Baja California, an area to which some attention had been paid in the abortive plans of 1908.[42] This decision proved to be the most fateful ever taken by the Mexican Liberal Party: it determined the movement's subsequent part in the anti-Díaz struggle, and had an important effect on its over-all place in the Mexican revolutionary sweep of 1910 to 1920. Attention must therefore be accorded the development of both Californias prior to their role as stage and staging area.

CHAPTER II

The Two Californias

Alta and Baja California have had an interesting history. Discovery of Baja California was one of the lesser ventures of the great Hernán Cortés, who in 1539 dispatched an expedition that reached the mouth of the Colorado. Because the peninsula consisted primarily of desert wastes, rugged mountains, and interior wilderness, settlements were few until the twentieth century. During the Spanish colonial period, the English freebooters Drake and Cavendish conducted raids, various explorations were undertaken, and for a time pearl-fishing was a lucrative occupation. The chief settlements throughout the eighteenth and early nineteenth centuries were the Jesuit and Franciscan missions in the south, serving the needs of the Indian population. For more than a century following Mexican independence in the 1820's, the remoteness of the peninsula and the difficulty of access presented grave problems for the central government.

Alta California, on the other hand, after small-scale settlement from Mexico in the latter part of the eighteenth century, proved much more adaptable to rapid, large-scale settlement. After the Mexican War the United States annexed the area, whereupon the population swiftly rose, with the Gold Rush as an initial stimulus. Despite overland travel difficulties,

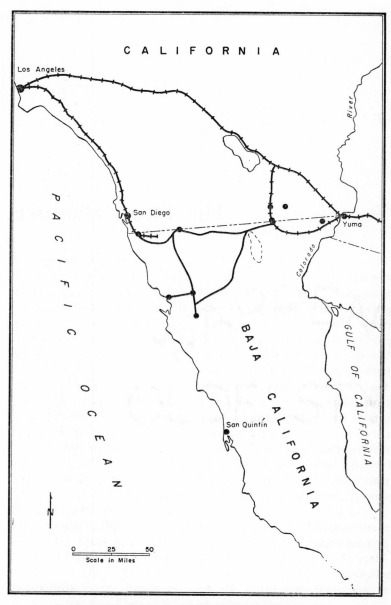

Southern Alta California, Northern Baja California, 1911

American California after 1848 was never isolated from trans-Mississippi America to any degree resembling the isolation of Mexican California from Guadalajara and population centers to the east and south.

Out of these geographical and demographic conditions there evolved an unhealthy, unbalanced relationship between the Californias, which, in turn, was representative of the disproportion between the United States and Mexico.

Though the partial military penetration of Lower California during the Mexican War might have enabled the United States to acquire it, the peninsula was not included in the Treaty of Guadalupe Hidalgo. A few years later, on second thought, the United States evinced somewhat keener interest during the negotiation of the Gadsden Treaty, but, in the end, recoiled from potential complications and contented herself with purchase of the southern parts of present-day New Mexico and Arizona.[1]

If the government vacillated as to the merits of further West Coast expansion, the appetite of various private parties remained unassuaged. A number of adventurers, known in American history as filibusters, undertook small military expeditions during the 1850's against unprotected areas to the south of the United States. One of their favorite targets was northwest Mexico.

Actually, these filibusters were merely following in the footsteps of earlier ambitious free-lancers. At the beginning of the century, a tradition of filibustering had grown up. Its origin antedates Mexico's independence from Spain. Aaron Burr, adventurer and crypto-renegade, conceived the first filibuster in his projected Southwest Empire, which was to have been carved out of newly acquired American territory and the northern part of Spanish Mexico. His stillborn scheme represented a greater danger to Mexico than it did to the young but rapidly growing northern republic. The Burr conspiracy served as a symbolic precedent for adventurers raiding Texas about 1820.[2]

The first suggestion of filibustering in California came at the beginning of the Mexican War when the John C. Frémont expedition engaged in some disingenuous maneuvers that helped to lead to revolt by American settlers and to annexation.[3] However, only between 1851 and 1857, the period before and after the Gadsden Treaty negotiations, did filibustering burst into full bloom. At that time, a group of adventurers, using as their base San Francisco, then swarming with disappointed gold-seekers, launched a series of attacks on Baja California, especially Sonora. They stamped an indelible impression upon the Mexican mind.[4]

Among the apostles of trouble were two Frenchmen, Charles de Pindray, who was possibly not consciously a filibuster, and the celebrated Raousset-Boulbon, who united a force of his own with that of Pindray after the latter's mysterious death in 1852, definitely making the combined force into a filibustering expedition. In 1854, Raousset-Boulbon led still another group into Sonora. The other leaders were Joseph Morehead, who landed briefly in southern Baja California in 1851, William Walker, famous also for his later Central American filibustering, whose initial exploit took the form of a descent upon the peninsula in 1853 and 1854, and H. A. Crabb, a Walker disciple, who led still another force into Sonora in 1857. The odds against the success of these ventures were demonstrated by the fate of their leaders: Pindray was assassinated or committed suicide, Raousset-Boulbon faced a firing squad, as did Crabb and almost his entire party, while Walker survived only to die in exactly the same fashion in Honduras in 1860.[5] Nevertheless, during the first Raousset-Boulbon incursion and the Walker raid, the adventurers' spectacular, albeit short-lived, victories seemed to augur the severance of the northwestern areas from Mexico. After 1857, except for a brief flurry of verbal filibustering at the close of the 1880's,[6] the evil seemed to have abated. The terrible punishment meted out to the Crabb party—one youth survived to tell the story[7]—was a forbidding lesson for would-be intruders.

Between 1906 and 1907, the Liberal Junta, in the course of its wanderings, settled for the first time in Alta California, an area that had undergone vast development following the earlier age of the Gold Rush and the Filibuster. As the Gold Rush had drawn people to the north, the second half of the nineteenth century saw a rapid population influx into the fertile coastal regions of the south. With the land boom of the 1880's, Los Angeles became a large, cosmopolitan city, and San Diego grew apace. The state as a whole turned into a major center of agricultural production, commerce, and export trade.

The nation's westward movement during the first decade of the twentieth century resulted in yet another spectacular population increase. This was especially true in the southern portion of California, where abundant fertile land, oil production, hydroelectric power, and sheer ballyhoo acted as magnets. In 1900 this region had had fewer than 350,000 inhabitants, in contrast to the more than 1,000,000 in the north; but in ten years' time the respective totals had changed to 815,000 and 1,500,000. San Diego was keeping in step, having reached almost 40,000 by 1911. The figures for the state's two largest cities were striking. San Francisco, recovering from the earthquake, had a population of 416,000 in 1910. Los Angeles was catching up swiftly, with a figure of 319,000, having more than trebled its population in ten years.[8]

The economic, political, and cultural life of southern California then, as later, centered about the City of the Angels. That the Junta should settle there is understandable. For a group forced to live in exile, no more stimulating locale could have been found. Even then, in the pre-Hollywood and pre-smog days, Los Angeles attracted attention. The city had an excellent climate. There was an active civic life. Amidst its hustle and bustle, every human type and every national and racial strain could be observed. Of interest to the Junta was the existence of a Mexican neighborhood in one section of the city. Approximately, the headquarters of the Liberals at 519½ East Fourth Street were in a dingy industrial area inhabited by semi-employed laborers and discontented drifters.[9]

So much growth and change engendered sharp conflict between capital and labor. In the process of developing the new land, the leaders of capitalism acquired enormous influence. Of especial concern here were three powerful interests that loomed large not only in American California but in Mexican California as well. These were the Southern Pacific Railway, the Spreckels family, refiners of C & H sugar, and General H. G. Otis, of the *Los Angeles Times.*

For years, the Southern Pacific, headed by E. H. Harriman, was the most potent vested interest in California. Its lobbyists consistently prevented the imposition of legislative impediments upon railway projects. By 1910, however, steadily unflattering publicity had made the road's Sacramento representatives slightly apologetic and a little less than omnipotent.[10] Nevertheless, the tentacles of the Southern Pacific still had a wide spread. One of its smaller arms reached into Lower California.

The influence of the Spreckels family had a similar range. In San Francisco the family had long been prominent. One of its members, John D. Spreckels, visited San Diego in the 1880's, found the youthful southern city charming and inviting, and, as a result, transferred his activities and the family patronage as well. He was instrumental in erecting the Coronado Beach Hotel and the city's street-railway and water-supply systems; he acquired an interest in two other hotels and new office buildings; and he promoted the beautification of Balboa Park. Only the *San Diego Sun,* owned by the liberal editor E. W. Scripps, prevented Spreckels from monopolizing the public print, for both the influential *Union* and the *Evening Tribune* belonged to him.[11] In addition to looking after his interests in San Diego, John D. Spreckels was instrumental in constructing a railroad, part of which ran to the south in Lower California. He was both benevolently paternalistic and very conservative.

Probably the most influential individual in the California Southland of the time was General Harrison Gray Otis, who, rich as he was, owed his great power less to his wealth than to his editorship of the widely read *Los Angeles Times.* Born in Ohio in 1837, he epitomized extreme conservatism and rugged individualism to the day of his death in 1917. In his politics, he was an ultraconservative Republican. A veteran of the Civil and Spanish-American Wars, he moved to California in the seventies and gained full control of the *Times* during the expansion of the eighties. Among his other properties was a valuable tract of land in Baja California, obtained just after the turn of the century. In Los Angeles, the *Times* led by far in circulation and influence among the city's four mass-distribution newspapers; and one of its quondam competitors, the *Herald,* was at times controlled by Otis.[12] Whereas in San Francisco labor and capital were fairly evenly matched, Otis, a foe of labor and an advocate and practitioner of the open shop, greatly enhanced the reputation that Los Angeles acquired as a hub and hotbed of reaction. In every direction, Otis exercised his influence to the utmost, hated with abandon, and pursued his goals courageously and relentlessly.

By the early years of the new century, after a long period of union-baiting had prevailed, labor in southern California began to organize against a backdrop of powerful capitalistic forces. In Los Angeles, in particular, a determined effort was made to break the city's open-shop tradition. After several setbacks, success seemed at last within grasp by 1910 and 1911, a period when the mounting need for construction workers and field hands spurred unionization. With the help of capable and enthusiastic organizers from San Francisco, the expanding American Federation of Labor had organized the workers in many Los Angeles trades by 1910. The growing labor movement attracted both native Anglo-Americans and members of minority groups. In the ranks were quite a few Mexicans; some of them had resided in California for several years, others had recently come from Baja California, Sonora, and regions farther south in Mexico.[13]

Shortly after Flores Magón, Villarreal, and Rivera had returned to Los Angeles, the city's labor-capital strife came to a shattering climax when, on October 1, 1910, the *Los Angeles Times* building was blown up, killing a number of people. The chief perpetrators were J. J. and J. B. McNamara and Ortie McManigal of the International Association of Bridge and Structural Iron Workers, AF of L. In the midst of their trial in December, 1911, the defense attorney, Clarence Darrow, had to reverse the plea to guilty. The *Times* bombing did enormous damage to labor's cause for years afterward, as Los Angeles reverted to the open-shop tradition, and General Otis was able to expound with even greater zest on the dangers of the labor movement.[14]

The blowing-up of the *Los Angeles Times* represented an outburst of extremism, partly induced by a long-standing denial of labor's rights. A similar reaction was the swift rise of the radical competitor to the AF of L, the Industrial Workers of the World, which first made a strong impression in California between 1910 and 1912. Though with their eleven locals in eight California cities, plus their at-large membership, they were in 1910 much smaller than the AF of L, they had a considerable impact. The "Wobblies'" main success lay in organizing migratory labor in mining, lumbering, and agriculture. The incendiary slogans in their weekly *Industrial Worker* and their unorthodox tactics created a furor. In particular, the Fresno and San Diego Free Speech rows of 1910 and 1912, which were marked by months of hectic haggling, riots, irresponsible boasting on the part of the Wobblies, and unconstitutional reprisals on the part of the city officials, focused attention on this branch of organized labor.[15] In their contacts with American workers, the Liberal Junta found the IWW, with their anarcho-syndicalist orientation, more attractive than the AF of L.

So much ferment, growth, and change could not fail to bring about a shift on California's political scene. All across the land the Progressive Era was under way. In the state, just as in the country as a whole, powerful interests met serious opposition from moderate reform. Progressive Republicans managed in 1910 to push aside the old state machine, and elected as governor Hiram Johnson, a man who, at the time, was widely believed to be a liberal. In that campaign, the Democrats also ran a liberal, Theodore A. Bell, who lost to Johnson by only 22,000 votes.[16] Still another interesting political development was the growth of a moderate Socialist party under the leadership of Job Harriman. Its main strength lay in Los Angeles, where there took place frequent collaboration between the heads of the party and some union leaders. It was some of these men who had helped the Liberal triumvirate make a fresh start after their return from imprisonment. The Socialists' growth reached its peak in 1911, when Harriman sought election as mayor of Los Angeles. His chances were good until the McNamara debacle caused a strong public reaction at the climax of the campaign.[17] After this, Socialism declined substantially in California.

The Junta's decision to concentrate on garnering a base in Baja California and starting the campaign at Mexicali, in the eastern part of the territory, was bound to have wide repercussions on the American side of the frontier, for the area in question was the Colorado River delta, a vast desert bisected by a boundary representing no more than an artificial political line. Since the territory on both sides of the frontier had been recently developed, with the impetus largely from the American side, the Liberals could not act without becoming embroiled in the pre-existing interrelationship.

Between 1900 and 1910 the southern Colorado delta was the stage on which California's statewide drama of expansion was re-enacted *en miniature*. In one decade the desert was made to provide habitation and gainful agricultural employment for ten thousand people.[18] This minor miracle was the direct result of the harnessing of the Colorado. Since the soil was extremely fertile, the only needs were an irrigation system and publicity to attract settlers. Both were promptly furnished by a striking combination of initiative, imagination, skulduggery, and perseverance in the face of discouraging obstacles.

The pioneers in developing the area were Dr. Oliver M. Wozencraft, a native of Texas and member of California's constitutional convention, George Chaffee, Charles R. Rockwood, Anthony Heber, and Dr. William T. Hefferman. Dr. Wozencraft first envisioned the region transformed by means of irrigation into a fertile and habitable place, but did not live to see this. The others, who were engineers and promoters, sometimes in collaboration, sometimes at odds, built, in

1900 and 1901, the main channel of an irrigation system, most of it on the Mexican side. Chaffee sometimes is credited with naming the first permanent settlement "Calexico" in honor of the adjoining jurisdictions.[19]

News of the canal project quickly aroused interest. People became curious, largely through exposure to the publicity of the Colorado Development Company, a shaky corporation established by Rockwood. The company named the desert Imperial Valley. People flocked in, recovered from the shock of their first dismal impression, acquired cheap land, mainly on the American side, and soon succeeded in making a substantial living off the irrigated soil, despite a series of crises. Before long, the frontier towns of Brawley, Imperial Valley, Holtville, and El Centro had sprung up. Through bisection of the region's first settlement, Mexicali emerged as a Mexican town hardly distinguishable from Calexico.

Settlers and rudimentary towns were followed by political organization and a few of the appurtenances of civilized existence. Because the legal services and police protection of San Diego County proved inadequate for a population center 125 miles from the county seat, the local inhabitants, with the eager approval of San Diego, gained the right to constitute Imperial County. After a time, banks were opened, water and light facilities provided, and newspapers founded. Important in this connection was one of the early settlers, W. F. Holt, a shrewd, independent businessman from Missouri, who financed indigent farmers, built most of the Valley's public utilities, and helped establish the first newspapers. Transportation was improved when the Southern Pacific built a branch south into the Valley from its Los Angeles–Yuma line; for a time, a Holt-built, rickety interurban trolley ran from Holtville to connect with the railroad at El Centro.[20]

For two years, from February, 1905, to February, 1907, the region was blighted by a major catastrophe. Several disastrous floods on the Colorado severely threatened the Valley's economic potential. With tons of water engulfing the sub–sea-level area, the drainage provided by the canal and the Colorado-control system proved to be insufficient. This was the origin of the Salton Sea. Among the victims of the swirling water was the semiliquid California Development Company. To prevent bankruptcy, it was absorbed for a time by the Southern Pacific. By means of an outlay of $6,000,000, for which it was later partly reimbursed by the federal government, the Southern Pacific managed to stay the flood and restore some degree of normalcy to the Valley. As receiver for the California Development Company, the Southern Pacific gradually disposed of most of the Rockwood corporation's tangible assets. A Valley project, the Imperial Irrigation District, was soon set up for the purpose of acquiring water and land rights from the railroad. Eventually this led to local control.[21]

By 1910, the Imperial-Mexicali Valley area was booming once more. Since there was fear of flood recurrence, public confidence was boosted by reports that the federal government intended to seek Mexico's permission to construct more substantial dikes south of the boundary.

As a group, the population had many of the virtues and defects that had characterized earlier American frontier communities. The settlers were aggressive, confident, and equalitarian. As contradictions abounded, conflicting interests grated upon one another. The democratic spirit was typically demonstrated in the constant attacks on General Otis, a Valley landholder, who symbolized absentee landlordism, entrenched corporate wealth, and an obsolescent social outlook.[22] Though the settlers opposed Otis' aggressiveness, they themselves had expansionist tendencies, as reflected in their eager interest in the purchase of the lower Colorado delta from Mexico.[23] A similar contradiction was revealed when a few members of the IWW drifted in and met with a cool reception,[24] although it might have been expected that the Wobblies' clamorous self-assertiveness would harmonize with the generally raucous tone of the Valley.

While Alta Califronia witnessed such spectacularly rapid growth, Baja California was developing with painful slowness. In contrast to American California's early promotion to statehood, Mexican California's inhospitable terrain and sparse population compelled the government to keep the region at territorial status indefinitely. Late in the nineteenth century, the Porfirio Díaz administration divided the region into Northern and Southern Territories. Throughout the 1800's the population in the southern half outnumbered that of the north. In 1890 about forty thousand persons inhabited the peninsula, approximately seven thousand of whom lived in the north. Ensenada, the chief northern coastal port and at that time the territorial capital, numbered a little more than one thousand souls. In the 1870's and 80's Real del Castillo and El Alamo, mining centers to the east and south of Ensenada, grew temporarily to several thousand. As operations slackened, the miners departed, leaving the area as underpopulated as before. Thirty years after the filibuster days, relations between the United States and Mexico had improved sufficiently to cause Díaz, who desired foreign investment for the speedy development of Mexico, to permit Americans and others to purchase land and access to natural resources in the peninsula.[25] The manifest amiability of the 1890's cloaked latent sources of discord and trouble inherent in the continued isolation of the peninsula from mainland Mexico, the growing American investments on the Mexican side of the border, and the constantly mounting population-differential between the two Californias.

Between 1900 and 1910 the Northern Territory of Baja California, still an uninviting frontier, at last began to evince portents of impending rapid change, parallel, on a reduced scale, to what was happening north of the boundary. Among other things, there was a small but significant population increase. Because the interior, from the head of the Gulf of California west and north, consisted of a vast, mountainous desert, the population huddled along a triangular expanse bounded on the west by the Pacific and on the north by the American border. Among the population centers on the Pacific side were Ensenada, the only town with a population regularly in excess of one thousand, San Quintín, a smaller port further to the south, and El Alamo, a decaying mining site. Ensenada,

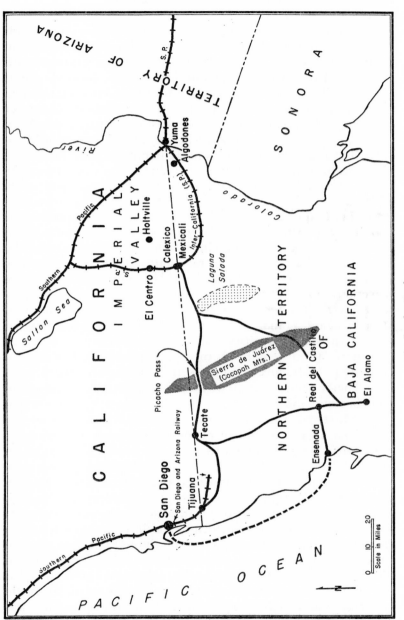

The Border Region

approximately seventy-five miles south from San Diego, was not then connected to it by a serviceable road. Along the American border, the two larger towns were Tijuana, with five hundred to one thousand inhabitants, located about fifteen miles south of San Diego, and the recently established Mexicali, with about the same population. Two other border sites were Tecate, thirty-five miles east of Tijuana, and Algodones, near the Colorado River, thirty-five miles east of Mexicali. The coastal area enjoys a pleasant climate, but the eastern part swelters in the blinding desert heat for six months of the year, with modest rainfalls during the winter and early spring.

Roughly four groups made up the more or less permanent population. Among the Mexicans there were, first, small businessmen, traders, ranchers, and fishermen along the coast, as well as a number of merchants at Tijuana and a few at Mexicali. Second, an Indian population numbering perhaps several thousands lived in the mountains and in a few isolated fertile valleys. These illiterate and poverty-stricken Guaycure, Cocopah, and Yuma Indians, who fared harshly at the hands of the territorial authorities, had but intermittent contact with the population centers. A third group consisted of several hundred Americans.[26] Whereas the Americans inland from the Pacific shore were chiefly middle-income operators of ranches and mines, some powerful interests were conspicuously invested around Tijuana and more especially in the Mexicali area. The fourth element comprised various other foreigners, ranging in status from the representatives of an English land company to Chinese coolies turned ranch hands.

Peninsular transportation facilities were limited. The infrequent early automobiles were practically useless for lack of serviceable roads. Various trails, used by horses, wagons, or occasional coaches, extended into the interior. One led from the flat Mexicali valley up the mountainous plateau to the west and onward to Tijuana. Another headed in the direction of Real del Castillo, Ensenada, and El Alamo. A third, travelled by a stagecoach, ran from Ensenada and Real del Castillo to Tecate and thence to Tijuana. Ocean transportation was more reliable. A coastal shipping line, the Meteor Company, operated a small gas-engined ship weekly between San Diego and Ensenada. Sometimes the craft of the Mexican merchant marine stopped at peninsular ports, and infrequently a ship of the Mexican navy docked at Ensenada.[27] This isolated population had more outside contacts with the United States than with central Mexico. It was sometimes easier to travel from one part of the Northern Territory to another or from another section of Mexico to a point on the peninsula via American California than to traverse the region. Though politically Mexican, the area was economically subjected to the powerful gravitational pull of the United States.

Foreign interests, mainly American and English, loomed large. Along the eastern boundary there was brisk activity as part of the American development of Imperial Valley. It was in this region that Harrison Gray Otis had his Mexican holdings. In 1900, as the irrigation project got started and as land values were about to rise sharply, he had purchased an immense tract of 832,000 acres with most of the best land in the area in it. The domain extended all the way south to the Gulf of California. The *Times* editor had purchased the land from General Guillermo Andrade of Baja California. The latter, a Díaz supporter, had obtained it in 1874 in partnership with Thomas Blythe, a San Francisco capitalist, with the intention of irrigating, but had never done so. Of these 832,000 acres, only 6,935 close to the United States boundary were under cultivation in 1908. More of it was used for cattle. The Otis properties were known as the California-Mexico Land and Cattle Company.

The editor and his prominent son-in-law, Harry Chandler, preferred to lease the valuable land rather than to sell it. However, 16,000 acres had been disposed of to G. C. Cudahy of the Chicago meat packing family.[28] In addition to the Otis-Chandler and Cudahy properties, there were various smaller American owned or leased ranches. While some crops, especially sugar beets, were raised on all of these, the farmers on the American side of the boundary were the chief beneficiaries of the canal's irrigation facilities. Because the Mexicali Valley's ranching and agriculture were sufficiently productive to warrant export facilities, the Southern Pacific had built a branch, known as the Inter-California Railway, extending from Andrade, ten miles west of Yuma, in an arc through Mexican territory to Mexicali-Calexico, where it connected with the railroad's north-south arm, which in turn extended through the Imperial Valley, to the Los Angeles–Yuma main line. The land on the Mexican side, from the railroad to the border, was owned by the Southern Pacific.[29]

Over on the Pacific side, there were two prominent foreign holdings, one American and one British. The first was the new railway project, the San Diego and Arizona, undertaken by John D. Spreckels. Spreckels had availed himself of the services of Robert Sherer and Sons of Los Angeles, a widespread railway-contracting firm. Between 1909 and 1911, thirty-five to forty miles of track had been laid. When topographical obstacles on the American side proved insuperable, Spreckels obtained personal permission from Porfirio Díaz to build about forty-five miles of line on the Mexican side, east of Tijuana. The chief purpose of this undertaking was to provide San Diego and northern Baja California with a direct rail link to the East, and, conversely, to make readily available to the agriculturally affluent Imperial and Mexicali Valleys the port facilities of San Diego. The existent rail connection to San Diego via Los Angeles was obviously inconvient and accordingly a hindrance to San Diego's progress. This line, therefore, was planned to run from San Diego to Yuma, or failing that, to link up with the Southern Pacific.[30]

The second important foreign holding in the Pacific area was the Mexican Land and Colonization Company, an English syndicate that owned much land extending north-south throughout the Northern Territory. Years before, the Mexican government had permitted an American land and colonization syndicate to obtain 18,000,000 acres. Finding it difficult to attract lessees or purchasers, the concern sold out in 1890 to the English group, which in turn failed to interest many investors at the time.[31] However, by the early 1900's many of the farmers and ranchers between Tijuana and Ensenada, some of whom were Americans, had leased or purchased land from the Mexican Land and Colonization Company.

The *Jefe Político,* or territorial governor, who held forth in his tiny capital at Ensenada, was the political ruler of northern Baja California. In 1910 and 1911, the incumbent was Colonel Celso Vega, a middle-aged army regular. Vega's tasks were to maintain order and ensure protection to foreign interests.[32] He was assisted by Prefect José María Larroque at Tijuana and a few customs officials stationed at Mexicali and other border points. Not only was Celso Vega devoted to the Díaz dictatorship, an important prerequisite for holding responsible public office, but in addition he was by nature endowed with many attributes that made for a small-scale Porfirio. The virtue of Vega's ample courage was offset by the twin vices of obstinacy and extreme irritability. Even the maintenance of orderly conditions, which he viewed as his primary function, was not easy, for he was supplied with a military-police force of about one hundred men, which, in an emergency, would hardly suffice. His faithful protection of American and other foreign interests was due more to his own narrow conservatism than to a dream of a golden economic future for the territory, or a desire to court wealthy foreigners. He was not adept at encouraging the small Mexican business interests at Ensenada and elsewhere, and was generally not well liked. He wasted no time or effort worrying about the plight of the Indians in his territory. Enforcement of the status quo satisfied this epitome of latter-day Porfirismo.[33]

With a revolution erupting in Mexico, Vega happened to occupy the governor's chair at a most critical time. The few thousands in Baja California felt the stirrings hardly less than others. In such a time and under such circumstances, a governor far more imaginative and capable than Celso Vega could not have formulated effective responses to the groping desires of the people in the face of the immense problem of absentee, foreign landownership. When the storm broke, the colonel simply met force with counterforce in what became a frontier civil war. No alternate course could have been expected, and in his circumstances no other was possible.

Such were the conditions in the two Californias when Flores Magón and his companions decided to direct their efforts to the immediate south. It should have been obvious that without a large, well-organized force, determined to carry out specific, inclusive plans, the powerful interests invested in the peninsula, as well as the popular memory of its history, would become almost insuperable obstacles. However, Flores Magón, in his revolutionary optimism and his anxiety to overtake Madero, plunged ahead. It is not difficult to surmise his thinking: In California, the spirit of the Progressive movement would provide a sympathetic atmosphere for the Liberal cause. Help might come from the Junta's connections with some of the state's labor elements. Baja California was Mexico, and Mexico was in revolt. Surely, only a small stimulus was needed to arouse the people. While Liberal action in the main theatre seemed likely to be temporarily overshadowed by the Maderistas, in the peninsula, where Flores Magón's name had been fairly well known ever since his arrest of 1907, and where there was no sign of Anti-Reëlectionist activities, there might be an opportunity for a quick triumph. Since it was geographically close to the Liberals' headquarters, no difficulty was anticipated in controlling the course of action. It was a foregone conclusion that Díaz would not be able to defend the peninsula easily because of its isolation. Assuming a successful campaign, the Liberals would use the peninsula as a base and recruiting ground for further action in all of northern and western Mexico. Finally, the Junta would then move there to direct operations, transferring themselves further southward with the sweep of subsequent victories.[34] In December, *La Regeneración* prophesied for its readers the Junta's prompt reconstitution on Mexican soil.[35] This was never to happen.

According to plan, the party made preparations on both

sides of the border for a strike at Mexicali. On the Mexican side, arrangements were made by the Magonista scouts and agents Pedro Caule, José Cardoza, Fernando Palomárez, and Camilo Jiménez. Since the population was small, scattered, and hesitant about committing itself to an open display of opposition to the Vega administration, recruitment was disappointing. The scouts' mission was useful, however, for, at considerable risk, they gathered information concerning roads and trails, water supply, mountain passes, and ranches. In addition, they learned that Mexicali was weakly garrisoned.[36]

As it appeared that an attack did not require a large force, a surprise move by a guerrilla unit was prepared. On the United States side, four individuals helped to complete arrangements. Two Mexicans, José María Leyva and Simon Berthold, a veteran Magonista who had been active in Los Angeles labor exertions against Otis, journeyed to the Imperial Valley to lead the expedition. They lingered at IWW headquarters in Holtville for a few days, conferring with Antonio Fuertes, who maintained contact with Jiménez on the Mexican side, and with Stanley Williams, an American IWW, whose interest had been aroused by the impending events, but who did not take a direct part in the seizure of Mexicali.[37]

After arms had been slipped across the border, Leyva, Berthold, and six others on January 27 crossed the boundary, a few miles east of Calexico-Mexicali. The group marched to Laguna Salada, a usually dry desert lake near a trail-crossing, about twenty miles southwest of Mexicali. There they met a twelve-man force, including several Indians, organized by Jiménez. After distributing the weapons, they marched on Mexicali, and easily captured the town in a predawn action on Sunday, January 29. The lone casualty was the jailer, who was killed during a scuffle while several Magonistas were being freed.[38]

At the moment, the capture of Mexicali was a big step forward for the Junta. It proved that the Liberals were able to take a strategic objective without assistance from another revolutionary group. Isolated Mexicali was the first port of entry taken by revolutionists. Its capture meant access to customs revenues and marked the first spot of Mexican soil which could be occupied indefinitely. The triumph was certain to provide a much-needed stimulus to the recruitment program. Insofar as the Liberal revolution had an inception date, the fall of Mexicali was it.

CHAPTER III

In the Field

To capture a base proved easier than to launch a campaign. If the Liberals seriously believed that there was some chance of carrying out a Mexican social revolution from northwest to southeast, a gigantic problem in military organization confronted them. Unlike the talented Trotsky, who was endowed with a rare combination of skills as a writer of theory and as a chief of staff, Flores Magón had no administrative ability whatsoever.

La Regeneración appealed urgently to Mexicans and to radicals everywhere.[1] Flores Magón managed to obtain extensive and sympathetic attention for the Liberals' activities from the radical press of the United States and other countries.[2] Direct calls for volunteers could not be made, lest the neutrality laws be violated. Obviously, increased Mexican support was a first essential. In his simultaneous appeals to radicals of all, and possibly clashing, hues, Flores Magón chose to overlook potential misunderstandings over the precise nature of the Junta's aims, and failed to foresee embarrassment should recruitment succeed among non-Mexicans and lag among Mexicans.

As it happened, the greater part of the radical support came from members of the IWW.[3] At first glance, nothing

seemed more apposite than the marriage consummated between the anarchist Junta and the syndicalist Industrial
Workers of the World. Despite the urban ring to their name,
the Wobblies in the West, at least, were a last manifestation
of the frontier spirit, for they were in essence vagabonds, capable of outbursts of feverish energy when aroused by novel
prospects or expectation of excitement, instantly resentful of
any form of authority, and exponents of a rough-hewn equalitarianism. As such, they were the radical pioneers and adventurers of American labor. To the Junta, their background
appeared nicely suited to fighting conditions in northern
Mexico. No importance was attached to the sizable socialistic
minority within the anarcho-syndicalist organization,[4] for the
Junta themselves were beset with an identical division of
sentiment. Nevertheless, an analyst of revolutions might have
warned the Magonistas that the alliance was bound to be tem-
pestuous. If the Wobblies' aggressiveness augured well for
their performance as soldiers, it also suggested that they might
soon weary of their circumscribed military role.

Interestingly, Jack London, the novelist, socialist, and onetime volunteer who marched with the unemployed in Coxey's
"Army," helped in forging the link between American radicals
and the Liberals. On February 5, a well-publicized meeting on
behalf of the Liberals was held at the Labor Temple in Los
Angeles. On that occasion, $140 was collected for the Mexicali
warriors.[5] Though London refused to deliver a speech,[6] he did
prepare a devil-may-care manifesto for the gathering of
"Dear, Brave Comrades of the Mexican Revolution:"

We Socialists, anarchists, hobos, chicken thieves, outlaws and
undesirable citizens of the U.S. are with you heart and soul. You
will notice that we are not respectable. Neither are you. No revolutionary can possibly be respectable in these days of the reign
of property. All the names you are being called, we have been
called. And when graft and greed get up and begin to call names,
honest men, brave men, patriotic men and martyrs can expect
nothing else than to be called chicken thieves and outlaws.

So be it. But I for one wish there were more chicken thieves
and outlaws of the sort that formed the gallant band that took
Mexicali.

I subscribe myself a chicken thief and revolutionist.[7]

This bumptious proclamation, which was the novelist's only contribution to the events of 1911, expresses the frame of mind shared by London and the members of the IWW. London's credo was a paradoxical one: an interest in socialism and the reformation of corrupt capitalist society blended with an obsession with individualistic brute force and the cult of the leader. His radical admirers at that time found it convenient to gloss over the Nietzschean aspect of his Social Darwinism. London himself drew a potentially dangerous line of discrimination; he was, he said, "first of all a white man and only secondly a socialist."[8]

The Wobblies lived this creed. There was an element of London's leadership cult in the admiration lavished upon their boisterous leader, "Big Bill" Haywood. Their class-conscious folk balladier and martyr, Joe Hill, frequently dwelt on the theme of the radicals' purity, simplicity, and resistance to the wiles of capitalism. On occasions, a trace of Social Darwinism would appear in the *Industrial Worker*, with its confident allusions to capitalism's imminent demise and its contemptuous denunciations of the decadent "plutes" and "parasites" of the outmoded order.[9] Assuredly the IWW emphasized co-operation, although the members frequently found the principle more difficult to apply than to believe. In view of the repeated displays of impatience vented on the Mexicans by the IWW's who went to Lower California, there was even a slight hint of London's attitude that socialism was for favored peoples at the expense of the less fortunate, or, in this case, the less reckless.

Neither in *La Regeneración*'s editorials of 1910 and 1911, nor at any later date, were these ideas to be found in Flores Magón's writings. Whatever dangers were inherent in his Machiavellian methods, his over-all philosophy was free of all elements of cultism, violence for its own sake, anti-intellectualism, or selective anarchistic Social Darwinism. Early in the 1900's no radical thinker could have been expected to divine these various pressures within the IWW; they have become evident only with the passage of time. Nevertheless, the Mexican revolutionist too willingly ignored the obvious menace in the Wobblies' penchant for heedlessness.

In seeking IWW help, Flores Magón and his associates had logic on their side: whatever the practical disadvantages of an alliance between exiled Mexican intellectuals and anti-intellectual American direct-actionists, the two at least had a common ideology capable of surmounting numerous mundane irritations. This was not the case, however, with other military assistance garnered by the Junta. In their haste to obtain manpower, the Los Angeles leaders took the risky step of permitting any and all comers to join the army,[10] as long as verbal assurance of good intentions was proferred. Before long, a growing number of drifters and free-lance soldiers had found their way into the Liberal ranks. As a student of revolutionary history, Flores Magón should have known that rapid disintegration befell social experiments in which the members' allegiance was not carefully checked.[11] However, his historical lessons were drawn exclusively from the record of capitalist blunders. As enlistment proceeded, the Magonistas found it difficult to distinguish adventurers from aggressive social reformers, partly because various unemployed soldiers of fortune, casually noting the IWW's combative proclivities, joined the organization to escape boredom during the intervals when their professional services were not in demand.[12] Although the adventurers presumably were indifferent to social questions, and the IWW's were thoroughly class-conscious, the two groups associated amicably for a time during the campaign that followed. The adventurers were satisfied to find fellow enthusiasts for the risks of battle, and the Wobblies were preoccupied with a social creed. As for the Junta, thinking always in theoretical terms, they did not bother to ask themselves whether these two sets of imported allies would harmonize with the Mexican troops.

Significantly, the Junta's appeals for help to Mexicans tended to differ from those directed to foreigners. Mexicans were usually urged to cast off their chains of tyranny and peonage in expectation of subsequently sharing the fruits of their labor with their fellows.[13] Non-Mexicans were not only encouraged to fight for liberty, but were also given verbal promises of a more tangible reward: should the Magonistas win, each soldier would receive 140 or more acres of land, and a bonus of $100 to $600.[14] These assurances were usually given by the army leaders or by recruiters to be found at the *Regeneración*'s 519½ East Fourth Street offices in Los Angeles or in taverns and other public places in the larger cities on the West Coast, not by the Junta leaders themselves.[15] Whether Flores Magón realized that his representatives made such commitments is not clear. At headquarters, there often was a surplus of self-appointed spokesmen ready to give out unauthorized statements.[16] At any rate, the effect was to encourage foreigners to join the Magonista army.

In only one phase of military preparations did the Junta display shrewdness. Bitter memories of the 1908 convictions under the neutrality laws made the leaders extremely cautious in sending men and arms into Mexico. Each volunteer was carefully instructed to cross the frontier carrying no weapons, while at the same time the transportation of arms to the Mexican side was arranged. A simple system was devised whereby arms in boxes with such labels as "electrical equipment" or similar designations were sent to railroad freight stops near the border, then smuggled across.[17] The subterfuge proved fairly effective.

If the Liberal leaders' method of building an army suggests a certain inexperience and organizational ineptitude, their handling of revolutionary finances reinforces this impression. In the six months following their release from prison, the leaders advanced Liberal fiscal affairs from a state of virtual bankruptcy to a level of sizable revenue. Through an energetic campaign, helped by the outbreak of fighting in Mexico, *La Regeneración* steadily attracted more readers. In April, two months after party activity began in Lower California, subscriptions numbered 27,000.[18] At the rate of $2.00 per year or $1.10 for six months, income from this source reached several hundred dollars per week. Moreover, funds were also raised at rallies. Thus, in February alone, meetings in Los Angeles, San Francisco, and San Diego yielded another $300 to $500.[19] After printing costs were defrayed and *La Regeneración*'s ample staff was remunerated, a substantial sum remained.

The Junta might have been expected, at least during the

precarious opening phase of military operations, to sink every available penny into the army. This was not the case. At first moderate sums were spent on supplies and ammunition,[20] but the amount of money expended for that purpose soon slowed down to a trickle. In part, this was caused by the American government's strict enforcement of the neutrality laws, making smuggling more difficult: rather than risking confiscation, which might set the government on the leaders' trail, the Junta followed the shortsighted policy of supplying their army inadequately. In any event, their "General Instructions" specified that the army was expected to be self-supporting, and the leaders were so sanguine as to hope the field commanders would send surplus confiscated funds back to headquarters. The monies that might fruitfully have been spent on the army, whatever the risk, were invested in an elaborate propaganda campaign. Crates of books, such as Kropotkin's *The Conquest of Bread,* were mailed out, printing costs were paid for articles appearing in hundreds of journals in all parts of the world, and expensive manifestoes were run off and distributed.[21] These outlays succeeded in obtaining for the Liberal cause an amount of space in the American and foreign press disproportionate to its actual military accomplishments. If a properly supplied army had been able to undertake an offensive equal to the propaganda bombardment, the peninsular Liberals would have scattered the Federals in a trice.

Two outstanding contributors to the efforts of the Liberal movement to organize and to obtain money and publicity were an American couple, John Kenneth and Ethel Duffy Turner, both attached to the Junta in a voluntary capacity. The former was a socialist-minded journalist whose interest in the Liberal cause had been aroused in 1908 when he interviewed Flores Magón, Villarreal, and Rivera in the Los Angeles jail. After an investigatory trip to Mexico with Gutiérrez de Lara in 1909, he published a series of articles in the *American Magazine,* then at the height of its muckraking period, exposing the tyrannic excesses of the Díaz regime.[22] In book form[23] these helped considerably in undermining further the dictator's dwindling popularity in the United

States. Turner was a contributor to such Socialist journals as the *Appeal to Reason* and the *International Socialist Review*, and had covered some of the IWW Free Speech riots. This background made him very helpful in spading the most fertile soil for the propagation of Liberal ideas, in appealing for funds, and in searching California's labor circles for volunteers.[24] A fairly careful study of past court decisions involving the neutrality laws enabled him to function as the Junta's lay counselor in this hazardous area of the law. Mrs. Turner, after Sanftleben's resignation, became editor of *La Regeneración*'s English page.[25]

In the meantime, the tiny Magonista force prepared for further action. Though the capture of Mexicali did not lead to a species of inter-California *levée en masse,* as Flores Magón had hoped it would, it nevertheless provided a lively stimulus to recruitment. Within two days the original force of eighteen men had swollen to sixty, and within a fortnight this figure had doubled,[26] despite efforts by a small contingent of American army troops to prevent enlistments. The four elements that were to make the little army unique in the history of border warfare were present from the beginning. Its nucleus consisted of Mexicans from the Mexicali region, aided by a valuable scouting force composed mainly of Cocopah Indians. A number of IWW's, who had been assisted across the border by their Holtville local, constituted the third element. In the months that followed, Imperial Valley was to hum with Wobbly activity, as many itinerant IWW members, attracted by the border excitement, drifted into the region. A few soldiers of fortune who joined at the same time as the labor radicals comprised the final component.[27]

The new force was headed jointly by Leyva and Berthold, neither of whom possessed conventional qualifications for military leadership. Little is known of Leyva's life prior to 1911, other than that he was of Mexican birth and upbringing and had lived for a time in Los Angeles. Even allowing for the personnel shortage, the Junta's selection of Leyva as commander seemed risky, since he was by occupation a plasterer (a member of the American Federation of Labor's Hodcarriers Union), not a soldier.[28] Nor did Berthold seem a better candidate for command. Born in Sonora and abandoned by his German parents, he was brought up as a Mexican by the woman who adopted him. After moving to Los Angeles about 1905, Berthold became involved in the city's anti-Otis labor activities. He worked as a truck driver for the fuel company of Perry and Skid, was active in the Teamsters Union, and gained some prominence as a labor organizer and an IWW enthusiast.[29] Whether his union activity, though militant, would prove a satisfactory equivalent to training specifically military appeared highly problematical. Berthold's wide contacts and his knowledge of Spanish and English, essential in the bilingual army, made him equal in importance to Leyva, despite his official status as second in command.

The coleaders inaugurated their administration by trying to establish the Magonista political and occupational policies, and, at the same time, by attempting to hasten preparations to take the field at the earliest possible date. They enjoyed greater relative success in the first endeavor.

From the outset Berthold strove to create a favorable public opinion in the area where they were operating. Acting as the Magonista spokesman, he declared in a message sent across the boundary that the people of the Valley "must bear in mind that we are not a mob. We are fighting for principles."[30] Moreover, he maintained that the local action was part of a nationwide movement, and that the Mexican Liberal Party, of which the Mexicali men were a part, was "the same as the Socialist party in the United States": it aimed at freeing Mexico from the Díaz tyranny, including its "intolerable" officialdom, in order to make it "a land for the poor people who have heretofore been treated like so many cattle." Specifically, he reminded the public that all saloons had been ordered closed, that women and children would be well treated, and that American citizens would be accorded respect: "We are rioting without riot, bloodshed or debauchery."[31]

Insofar as the Liberals sought to participate in the general movement against Díaz and to create a better life for the Mexican poor, Berthold was substantially correct. The statement that Mexicali soloons had been closed was also accurate, and it was likewise true that at this moment, and most of the time thereafter, Americans were treated well, although this consideration applied more to their persons than to their property. But the view that the Liberals were identical with the American Socialists was certainly inexact. The inaccuracy was probably unintentional, for Berthold simply expounded the Liberal objectives as he understood them.

Subsequently, the Magonista spokesman sought to clarify other matters of general interest. Americans were assured of the integrity of their Mexican properties. Also, they were promised that, contrary to rumor, the canal system running from the Colorado River through the Mexicali-Imperial Valley would not be dynamited.[32] Concerning the army's movements, there was an optimistic announcement that as soon as the Mexicali soldiers were joined by a rebel group from Ensenada, the joint force would depart for action into Sonora.[33]

In this fashion Berthold fulfilled the Junta's "General Instructions" with regard to announcement of aims, protection of foreign neutrals, and assurance of personal security to noncombatants. Furthermore, the two leaders made an interesting assay at carrying out the Instructions' self-financing clause. In capturing the border town, the victors took, as a matter of course, possession of the customs revenues, which amounted to only $200. When a storekeeper took exception to the new regime, a $285 fine served the dual purpose of guiding this recalcitrant's political re-education and of improving army finances. Additional funds were obtained by means of the temporary incarceration of a disgruntled, slow-moving Federal official, Gustavo Terrazas. While one of his acquaintances who had joined the Liberals, Rodolfo Gallegos, acted as a hostage, Terrazas was permitted to visit Calexico to get $500 from other Mexican acquaintances.[34] After the money was delivered, Terrazas carefully avoided returning to Mexicali while the Liberals held it. With almost $1,000 in cash, the officers placed the new army on a sound financial footing for the time being.[35] For good measure, the assessment principle was extended to include a small levy on all commercial enterprises in Mexicali.[36] Since at that time 90 per cent of the businesses were American-owned,[37] the possibility became manifest that relations with the neutral foreigners might increase in delicacy.

In the strictly military sense, the Liberal leaders ran into obstacles concerning materiel. From February 12 on, the United States Army detachment at the border halted rebel purchases of supplies on the American side.[38] Realizing that overt attempts at buying and transporting military equipment would be foolhardy, Leyva and Berthold had expected to purchase other supplies, notably foodstuffs. Since they had previously smuggled food and provisions across in fairly large quantities, and had been able to make small purchases in Mexicali,[39] the army did not feel the full impact of the decree for several weeks. At the moment, the army's new-found dollar-prosperity was more illusory than real. A little later, after foodstuffs were nearly exhausted, the problem became acute, because whatever effort was spent on smuggling had to be devoted to getting ammunition across in the teeth of a more careful surveillance. Eventually the Magonistas would be forced either to fight a war without victuals and clothing or to live off the land.

At Ensenada, meantime, the news from the northeastern border prodded Colonel Vega into action. Before the capture of Mexicali, the governor, like most Díaz officials elsewhere, had complacently assumed that the established order was secure. Though he had been apprized of a possible movement through the arrest of several Magonistas before January 29,[40] he made no effort to send any troops to the border posts for the protection of his customs officials. Then, alerted by the Sunday's news from Mexicali, Vega marched the next day out of Ensenada at the head of a force that eventually numbered a little over a hundred men. His army was composed of a few

Mexican regulars, many impressed "volunteers," and some Indian scouts.[41]

Proceeding north along the trail to Tecate, the colonel covered the first half of his trip in a short time. At the border hamlet, however, his advance was delayed for more than a week. Some reinforcements from the small garrison at Tijuana arrived and were drilled in the Tecate Valley. During this pause the Federals scouted the rebels. Unexpectedly, heavy rains at this time drenched the region to the east of Tecate. More significantly, Vega was troubled by a number of desertions from the ranks of his volunteers. On top of this, the commander fell ill, and had to be borne on a litter for several days. The situation brightened for him when, on February 8, a hard-fought Liberal-Federal skirmish resulted in the dislodgment of the Magonistas from Picacho Pass in the Cocopah Mountains, thus opening the way to Mexicali. Though there were reports of numerous casualties, the Vega men took no prisoners in this or any other fight.[42] Resuming his march, the colonel slogged toward Mexicali in the pouring rain.

As the Federals drew near, the rebels were making preparations. On February 15, an important clash took place a short distance southwest of the town, along the canal bed, on a ranch owned by an American, Louis Little. Habitually overconfident, Vega had pressed forward with no attempt at concealment. Leyva's men, entrenched along the canal banks, poured a steady fire into the Federals.[43] In the midst of the fighting, several more Vega volunteers deserted. The coup de grâce came when the colonel, directing his troops in the open, was felled by a bullet in the neck. In a short time the battle turned into a rout. The Federals retreated toward Ensenada, with their leader once more on his litter.[44]

After a battle such as this, a desert Napoleon would have driven his men across the cold sands and up the high plateaus to Ensenada, beating the shattered enemy back to the undefended capital, in expectation of a spectacular victory. The easygoing Leyva, however, felt, with some reason, that enough had been accomplished by the dispersal of the Federals from the vicinity of Mexicali.[45] Berthold, who was on a trip to Los Angeles, missed the action.

The first battle of Mexicali, then, turned out to be of great immediate importance to the rebels. Even though they failed to exploit all the opportunities presented by their victory, they reaped a harvest of prestige along the border at a time when it was an asset of considerable value.

CHAPTER IV

Outside Influences

The startling developments in Mexican California stimulated curiosity in various places and among various groups. These newly aroused interests, it soon was evident, would have a significant impact on happenings in the territory.

For the United States government, the events of early February portended involvement in the Mexican crisis. The American neutrality laws, expected to prevent use of American territory as a base for revolutionary action in friendly countries, were generally enforced as a routine duty by the State and Justice Departments.[1] In the early phases of the action, the American government took minimal precautions. A few troops under a Captain Babcock were scattered along the border on both sides of Calexico,[2] and the laws were interpreted in a way which made it difficult for the Federals to purchase arms on the American side and impossible for the rebels to do so. But the number of border troops was small during the month of February, and the situation was roughly equalized, for the rebels were able to smuggle their arms across the long, then partially unmarked, boundary without great difficulty.

The situation in Lower California, however, was too complicated to be solved by a routine law-enforcement policy.

The American government's role in California international affairs started with the floods of 1905 to 1907. After the Southern Pacific had succeeded in temporarily halting the floods by means of emergency expedients, the people of the Imperial Valley clamored for a permanent solution. Accordingly, the federal government at first considered adoption of a Southern Pacific proposal, namely, to purchase the railroad's rights to the semibankrupt California Development Company, thus acquiring the company's canal property, and to construct dikes. The California Development Company, however, was a Siamese twin to a Mexican holding company whose shares could not be bought by a foreign government. Instead, the United States sought a less complicated way to dam the Colorado. After a survey, army engineers determined that it would be practicable to build a twenty-five-mile levee along the river on the Mexican side. Under this scheme, the dikes would have to be erected on the property of the Colorado River Land and Water Company, a holding company owned by General Otis and his son-in-law, Harry Chandler, of which the vast California-Mexican Land and Cattle Company was a subsidiary. Since Otis and Chandler were perfectly willing to have their property appreciated by dike construction, the government had only to obtain permission from Mexico to begin work. After Congress had voted a niggardly $1,000,000 to start building, the State Department in 1910 addressed itself to Mexico.

The Díaz government was asked to grant speedy approval in order that construction could begin by January 1, 1911, and the project be completed before the next flood danger, in May and June. At this point, the Díaz Foreign Office, with the painful memory of various nineteenth-century American encroachments on Mexico forever in the back of its mind, viewed a government-sponsored dike-building project as a potential infringement on the country's sovereignty. After much urging by Secretary of State Philander Knox, Mexico reluctantly granted permission in a note of December 1, accepted by the United States on December 3, 1910. This protocol stated that construction was officially to be undertaken by the Colorado River Land and Water Company, even though the American government chose to absorb the cost and provide the personnel. Significantly, it went on to specify that the United States government would "not acquire any right of ownership or easement or any right over any portion of the territory or the said works that may be executed on Mexican territory the real rights and all other rights to which spring from the jurisdiction and sovereignty of the Government of Mexico." As the State Department had already assured Mexico that the United States did not "want to secure for itself any rights on Mexican territory and only desires that American settlers be protected," it was glad to accept Mexico's terms.[3]

Hardly had construction begun, when the Liberal revolt complicated matters. To be sure, Berthold had promised that American property would remain unmolested. Nevertheless, the State Department, aware of another statement of his to the effect that the Magonistas would be "to Mexico what the IWW has been to Colorado, Idaho, and Nevada,"[4] was worried lest the dam work be endangered. Mexico was asked to protect the construction workers against attack. This request irritated the Mexican government, which reasoned that, if the original favor had not been granted, it would not then be in the peculiarly difficult position of being asked to provide troops to protect its neighbor's property in Mexico at a time when every soldier was needed against the revolutionaries. In view of this, the United States offered to provide "military co-operation" of her own. To Mexico, whose citizenry was sure to be instantly aroused by the appearance of American troops on Mexican soil under any circumstances, this was the worst possible alternative. Accordingly, Francisco León de la Barra, the Mexican ambassador in Washington, replied, in a neat bit of sarcasm, that Mexico did not "deem it necessary to have recourse to that benevolent disposition."[5] He did, however, tentatively agree to send a few troops from Sonora to the river delta, provided they were allowed to cross through American territory in the vicinity of Yuma, Arizona. The United States stretched her neutrality laws to permit this.[6] It subsequently turned out that the troops were unavailable.

Finally, Mexico notified the United States that Colonel Vega's expedition, after first clearing the rebels out of Mexicali, would proceed to the Colorado to protect the workers there. Mexico wanted Vega to purchase arms, ammunition, and provisions in Yuma, but the United States reminded her that the colonel could do so only if he subsequently used his force for constabulary, not military, duties.[7] At this stage, then, protection of the dam workers depended upon Vega's defeat of the Liberals. To the State Department's dismay, the Liberals were not defeated, leaving it with the unpleasant task of starting negotiations all over again, with every prospect of further delay. It was plain that the American government was unlikely to herald the Liberals as the saviors of Mexico. At the same time, the observant neighbor was troubled to note that the Díaz regime seemed unable to take efficacious protective measures in an area in which so many interests intertwined.

Aside from the United States government, the American public watched the cross-border events intently. The columns of the daily, regional, and radical press both stimulated and reflected general interest. The minority of the dailies and periodicals that catered especially to the well-to-do were consistently hostile to all of the revolutionaries, for President Díaz had long enjoyed the reputation of operating an orderly and stable administration that protected foreign visitors and vested interests. The majority of Americans were, however, sympathetic to the rebels, as editorials, letters to the editor, and interviews with observers attested.[8] In California, as distinct from the other American regions adjoining the border, the moves and beliefs of the Magonistas, rather than the Maderistas, attracted the lion's share of the public's attention.

Unlike the State Department, the people of California were not weighted down with multifarious legal and diplomatic responsibilities. They could, and did, react on the basis of emotions. Such spontaneity at times helped the Magonista cause and at other times set it back. In this particular area, pro- or anti-Díaz partisanship was largely determined by factors of geography and income. At first, majority opinion favored the rebels. In the state's principal population centers, the daily press reported regularly and fully on the events. Of the ten or twelve newspapers that regularly contained information, perhaps half, in the early phase, were open-minded, or warmly disposed toward the Magonistas. This probably represented a lesser degree of support than was given by the public at first.

By comparison, America's radical periodicals and newspapers initially almost unanimously supported the Mexican Liberals. Though they differed amongst themselves in their interpretation of particular incidents, they were usually in accord in criticizing the explanations offered by the bourgeois press.

The rather favorable press reaction at the beginning of the revolt constituted a potentially powerful propaganda weapon for the Liberals, provided they could retain indefinitely the support of a wide assortment of newspapers and periodicals. But they were not able to; first the commercial press, and eventually most radical organs as well, grew cool toward Magonism.

By mid-February a familiar specter returned to haunt Mexico: filibusterism. Mexicali had been captured by soldiers, many of whom came from the United States. The composition of the growing Magonista army was unusual. No one knew the Junta's general plans for Mexico, nor why the Liberals failed to perform on any significant scale outside the peninsula. Singly, any of these doubts would probably not have done much damage. Taken together, however, they raised up a phantom that has never been exorcised.

In Mexico and in this country as well, critics of the Liberal Party, ignoring its part in the Mexican Revolution as a whole, and observing that it made a strong impact only in an area where American interests were conspicuous, have long claimed that the movement in Baja California was nothing but a disguised filibuster on behalf of American property-holders, the United States government, or both. The most rabid of these critics charge Flores Magón and his followers with betrayal of his country and abject collaboration with Mexico's deadliest enemy for the sake of personal gain.[9] On the other hand, the Magonistas have contended for many years that they were the innocent victims of a plot concocted by the Díaz regime, the Otis interests, and some lesser enemies. They maintained that they were blackened with the indelible stain of filibuster. Until very recent times their viewpoint has received relatively little attention in Mexico.[10] In this country these contrasting points of view have also been advanced.[11] Because of the intensity and persistence of the feeling, it is useful to observe the circumstances under which an association between the Magonista movement and filibustering arose in the minds of many people. Among the numerous contributing factors were irresponsible newspaper rumors; hasty, unsubstantiated charges filed by the Díaz government's territorial representatives; memories of filibustering; comic intrigue; overestimation of the Mexicali Valley landowners' direct power and influence; and the Liberals' own blunders.

From the outset, the California press did not consistently use the terms "rebels" or "insurrectos" to describe the Liberals, as they did for the Maderista revolutionaries. As early as February 1, the *Los Angeles Examiner,* taking the lead in loose terminology, referred to the Mexicali fighters as "filibusters" and, two days later, described them as "raiders" who sought to capture Ensenada in order to have "a port through which filibustering expeditions from the United States could operate." The *Los Angeles Herald* had a variation on this theme. It recounted that there was talk in Calexico of organizing a corps of Americans to march across the border to establish "the Free and Independent State of Lower California."[12] The same item appeared in the *San Diego Union.*[13] Similar stories or rumors were repeated regularly thereafter, helping to create a vague association between filibustering and the Magonista movement.

That impression was not weakened when, later that month, the *San Diego Union* of Sunday, February 21, carried the following advertisement:

ATTENTION!

Spanish-American War Veterans
who served in the Philippines during
1898 and 1899 are wanted for mounted
service. Send copy your discharge
for particulars.

N. E. Guyot (First Colorado)
U. S. Grant Hotel, San Diego, Cal.

For several days thereafter, the *Union* reported on Guyot's
alleged effort to collect a force that would join the rebels south
of the boundary. Within a week Guyot had dropped from the
news, but an American using the alias of Harry Dell, re-
putedly in contact with him, was arrested and held incommunicado by Federal authorities in Tijuana.[14] From then on, public interest never was to slacken.

The *Los Angeles Times,* on the other hand, chose to emphasize the Liberals' supposed banditry rather than their
filibustering. A typical editorial denied any analogy between
Coxey's Army and the rebel force, on the ground that the
famed Coxey had merely been a "harmless idiot," while the
Magonistas were guilty of "murder, arson and robbery."[15]

Simultaneously, the Mexican authorities made haste to
pin on the Mexicali men the charge of filibustering, as the
most effective means of discrediting their movement before
it could gain a more secure foothold. Colonel Vega, on his advance on Mexicali, issued a communiqué, addressed "to the
people of the United States," in which he strongly implied that
the lawless men he was seeking were both robbers and filibusters, and added: "The difficulty is caused by irresponsible men,
citizens of no country and friends of no one. I place the blame
for the dissatisfaction, if any, on the Americans and their
newspapers and their Socialists." As for "a so-called rebellion," he categorically declared: "There is none."[16]

Waxing subsequently bolder, the governor claimed to
have proof positive that the rebel effort was being financed
by Americans resident in Mexico.[17] In Mexico City, where
news of the distant peninsular troubles usually was supplied
by the California newspapers and the Associated Press, the fili-

buster thesis soon became a reportorial fixture.[18] On April 1, it was elevated to the rank of official doctrine when President Díaz, addressing Congress, stated that in Baja California "groups of Communists, among whom [were] many American filibusters," were trying to set up a "Socialist State."[19]

The Magonista campaign was scarcely a week old when sensational reports from San Francisco spread word that an American, Dick Ferris, proposed to obtain Lower California from Mexico by purchase or by force.[20] In the ensuing months, the newspapers' delight in associating Ferris, a well-known West Coast personality, with peninsular developments did much to shape the rapidly growing popular impression that a connection existed between the Liberals and filibustering.

The turbulent life of Richard Wells Ferris, actor, promoter, intriguer, and clown, began in the nation's capital in 1867. After a variegated career all over the United States as actor, manager, and promoter, Ferris moved to Los Angeles in 1905 with his second wife, Florence Stone, who for a time was his leading lady, and who helped him considerably in his different ventures. Gradually, he expanded his managerial activities, earning fame as a promoter of automobile and airplane races along the West Coast. Viewing politics as a vast outdoor spectacle, with the entire populace as an audience, Ferris took to the public stage in the election campaign of 1910, running for lieutenant governor of California on the Democratic ticket. He lost the primary to his opponent, a professional politician, by only 6,000 out of approximately 100,00 votes cast.[21]

Even more than his interest in politics, Ferris' skill as a publicity agent led him to turn his attention to Mexican California, with resultant complications for the Liberals. By February, 1911, Ferris, in addition to his other activities, was directing from his headquarters in San Francisco the "Panama-Pacific" auto race, and had been appointed manager of a forthcoming groundbreaking carnival and pageantry celebration to be held in Balboa Park in San Diego to arouse advance interest in a great "Panama-California Exposition" that was to coincide with the completion of the Panama

Canal.[22] For the latter, Ferris had promised in San Diego on February 13 to "dream up" some "live publicity stunts" with which to hold the public's attention indefinitely.[23]

Of the possibilities of Lower California, Ferris was already aware. In previous years, he had counted the region among his manifold interests. Thomas S. Phelps, Jr., a retired naval officer; Harry Stewart, a personal friend; and Max Ihmsen of the *Los Angeles Examiner* had called his attention to the sparse population, the barren sands, and the natural harbors, and helped to confirm in him the conviction that the territory was indispensable to the United States.[24] With the skilled actor's sense of timing and the promoter's facility for attracting attention, Ferris immediately seized upon the capture of Mexicali to display his mastery of the art of publicity.

The promoter swiftly concocted an elaborate scheme for American annexation of the peninsula, with just enough semblance of reality to appear faintly plausible. Ferris and a friend, Richard Cords, an official of a fishing corporation, had supposedly gathered a group of businessmen who desired to purchase the area from the hard-pressed Díaz regime. The voluble Ferris then proceeded to engage in some name-dropping, giving the impression that he proposed to make contact with multimillionaires like James Hill and J. P. Morgan, should Díaz indicate interest. In the same vein, Dr. Plutarco Ornelas, the Mexican consul in San Francisco, was approached with a view to making the requisite connection with Díaz. Plans called for the new state to be named "The Republic of Díaz," and, after a decent interval, to be resold to the United States at a neat profit for the sponsors of the transaction.[25] Should the Mexican president display an unwillingness to sell, he would be confronted by the formidable threat of a Ferris-led filibuster.[26] In order to make the threat seem authentic, and still not to fall afoul of the neutrality laws, the promoter shrewdly arranged for a New York cohort, a man named Leslie, to have an advertisement inserted anonymously on February 14 in the *New York World,* the *American,* and the *Herald,* appealing for one thousand men with military experience to join "General Dick Ferris," who would pay the

travel expenses of those found acceptable.[27] Earlier in the
month, on February 5, an important promotional bombshell
had been launched, with a telegram of inquiry to Díaz and
one of menace to Pascual Orozco,[28] the Maderista general who
had declared that the revolutionists would sweep all of Mexico, including Baja California. To Orozco Ferris had wired:

> This peninsula rightly belongs to our country, and must, in time,
> be a part of it. Our occupation is a legitimate conquest in the
> cause of civilization and the ambition of patriotic American citi-
> zens who recognize its geographical importance to this country
> in view of the completion of the Panama Canal. . . . Unless peace-
> fully ceded . . . , the Panama Pacific Expedition will sail from
> San Francisco at an early date.[29]

Hardly since the Ostend Manifesto had there been a more
blatant enunciation of the creed of Manifest Destiny.

As he had hoped, the actor reaped an abundant harvest of
publicity from these telegrams. For ten days the *San Francisco
Chronicle*'s columns overflowed with Ferris news. The headline on February 7 announced, "Díaz hasn't answered Ferris—Lower California is intact," and a doggerel:

> Telegrams come and telegrams go,
> Over the Wires to Mexico,
> Ferris the bold, is keeping them hot,
> But Diaz, the diplomat answers not

accompanied a story on the same theme.[30] The next morning,
the *Chronicle*'s readers learned that Díaz had made the mis-
take of dignifying the actor's stunt with a caustic rejection.
Ferris was delighted, treating "the message as [coming from]
the leader of a world power to the possible head of a possible
near republic."[31] The news contained in the recruitment advertisements aroused so much attention that the hotel where
Ferris was staying, the plush St. Francis, reportedly had to put
on "an extra telephone girl and increase the number of mail
clerks in order to accommodate the great number of queries"
from interested ex-soldiers.[32]

Since Ferris was known to be interested in the promotion
of gambling, the *Los Angeles Herald*'s version of the story
chose to emphasize a "sporting republic" as a possibility for

Baja California's future: "The Ferris platform . . . includes a liberal constitution guaranteeing to every citizen not only life and liberty, but the pursuit of happiness, whether that happiness may take the form of horse racing, prize fighting, bull baiting, or betting where the little ball will fall." It added that "as a result of Dick's ready letter writing . . . , it is rumored . . . that the entente cordiale between the Díaz and Ferris dynasties is a trifle strained, not to say bent."[33]

In Mexico City, the reaction of the newspaper *El Imparcial* was a mixture of sarcasm and intense irritation. A news item that mentioned Ferris' desire to employ a celebrated painter to design a flag, a poet to compose a national hymn, and a conductor and orchestra to perform at the dedicatory ceremonies was dismissed with a satirical comment. However, the paper seized upon Ferris' boast that he would soon begin his military operations if he did not promptly receive a favorable reply to his offer, and made the entirely unsubstantiated, but nonetheless damaging, charge that these operations had already begun, in the form of the "filibuster action of Berthold" and his companions.[34]

Obviously, the Ferris publicity effort had implications dangerous to the Liberals' campaign. Nevertheless, *La Regeneración* had astonishingly little to say about his activities. The San Francisco hocus-pocus earned no reference whatever in the Spanish pages, while on the English page, in successive weeks, Mrs. Turner offered only three comments. On February 11, after a brief description of Ferris' proposals, there followed the statement, "Don't be foolish, Dick." The next week's comment was: "If Dictator Dick, alias Ferris the Fearless, will only wait a little while before starting out on that filibustering expedition to take Lower California, he'll probably get Díaz to sell and sell cheap. But will Díaz be able to deliver the goods? We think not." The final observation appeared on February 25: "Ferris the Ferocious Filibuster is still making a wee noise like a 'sporting republic' for Baja California. But that noise has become very wee, indeed, scarcely more than the feeble peep of a new-born chick." As one who made merry at the expense of the downtrodden, Ferris would

appear to have been a convenient example of a capitalist ex-
ploiter against whom Flores Magón might have directed his
formidable powers of sarcasm. Instead, the Junta chose to ig-
nore him or to indulge occasionally in lightly jocular admoni-
tions that were neither bitingly satirical nor bitterly denun-
ciatory.

Well-pleased with his initial venture into Mexican revolutionary affairs, by late February the actor permitted himself
to be temporarily dropped from the news. Though there was
not the faintest evidence of large-scale preparations by the allegedly formidable Ferris military force, a sizable number
of hopeful free-lancers had contacted the promoter.[35] Disappointed in San Francisco and still unattached, some of them
may have drifted to Mexicali, where the Magonista policy of
admitting all comers could have made it possible for them to
join the several adventurers already in the Magonista army.

Newspaper headlines notwithstanding, the Liberal army's
future was far more apt to be undermined by the actions of
the influential Mexicali-Imperial Valley landowners than by
the posturings of Dick Ferris. The nature of the activities of
these wealthy ranchers lies at the heart of the bitter debate
over the Magonista movement. Did they seek, by supplying the
Liberals with money and infiltrating their ranks with adventurers, to transform them into a filibustering force with
which to acquire the peninsula? Or, on the contrary, fearful
of the Magonistas' radical ideas about landownership, did they
succeed in ruining them with the label of filibusters, the better to obtain Baja California for the United States by other
means? An ultraconservative Mexican historian, Rómulo Velasco Ceballos, Flores Magón's most tenacious intellectual
enemy, expounded the first of these theories,[36] and so generally
well-informed an observer as Carleton Beals has set it forth
in the United States.[37] The Magonistas have maintained that
the ranchers sought to discredit them, citing on their own behalf the filibuster talk in the press, the eventual revelation that
a spy, a former cowboy on the Otis ranch, had infiltrated their
ranks, the appearance of reports in 1911 to the effect that the
United States would like to purchase all or part of the penin-

sula, and the anti-Magonista pressure, supposedly Otis-inspired, that the American army units exerted along the border.[38] Actually, Otis desired, but could not obtain, military intervention to suppress the rebels. Otherwise, his influence was limited to his newspaper, which never mentioned the word "filibuster" in connection with the Liberals' activities. Both contentions are based on the incorrect assumption that the Mexicali landowners really desired American annexation. As such, they are prime examples of the leaky "conspiracy theory" of history.

In the third week of February, the War Department, aroused by the turbulence along the western border, ordered the then Brigadier General Tasker H. Bliss, commander of the Department of California, to conduct a personal check on conditions in the Imperial Valley. In the course of his tour, Bliss demonstrated a decided unfriendliness to liberalism or radicalism, but scrupulously confined himself to the duties assigned. He journeyed to the Valley from San Diego by the roundabout train route through Los Angeles. Along the way, he acquired as a travelling companion the belligerent H. G. Otis, whom he had known as an influential non-professional soldier in the Philippines. *La Regeneración* took note of their joint appearance, drawing the inevitable conclusion that the capitalist Otis had devised an anti-Magonista intrigue which he had directed his military lackey, Bliss, to carry out.[39] Nothing happened subsequently to confirm the validity of this exercise in Marxist logic.

In a preliminary, brief report, the future chief of staff addressed himself to the problems of American property. He pointed out that, except for the destruction of a railroad bridge two miles southwest of Mexicali on the Mexican side of the boundary, American property had not been destroyed. Moreover, he had received assurances from the Liberal commanders on that very day that "they would continue [the] policy of non-interference."[40]

Upon completion of his inspection tour, Bliss submitted an eighteen-page report to the War Department. The general's observations on conditions in the Valley, and especially on the

landowners' attitude as typified by their wealthiest representative, Otis, shed much light on the issue of the ranchers' behavior. Incidentally pointing out that the entire populace on
both sides of the boundary sympathized with the rebels, that
events had showed that a semiconstabulary force such as
Vega's could not dislodge the Magonistas, and that it was up
to the Mexican government to make a real attempt at oust-
ing them by using regular troops, the general went on to say:

Pretty much all of the valuable agricultural land in the northern part of Mexican Southern California is understood to be in
the hands of Americans. The Colorado River Land Improvement
Company and the Mexico California Land and Cattle Company
alone own a principality.

The land . . . acquired by various American interests was, prior
to the more or less recent change in ownership, held by Mexican
natives under old Spanish Land Grants, dating back to the early
days of Spanish occupation. These are the same kind of grants
which caused so much trouble in Northern California after its
acquisition by the United States from Mexico. But the conditions as regards settlement of titles are far worse in Mexican
Southern California than in Northern California. The original
grantees, or their immediate successors, intermarried with Indians, and their descendants, to remote degrees of relationship,
all lived on the same estate in relations which soon became those
of peonage to the recognized owner. In time the original Spanish
blood practically disappeared until the present occupants of the
soil have become Mexicans with varying strains of Indian or
Spanish blood, . . . mainly the former. Moreover, with the expulsion of the Jesuits who were in entire control in Southern
California until about the year 1767, the parish registers began
to cease to be properly kept. This continued until it finally became impossible to tell which one of the many hundreds of residents on a given estate was the legal heir to the property.

It is evident that such an owner can give no title to his land
that would be recognized under any other conditions than those
prevailing in Mexico. If Southern California were to become
American territory a shrewd lawyer could bring forward a hundred claimants who could prove as good a title to the estate as the
man who has been tacitly recognized by them, heretofore, as its
owner.

Nevertheless, it is from owners such as these that Americans,
who have crossed the border, have purchased at the price of a
few cents an acre vast tracts of land, which are thus coming to
be known as "American interests."

Under existing conditions along the border it is important to note this fact, because . . . it explains the different view which two classes of the people here take of the present insurrection. . . . California is honey-combed with the Socialistic spirit. Those forms of so-called "Labor Unions" which make Socialism their basic principle are strong here. These are the men who are particularly active in their sympathy with the present insurrection. . . . The labor organization known as the I.W.W. . . . is especially active in fomenting the present trouble.

On the other hand, the owners of large American interests in Mexican Southern California view with great apprehension the growth of the existing movement. They do not wish the present separation of Southern California from Mexico either by direct annexation to the United States or by the creation of an independent government there which, they think, would be promptly followed by annexation. They believe that their present interests are better subserved by the Mexican Government than they would be by the United States. Among other things I think it very possible that they wish to cure their present defective titles by acquiring one from long and undisputed possession under present conditions. This class of people ardently desire the intervention of the United States to put a stop to the insurrectionary movement in Southern California before it gathers further headway.[41]

General Bliss's special vantage point gave him the accurate understanding of the ranchers' position that others lacked. Neither the ordinary, uncommitted local observers along the border nor the Liberals grasped that the landowners did not desire a change in Baja California's national allegiance. The possibility of a filibuster, with the ranchers as instigators, seemed plausible to both groups. At the same time, wealthy farmers and businessmen, struck by the fact that an overwhelming portion of the Magonista effort was directed at the northwesternmost part of Mexico, concluded that this localized radicalism amounted to a novel version of filibusterism. The situation, then, was extremely complicated. It might have been clarified at this point by an unequivocal enunciation of aims by the Junta. But for them to admit publicly their connection with the military effort meant courting immediate arrest. The clarification of objectives was accordingly left to the leaders in the field. Berthold and Leyva, however, did not possess extensive knowledge of political theory, nor had they been kept well informed by the Junta; and they proved unequal to the task. Upon repeated questioning by reporters, they offered, on February 21, a résumé of the Liberals' aims: The Magonistas were independent of Madero, and bent upon establishing a utopia in the form of a socialistic, or cooperative, commonwealth.[42] This statement proved to be a disastrous blunder, for it seemed to provide another bit of evidence to substantiate one form of the filibuster talk. At the heart of the error lay the juxtaposition of the words "independent" and "commonwealth." "Commonwealth" usually denotes a separate entity, and hence the manner in which these terms were interpreted was grist for the mills of those who wished to believe that the Magonists were filibusters, and explains the reference to the "present separation of Southern California from Mexico" and "the independent government there" in General Bliss's report of February 24. The Leyva-Berthold statement was to echo resoundingly from Calexico to San Diego, Los Angeles to San Francisco, and New York City to Mexico City.[43]

Actually, the leaders merely meant to explain that the Liberals aimed at utopian political and socio-economic goals, not only in Baja California, but wherever they might prevail. The term, "co-operative commonwealth," then a stock expression in the leftist, and especially IWW, jargon, came readily to their lips. Radicals used it loosely to describe their prospective ideal non-capitalist society.[44] However, when applied in the specific context of the situation in Baja California in February, 1911, by political novices who were unable or unwilling to translate its meaning into conventional terms, it was almost inevitably bound to give rise to a misconception.

Flores Magón was in a painful dilemma. Never anxious to specify openly his exact political aims, he now had the choice of either continued silence at the price of dangerous misinterpretation of the nature of Magonism or detailed correction of his subordinates. Public acknowledgment of his sponsorship of the movement would in all probability result in his speedy return to prison and the collapse of his revolution. As a matter of course he chose to remain silent; the misunderstanding was perpetuated.

Amidst so much confusion, the first month of the Liberals' entrenchment in Lower California drew to a close. The start had been fairly promising, but the developments that followed were disturbing. Flores Magón, by setting off a rebellion in one country from an underground haven on the soil of its powerful neighbor, had pried open a veritable Pandora's box.

CHAPTER V

Fighting on All Fronts

Throughout March and early April, much of the tension at the core of Magonism became evident to observers. Strife increased both at headquarters and on the battlefields. Simultaneously, the peninsular Federals launched a fresh offensive; there was a sharp increase in vexation between the Mexican and American Foreign Offices; the United States Departments of War and Justice commenced playing a larger role in border developments; and the newspapers continued to provide unfailingly lively, though not consistently accurate, reports.

The Los Angeles Junta decided to strike once again in distant Chihuahua, where an organized force had been lacking since Praxedis Guerrero's death during the late December fighting. There, and in several other states, only scattered bands of Liberals had been operating.[1] Accordingly, the customary small Magonista striking force was formed, with the usual hope of stirring up support in the field. The leaders were Prisciliano Silva, a veteran of several border actions, including the Guerrero raid, Gabino Cano, and Lázaro Gutiérrez de Lara,[2] who, like Guerrero, had come to prefer field action to the friction at 519½ East Fourth Street. On February 11, the Liberal force captured Guadalupe, a village on the Río Grande southeast of Juárez.

At the same moment, the Anti-Reëlectionist revolution moved into a more active phase. On February 14, Madero crossed the boundary, claimed leadership of all forces fighting in the state, and prepared to attack the town of Zaragoza. As Silva and his separate force did not automatically recognize Madero's primacy, they represented the first outright challenge to his leadership on Mexican soil. A clash followed. According to the Magonistas, Madero, after requesting their assistance in the capture of Zaragoza, seized a convoy they sent him. Apparently, both free choice and force were involved, for Gutiérrez de Lara, who headed the reinforcement party, joined Madero willingly. When, at one point, Madero conferred with Silva and ascertained his connections, he denounced the Liberal Party as radical and riddled with personalism. After this, Silva was arrested, and Cano was driven to the north side of the river and exposed to the American authorities.[3] The Magonista Chihuahua force was thus swiftly smothered. Incidentally, the damage done by the Berthold-Leyva statement of February 21 was partly the result of this episode: had it not occurred, less stress would have been placed on the "independent" character of the Liberal movement.

The incident so infuriated Flores Magón that he immediately wrote a bitter editorial denouncing Madero as a "Traitor to the Cause of Liberty." In it he contended that, during the Junta leaders' most recent imprisonment, the Anti-Reëlectionists had falsely created the impression that the two groups were in close accord, thus insidiously weakening the Liberals by inducing many of their number to join Madero. The basis of the difficulty was a fundamental difference between the two strategies. The Liberals desired no more than a minimum tactical co-operation for the purpose of overthrowing Díaz, followed by an open competition to determine Mexico's future system. Madero, on the other hand, assumed that his energetic bid for the presidency in the rigged election of 1910 entitled him to leadership over all revolutionary groups. According to his thinking, other factions, after first recognizing his primacy, should co-operate with his movement in a subordinate capacity. This Silva would not do. In Flores Magón's opinion, there was no reason whatever for Madero's assumption of general leadership. Since he did not accept the principle of presidential elections, a victory for Madero in the election of 1910 would have been no more relevant than a defeat. He based his own claim to equality, if not primacy, on the much greater age of his revolutionary movement, and the more severe persecution it had endured, as well as Madero's onetime association with the Liberals. Flores Magón's editorial of February 25, after criticizing the Anti-Reëlectionists' "millionaire propaganda," denounced Madero for allegedly issuing a circular entitled "The Public Dictamen," in which he represented himself as "provisional president" of Mexico, and Flores Magón as "provisional vice president." The writer concluded with a significant reaffirmation of his anarchism in the statement that "all governments are bad," whether they be called "absolute monarchies or constitutional republics."[4]

At the same time, the Junta revised their January 3 "General Instructions" to their field leaders. The revision, dated February 24, and still issued under the 1906 slogan of "Reform, Liberty and Justice," declared that, in view of the treachery to which the Liberal fighters had been subjected by Madero, Clause 11, which provided for avoiding conflict with the Anti-Reëlectionists and for trying to convert them peacefully to Liberalism, was thenceforth abrogated.[5]

The split had far-reaching repercussions. With Díaz still quite strong, this public admission of division, and the attendant bitterness, seriously damaged the forces opposing him.

As the weaker group numerically and the more radical politically, the Magonistas immediately felt the adverse effect of the dispute. Henceforth, their radicalism attracted increased attention. Worse yet, the Maderistas greatly extended their advantage in Chihuahua.[6] Had not the Silva group been broken up so abruptly, it could conceivably have grown into a sizable unit, active in the field and recognizable as Liberal. Such a force might have dispelled the growing public notion that the Liberals were concerned exclusively with Baja California. As it was, despite the Junta's abrogation of the non-aggression clause involving the Anti-Reëlectionists, some revolutionaries who had in an earlier day been Liberals, or at least readers of *La Regeneración,* fought from this time on with the Maderistas. They preferred to carry on the fight against Díaz regardless of party feuds; some of them did not know or understand the Liberals' new policy. This hurt Flores Magón. He would occasionally claim in *La Regeneración* that certain military accomplishments in different states were the results of Liberal efforts,[7] but usually he was able only to describe the action. To call attention to the fact that some of his followers were fighting alongside the other revolutionaries would have been tantamount to admitting that his orders to fight the Maderistas were being ignored. Because of these circumstances, then, Madero, in addition to the reward of his own endeavors, succeeded in reaping a considerable part of the harvest from the seeds planted by Flores Magón and others in the previous years.

Furthermore, the episode finally brought on the rift that had long been gestating in the Junta. Antonio Villarreal resigned, or was dismissed, and departed for Chihuahua to join Madero. With Villarreal and Gutiérrez de Lara gone, the Turners, who were influential but were not policy-makers, remained as the only Socialists in the Junta entourage. Though an irritant had been removed and anarchist policies could thereafter be pursued without the confusing socialist undercurrent, the loss was disturbing. Villarreal was so popular that Flores Magón felt he had to warn his readers not to listen to the former's version of the split, nor to join with him. In particular, an anti-Flores Magón manifesto by Villarreal, published in *El Paso del Norte,* El Paso, Texas, was denounced as a pack of lies.[8] After a month the dispute was taken up in the American radical press, with even graver consequences.

The lack of harmony at the Magonista headquarters was dwarfed by the dissensions in the field. The advantage gained in the Battle of Mexicali was soon frittered away in inactivity.

Talk of reinforcement from Ensenada had come to nothing, as had the expectation of an imminent advance to join forces on the mainland. The Magonistas seemed rooted to Mexicali. Now the cool desert air echoed the sounds of furious blows, harsh words in several tongues, and angry bursts of gunfire that did not come from the outposts watchful of an enemy approach. There occurred such incidents as the shooting of W. E. Clark, an IWW from Cincinnati, Ohio, who was seriously wounded, either accidentally by his own hand, as Berthold averred, or by a Yaqui Indian, as consensus had it. In retaliation "Wild Bill" Hatfield (allegedly one of the famed Kentucky Hatfields) then killed a Mexican by a shot in the face. Despite threats of dire punishment, the incident concluded with neither the Yaqui nor Hatfield court-martialed.[9]

The come-one–come-all recruitment program had much to do with the friction. By late February, the proportion of non-Mexicans had reached no less than 50 per cent. Americans, several of whom were Negroes, made up the largest contingent of outside help. A scattering of English, Australians, Boers, Russians, Germans, and Frenchmen were also on hand.[10] The delay in advancing on Ensenada, failure to fulfill the verbal promises to pay the recruits, differences in language and national habits, and a conspicuous lack of confidence in the dual command were the ostensible reasons for the arguments.[11]

At the core of the controversy glowed the fast-rising star of a man usually called either William Stanley or Stanley Williams. A colorful member of the IWW, his origins were vague; he was also identified as Cohen, and again as Robert Lober of Cleveland, Ohio, which may possibly have been his name. Williams had served in the American army during, and for some time after, the Spanish-American War, had wandered and worked his way through every tough locality in the West, and had participated in the Free Speech riots of 1910.[12] Because in him intelligence, the proper shade of political radicalism, fearlessness, recklessness, and irresponsibility were combined in equal proportions, it would take the Delphic oracle to determine whether he was an asset or a liability to the Liberal army. As one of the original group of planners in Holt-ville, he had been too closely watched to participate in the capture of Mexicali. About a week later, however, he suc-ceeded in crossing the boundary. After playing a prominent part in the engagement of February 15, he secured from Leyva reluctant permission to form an auxiliary force containing a large number of the non-Mexican volunteers.[13] As Leyva had suspected, the irresponsible Williams acted autonomously as often as he co-operated with the main body. On the night of February 21, the Williams daredevils, after capturing an Inter-California freight train, opened the engine's throttle and roared into Algodones, a hamlet to the east of Mexicali, with guns blazing at the handful of startled Federal customs of-ficials. Thus, the Magonista possession of the area east to the Colorado was assured in a twinkling. The exploit drew head-lines.[14] About three weeks later, the Mexican government or-dered an indefinite suspension of train service on the line.[15] By early March, Williams, weary of Leyva's Fabian leader-ship and probably not averse to occupying the top-command post himself, brought the discontent to a head by agitation for change.

Williams saw his chance in the equalitarian principle of election of the commander. Alleging pusillanimous leader-ship and misappropriation of funds against Leyva, Williams on March 4 proposed the election of his admirer José Cardoza as the nominal new leader. Though most of the Mexicans still preferred the Leyva-Berthold team, a minority joined the solid bloc of foreigners in voting to unhitch it. Shortly after the vote, however, the malcontents, who had stacked their rifles prior to eating, found their weapons confiscated by Berthold, and themselves surrounded by his followers with guns levelled. After an interlude in irons, Williams was for-cibly removed across the border.[16] The incidents touched off ten days of hectic arguing, during which Flores Magón's cher-ished dream of anarchism became a reality.

Berthold bought his victory dearly, for his resort to Bona-partism constituted a gross violation of the sacrosanct principle of democratic election. It quickly brought a flurry of desertions. Since most of the deserters were Americans, the loss perhaps had its compensations. But among those who left were forty-five Mexicans, led by the disappointed Cardoza, who drifted east to the dike-building area, and thence, after a few days, to Sonora to join the Maderistas. The Junta dispatched their trouble shooter, John Kenneth Turner, to mediate the differences. When he arrived on March 8, the Mexicali army seemed on the brink of dissolution. Among the force, numbering about 140 troops, only about 40 staunch Berthold followers were permitted to carry arms.[17]

Turner's mediation began with a conference with the diarchy, "marked by loud talking and violent gestures."[18] Another ballot was taken, with yet another vote adverse to the incumbents. Had the Federals been able to seize the initiative then, they might easily have dissolved Magonism in the midst of a ballot. A semblance of order was restored by means of a harmony meeting in which Williams returned as witness for the dissidents. Berthold won support by an impassioned speech promising submission to the voters' will, should he and Leyva fail to undertake an early advance on Ensenada. Williams and other IWW's, as well as miscellaneous hangers-on, were again forced to abandon the movement and cross the boundary. Simultaneously, some fifty to one hundred Mexican recruits arrived, enabling the dual leadership to legalize their coup.[19] Leyva and Berthold had developed an understandable desire to eliminate the disturbance, not to say danger, inherent in the presence of so many foreigners in the ranks.[20]

Williams partly succeeded with a countercoup. After hastening to Los Angeles, probably in the company of Turner, he induced the Junta to approve his appointment as commander of a separate new unit. The ambitious Williams furthermore let it be known that soon he would be generalissimo, but the Junta did not indicate approval of the forecast.[21] Though he never did attain to the supreme military post, he returned on March 12 to head his autonomous command. This force, composed of the supposedly expelled Wobblies and soldiers of fortune, and usually dubbed the "Foreign Legion" by the press, was assigned the sector east of Mexicali. A smaller number of non-Mexicans rejoined the main force. Turner, who reportedly felt that extensive foreign participation increased American sympathy for the movement,[22] may have exerted his influence to obtain the Junta's approval of this solution. The problem was complicated because Leyva and Berthold, though they adequately reflected Mexican revolutionary aims, were of dubious competency, but Williams, who was militarily capable, was of dubious reliability. The dispute ended, then, with a greater autonomy for Williams, a deterioration in the authority of the dual command, and a noticeable increase in lack of rapport between Mexicans and foreigners.

Events had also taken a new turn amongst the Federals at Ensenada. After his defeat, Colonel Vega had retired to his capital to sulk and to recuperate from his wounds. With little or nothing done to prepare defenses, the population grew restless, and the governor became very unpopular. Then, early in March, the Mexican Department of War and Navy ordered Colonel Miguel Mayol, commanding a force of 500, known as the "Fighting Eighth," to Ensenada. This was the largest and best-trained unit that had yet appeared on the peninsula. Largely because of the State Department's pressure, Mayol had been commanded by his superiors to proceed to the Colorado to protect the waterworks. Governor Vega, as could be guessed, hoped that he would attack the rebels en route.[23] The Eighth set forth without a clear determination of whether it had a single or dual mission, but, since the revolutionists were between the dikes and Ensenada, the force might have been expected to attack them.

At the same time, the Magonistas managed to strengthen themselves elsewhere along the California border, despite the quarreling at Mexicali. Guerrilla bands, headed by Luis Rodríguez and Francisco Vásquez Salinas, raided for a time between Tecate and Tijuana, and Rodríguez with twenty men captured Tecate on March 12, not long before Mayol's arrival.[24] This village, located in a fertile valley high above

the desert, was a valuable acquisition; its possession represented a potential threat to Tijuana.

With Mayol and the Fighting Eighth bound to arrive before long, Leyva and Berthold finally decided to march out
of Mexicali at midnight of March 14.[25] Though imminent
danger appeared to warrant the services of Williams' fighters,
the scrappy Foreign Legion was left behind to scour the
eastern area in the unlikely event of a second Federal approach
from Sonora. After moving slowly to Laguna Salada, Leyva de-
liberated, and on March 16 committed the ghastly blunder of
splitting his force. Berthold, with a mixed contingent of sixty
to seventy Americans and Mexicans,[26] marched south to El
Alamo, where a series of adventures awaited them. The reasons for so startling a tactic may only be surmised. It may
have been an aftermath of the quarrels, an ill-timed attempt
to seek new recruits in the south, a wish on Leyva's part not
to commit his entire army against the Federal advance, or a
tentative move to offset the threat to Mexicali by a counterthreat to Ensenada via El Alamo.

Having halved his own striking potential in the face of his
powerful enemy, Leyva drove up the mountain westward toward Tecate, where the small Rodríguez force was by this
time encircled. Too much precious time had been lost. Early
on March 17, Rodríguez and his men were completely wiped
out by Captain Justino Mendieta, commanding a detachment of the Eighth.[27] Leyva stumbled into view at dawn on the
nineteenth. Despite the disaster, he stood a good chance of at
least regaining the strategic site, for Mayol's main body was
nowhere to be seen, and the 150 rebels had a nearly two-to-
one edge over Mendieta.[28] After three days of desultory fighting, Leyva lifted the siege. According to him, the retreat was
due to a shortage of ammunition and the need to cover
Picacho Pass to prevent Mayol from slipping through while
the Liberals were at Tecate. Upon discovering that Mayol had
not advanced by way of the Pass, Leyva dropped back to
Mexicali.[29] He had suffered a fairly heavy number of casualties
and desertions. According to his men, he had "retreated at full
speed on horseback, leaving his foot soldiers to their fate."[30]

This defeat ended Leyva's tenure as commander. Reluctant, however, to give up, he displayed in trying to retain his post a spirit that would have done him credit at Tecate had it been in evidence there. On March 29, a new Junta agent, Antonio de Pío Araujo, notified him of his dismissal, but he lingered until April 4, sometimes still claiming to be leader, asking for monetary contributions from Mexicali merchants, and talking of joining Berthold. Unwanted in Baja California, where he wished to be, and rumored to be wanted in Alta California, where he did not care to be, Leyva finally wandered off to join Madero, whom he had alternately disparaged and defended, depending upon his degree of security as Magonista leader.[31]

With Mayol presumably approaching the Valley, Francisco Vásquez Salinas, who had come to Mexicali after missing the Tecate massacre because he happened at that moment to be in the United States, was selected by the Junta as the new commander.[32] A letter dated March 28 notified him of his appointment. In it, Flores Magón insistently urged him to make the spirit of unity one of the prime objectives of his leadership. Simultaneously, even though the recent quarrels had been caused partly by an excessive autonomy permitted the different groups, the new commander was instructed not to curb the subordinate leaders' independence. Evidently, the Junta had wearied of the numerous requests for instructions, for Vásquez Salinas was informed that "in all cases the proper initiative of each chief of column would give better results than to be consulting every moment with headquarters."[33]

Under the circumstances, Vásquez Salinas displayed a disinclination to accept the honor. Several days of confusion followed, during which the reluctance of Vásquez Salinas to take the post was matched by the ambition of Williams, now revealed to be a deserter from the United States Army, to obtain it. A bewildered Angeleno correspondent described the situation thus: "With Leyva seeking funds to finance a safe exit from the zone of war, Salinas declining to command the insurrecto forces, and Stanley Williams, heretofore known as General Stanley, and now alleged to be a deserter from the United

States army, their commander-in-chief, the insurgents are awaiting the onslaught of the federals under Mayol."[34]

With so much open bickering, a full airing of the Liberals' difficulties seemed in order. Flores Magón's ability to explain the shortcomings of his own movement, however, was by no means equal to his talent for denouncing the failings of others. *La Regeneración*'s treatment of the army quarrels is illustrative, as are the activities of Antonio de Pío Araujo. Pìo Araujo, who had just been liberated from an American prison, shuttled along the border as a contact between headquarters and the forces and as a purveyor of judicious Liberal policy statements in the wake of the almost continuous misunderstandings. Pío Araujo's maiden effort was less than helpful: "There is no truth in the report that our forces in Lower California are not working as a part of the main forces in other parts of Mexico. They are, and in Gen. J. M. Leyva we have a soldier who is both fearless and efficient."[35] The first statement was misleading, and the second, fatuous. As to *La Regeneración,* it chose to deal with the issue of the quarrels by denying that they existed. Unwilling to admit publicly that Leyva had been dismissed, the paper announced that he had departed on an important mission for the Junta.[36]

Meantime, with Mayol approaching, the lonely desert turned into a busy thoroughfare. The colonel, desirous of avoiding a possible ambush at Picacho Pass, had marched on Mexicali in a wide arc to the south. Also on the move were reinforcements sent from Mexicali to El Alamo, as well as stragglers from the Tecate defeat heading southward.[37] Yet, these comings and goings brought no contacts, except three messengers involved in the Mexicali–El Alamo shuttle, whom Mayol apprehended at Laguna Salada. One of these was W. M. Ford, an Imperial Valley cattle-rustler. Disposing of this hindrance by means of the *ley de fuga,*[38] the colonel advanced to Little's Ranch to reconnoiter. Though this approach suggested that he intended to do battle, he saw fit, on April 8, to telegraph the War and Navy Department asking permission to do so. In his roundabout march through the desert he had exhausted his provisions, and his telegram suggests that he wished to attack chiefly in order to use Mexicali's supplies to restock his army.[39]

The Liberals' supply situation was not good, either. It had deteriorated as a result of a new policy of the United States government. Back on March 6, President Taft had abruptly ordered 20,000 troops to the American border,[40] thus maximizing the difficulties in obtaining ammunition, and making almost impossible the smuggling of food and other necessities. The rebels were therefore almost completely dependent on the resources of the peninsula for survival.

This emergency caused the Liberals to begin the appropriation of foreign possessions in the Mexicali area on a large scale, with Stanley Williams leading the way.[41] Williams, taking note of Mayol's unusually deliberate approach, determined to lead his troop of eighty-five in a daring attack on the enemy's five hundred. He may have intended, if successful, to march through to join the El Alamo party, and then to threaten Ensenada, for there is a reference to this plan in Flores Magón's letter of March 28 to Vásquez Salinas.[42] Accordingly, he began to requisition horses, mules, wagons, food, and any available ammunition from the Cudahy ranch and Otis' California–Mexicali Land Company ranch. As might well be expected, there were difficulties with the respective managers, T. P. Daly and Walter Bowker. Following the Junta's "General Instructions," Williams issued receipts, which were, however, refused or ignored. His men bullied Daly into fleeing across the border in his automobile, lest they appropriate the vehicle. Vásquez Salinas publicly disavowed Williams' acts, thus creating new issues over which to dispute.[43]

On April 8, the second Battle of Mexicali, or the Battle of Little's Ranch, took place. Since the reckless advance of the Foreign Legion caught Mayol by surprise, Williams' contingent managed to do considerable damage to the Eighth at first. But the Mexican commander's machine guns had the last word; Williams received a fatal wound; and the band had to flee back to Mexicali. Mayol did not attempt pursuit. Estimates of the losses varied widely. On the Federal side the toll was especially heavy. The Magonistas, counting wounded, dead, and deserters, probably suffered a 25 per cent loss, chiefly in desertions. Williams died the day after the battle.[44]

In retrospect, two small matters require attention. Though beforehand Mayol had intimated at times that he would fight and on other occasions that he would not, afterwards he announced that he did not pursue the rebels because his orders were to protect the Colorado works, not to fight.[45] Meantime, the Liberals clung to Mexicali. To the amazement of everybody along the border, after remaining stationary for a week, Mayol marched off to the river.[46] People concluded that the rebel band, though outnumbered, had intimidated him into a withdrawal. With the investers gone and the Magonistas still in possession of their base, the apparent setback had been turned into a moral victory.

Questions were also raised concerning Vásquez Salinas' inaction. The *Industrial Worker,* reflecting the IWW's resentment, thundered: "Stanley would have captured Mayol's machine guns and many men if he had had a few reinforcements, but all this time traitor Leyva [*sic:* an obvious confusion with Vásquez Salinas] was reposing in the trenches in Mexicali, waiting for Stanley and his men to be slaughtered."[47] Vásquez Salinas, for his part, explained that he had wanted the two groups to force Mayol to attack Mexicali proper, as they were strongly entrenched there, and pointed to the fatal outcome of the sortie as evidence of the soundness of his plan. Of Williams, he said, "I ordered him to go out, but only when he demanded it,"[48] a remark as deserving of inadvertent immortality as Ledru Rollin's observation that his people were on the march, and, because he was their leader, he must follow them.

The Magonista, and even more, the Maderista, movement exacerbated relations between the American and Mexican Foreign Offices. The indefinite length of the revolt necessitated an over-all policy for the United States. From the standpoint of the Mexican government, the vital objective was to induce the United States to enforce a very strict interpretaion of her neutrality laws.

A firm, clear-cut policy was a virtual impossibility for the battered Taft administration. It had to balance the desires of its wealthy backers and the European powers for stability in Mexico against the clamorous insistence of liberals and radicals that the revolutionists be permitted to operate freely. Knox's "Dollar Diplomacy" in Honduras and Nicaragua had drawn sharp criticism from Democrats and Progressive Republicans, who, heartened by their triumph at the polls in 1910, looked eagerly toward 1912, while public opinion took on a more and more liberal turn. Tugged, pulled, and bullied, the administration pursued a fitful course, conciliatory toward Mexico one day, unfriendly the next. As a result, no one is sure just what it hoped would be the outcome of the revolution.

The troop concentration of March 6 was Washington's most aggressive step. Fear that American lives and property might not be sufficiently well protected in the areas of fighting, Mexican complaints that the neutrality laws were not being adequately enforced, and, incidentally, concern over the Lower California situation all played some part in the decision. Important also in precipitating this ill-advised move was Henry Lane Wilson, the arrogant, Mexican-hating ambassador, who happened just then to be on leave in the United States.[49] Certainly, the effect of the decision was to undermine confidence in the Díaz regime. Whether this was the intent is debatable. For some time before 1911, the Taft administration for several reasons had not been altogether satisfied with the Mexican government. It seemed possible, accordingly, that, should a sizable rebellion occur, Washington would be willing to countenance, or, indirectly, to help, the overthrow of the dictatorship, by a move embarrassing to Díaz.[50] However, in view of the multifarious pressures to which the Taft government was subjected, and the administration's tendency to drift, then plunge into an abrupt action without weighing all probable consequences, it is just as likely, if not more likely, that the troop movement was only a ponderous attempt to safeguard American interests by frightening the revolutionists, and, thus, incidentally, a move to help, not injure, Díaz. In denouncing the action, the liberal-radical press expressed the quite widespread, and probably erroneous, conviction that this was a prelude to intervention in Mexico.

Partly on its own initiative, and partly prodded by reminders from California, the State Department continued to seek protection for the dike workers. Among newspapers, the *San Diego Union* and the *Los Angeles Times* were particularly anxious for the entry of American troops into the work area or for some sort of acquisition of special rights over the canal network.[51] Also, the California state legislature, on February 17, passed a resolution asking the President to take especial care to protect the Imperial Valley against peninsular disorders.[52] In private, Otis, who enjoyed direct access to several branches of the government, kept after various departments. As General Bliss failed to show a full appreciation of the *Times* empire's requirements, the editor began to write Secretary of the Interior Richard A. Ballinger. A message of February 16 advised that joint military action against the rebels was necessary, and specifically asked that Ballinger "please say as much to President."[53] A week thereafter, Otis wrote the State Department, urging that troops be sent to guard Colonel Ockerson's dike-building camps.[54]

After Vega's retreat, Washington asked permission for American soldiers to patrol the water-projects area. Foreign Minister Enrique Creel rejected this request promptly, on the ground that such a concession would only strengthen the revolutionists, because the entire nation would rise against a Mexican government granting it.[55] It was at this point that Mexico decided to send one of her regular army forces. On March 4, the American Embassy reported the departure of Mayol and his Eighth, predicting that they would be at the river ten days later.[56] This estimate missed the actual date by one month, not only because of Mayol's slowness, but also because of the resumption of an earlier dispute. Mexico once more asked for permission to transport troops over American territory. Within the context, the United States felt compelled to refuse.[57]

The controversy was the outcome of the dilemma posed

by the dike construction. Mexico deemed that the United States had asked first for the favor of building the waterworks, and then for the favor of having them protected. Actually, the United States desired a third favor—the elimination of the rebels who represented a potential threat to the dikes—but could not state this in a diplomatic context. In return for protection of the dikes, Mexico asked not only for permission to transport troops through American territory, but also for re-entry for the purpose of attacking the rebels who allegedly threatened the dikes. Anxious to live up to the stringent requirements of international law, and perhaps mindful of the domestic liberal storm should both parts of Mexico's request be assented to, the American government rejected the second part of Mexico's terms. Since this response, in effect, suggested that the United States was more interested in having the dikes protected than in seeing the rebels attacked, Mexico, in pique, proceeded simply to comply. This explains why Mayol behaved so inconclusively. Since the defeat of the Magonistas would have served the interests of the Mexican government even more than the United States, Mexico risked cutting off her face to spite the United States' nose. Mayol's behavior suggests that he might have attacked, had he really desired to do so. His failure reflects upon, among other things, his efficiency as a soldier. Finally, after he moved to the river in mid-April, protection for the building sites was *ipso facto* provided, and the matter became a dead issue.

The troop movement and the dikes dispute caused General Bliss to make a return visit to the Valley, in early April. He concluded that Mexico's tardiness in sending troops and the inefficiency, including the possible addiction to liquor, of her commander accounted for the continuation of trouble in the area:

It appears probable that Colonel Mayol was the officer to whom the Mexican government, on the repeated insistence of our Government . . . , gave the order to . . . protect our construction work on the Colorado River. At the time that order was given there were no insurgents worth speaking of at Mexicali or at any other point. . . . After an inexcusable . . . delay the Mexican federal force appeared at Ensenada. After a further long delay there they marched to Tecate and drove out the band of insurgents at that place. After a further inexcusable and criminal delay they appeared at a point five miles to the westward of Mexicali. After a delay of two days Colonel Mayol was attacked by Stanley and his band of American insurrectos. At no time that I was in Calexico was it found that the Mexican federals had outposts further than about one hundred feet away from the edge of their camp.

Colonel Mayol . . . reiterated the statement that his orders were to go to the Colorado River dam and that he had no orders to attack Mexicali. . . . I waited for a week in Calexico, hoping that something would eventually beat a little common sense into Colonel Mayol's head and that he would get busy with the insurrecto band in Mexicali.

In my opinion any increased disorder in Lower California will be due to the gross military incompetence of the Mexican Federal commander there.[58]

When it came to Mexico's complaints, the two countries entangled themselves in the complications of American neutrality legislation. With Madero and Flores Magón both within the confines of the United States during the winter of 1910 and 1911, the Mexican government hoped that both would be apprehended for conspiracy. After four months, the accumulation of circumstantial evidence against Madero was sufficient, in February, to warrant an order for his arrest. He, however, had crossed back into Mexico at the opportune moment.[59] Thereafter, Mexico redoubled her proddings concerning the Liberals, pointing out that publication of defamatory and anarchistic literature, as well as violations of the neutrality laws, had incriminated them. Ambassador de la Barra's messages habitually referred to the Liberals as "filibusters," "adventurers" without "cause or flag," and "fugitives from American justice."[60] In a modified form, a statement made by Knox on January 24 with reference to Madero was applied to the Magonistas. It was illegal, Knox said, to transport arms, ammunition, and munitions of war, to leave the United Staes to enlist in foreign service, or to transport persons from one country into the other. The key clause in the applicable neutrality law was intended "to prevent the use of the soil . . . of the United States as a *base*" from which to launch "military   expeditions   or   military   enterprises" against friendly neighbors.[61] Such were the general rules. But the replies of the State Department usually called attention to the lack of concrete evidence in the charges made by Mexico. Meantime, the United States authorities made concessions to Mexico's desires by not permitting the Magonistas to transport arms freely, and limiting their transportation of persons, precisely because they were suspected of using Los Angeles as their base. The Magonistas have accused the American government of pursuing them more persistently than the Maderistas. If so, it was only because they used an American base indefinitely, while Madero transferred his person and activities to Mexico after a time.

During the Foreign Office exchanges, the Justice Department commenced the arduous process of investigating the Liberal movement. A. I. McCormick, the United States District Attorney for the Southern District of California, and two Bureau of Investigation agents were placed in charge of gathering information. From February until June, their efforts consisted chiefly of ordering the temporary arrest of border suspects in hopes of unearthing incriminating documents, and of checking on the activities of stragglers observed around the dingy offices of *La Regeneración* at 519½ East Fourth Street.[62]

One of the potential neutrality law violators was Dick Ferris. The Mexican government, taking note of his New York advertisements of February 14 and of the San Francisco newspaper publicity, half-apologetically called the United States' attention to him. The Justice Department obliged with an investigation of the neophyte Garibaldi.[63]

In due course, Special Agent Clayton Herrington, assigned to Ferris, reported that he was a mere publicity-seeker. A check had revealed that he had enlisted no men and had been in receipt of no incriminating correspondence.[64] To test his findings, Herrington had sent an army veteran, Earl Carter, to enlist in Ferris' force. After several delays, Carter obtained an interview on March 10. Forewarned or foresighted, Ferris reverted to the incorrigible ham actor that he was, and prepared a farcical tableau for Carter's benefit. The agent was surprised to find that a lady whom he took to be an actress—obviously, Mrs. Ferris—was a third party to the conference held at the St. Francis Hotel. With the woman referring to Ferris in gushing tones as "the General" and the actor addressing her portentously as "the Madam," Carter found himself unable to hold down the conversation to a pedestrian level. He ascertained only that "the General," after claiming to have received thousands of applications, had employed not a single volunteer. Otherwise, Ferris spoke vaguely of San Francisco support, adding suggestively that "when a man like Spreckels would risk three ships it showed the expedition was going through." So ended the interview,[65] and Herrington's investigation. On the basis of it, the State Department was able to assure the Mexican Embassy that Ferris was "only seeking notoriety."[66]

On Sunday, March 12, during one of the duller periods on the Baja California front, an incident near Tijuana caused a ripple of excitement and laughter. Under the headline, "American Girl, Braving Soldier Lines, Hoists New Flag on Mexican Soil," the *San Diego Union* reported a surprising feat by a Los Angeles horsewoman, Miss Flora S. Russell. After "designing a silk flag of unusual beauty—of a field of blue, from which flashed a rising sun with brilliant rays of yellow and over which hung the scales of justice," Miss Russell had gained permission to ride across the border. Near Agua Caliente, she planted her flag, proclaiming:

Lower California, I claim you in the name of equal suffrage and of model government, which I hereby christen as the future "Republic of Diaz." May the Great Ruler of all things nourish the little plant typified in this flag that I raise over this troubled land, and in His goodness bring to fruition the hopes and dreams of my sex for fullest liberty, symbolized in the scales of equality and justice.[67]

The particular tone of the proclamation, in combination with the flag and the ride across the border, pointed to the "fine Italian hand of Richard Ferris," who had promised to provide San Diego with the "most comprehensive publicity he had ever seen" for the June celebration.[68] A short interview granted by Miss Russell confirmed the impression:

When I am rested from my long ride and have time to express myself I shall tell you why I did what I did today. I wrote Mr. Ferris a long letter last week and he must have divulged my secret. I did not try to do it for myself. I want equal suffrage to be written into a constitution, and Mr. Ferris' plan offers the best opportunity at this time. I barely know Mr. Ferris, so I cannot be accused of favoring his project for personal reasons.[69]

Amidst threats from Mexican consuls vowing to secure her arrest, Miss Russell fled back to Los Angeles. It turned out that she was a fan of the indefatigable promoter, and especially of his wife, an ardent suffragette.[70] The brief time that elapsed between the Herrington investigation and this incident indicates clearly that Ferris was not worried about the Justice Department. Having used Miss Russell to advance his promotional schemes, he permitted the suffragette to drop from sight, and, for his part, chose to remain out of the limelight for a time.

As one improbable event succeeded another, most newspapers had become convinced that Liberalism must be a new and occult form of filibusterism or separatism. Apparently seeking to strengthen the latter impression, the *Los Angeles Times* published a fantastically garbled article to the effect that the Liberals received their financial support from wealthy Chicago interests and intended to create a republic of those northern Mexican states in which there were large investments of American capital.[71] With slight variations and attendant confusion of filibusterism, separatism, Liberalism, and utopianism, this article was widely printed. Actual accounts of day-to-day happenings were much less inaccurate than most interpretive articles, though the assumption of filibustering was implicit in the majority of them. The Mexico City press held these views a fortiori.[72] Of the dailies, the Imperial Valley papers alone were comparatively friendly to the Magonistas. *La Regeneración* even went so far as to recommend the *Calexico Chronicle* as useful supplementary reading for Liberals.[73] The *Imperial Valley Press* credited only the *Express*, among Los Angeles newspapers, with consistently accurate reportage of Mexicali events.[74] The *Press* was the only paper to point out, with respect to the "co-operative commonwealth" confusion, that the Liberals had "made no declarations of independence and they fly the flag of Mexico, even insisting that the Mexican flag be flown above the American flag placed upon structures of the canal property."[75] However, as Magonista quarreling continued, the *Press* grew impatient, remarking that the "visionary Socialists" acted independently of events elsewhere, and did "little to harass the government and a great deal to paralyze their own efforts."[76] By April, only the numerous radical weeklies raised no questions concerning the motives of the fighters.

CHAPTER VI

The Anarchy of Anarchism

If the peninsular revolution followed a rocky course, it only paralleled the larger movement in the rest of Mexico. In the three months following Madero's reappearance on Mexican soil on February 14, the pace of the Anti-Reëlectionist revolt accelerated considerably. More decisive advances might have been made had not the leader displayed a willingness to negotiate in the midst of fighting.

In the military realm, one serious reverse occurred in Chihuahua, when on March 6 Madero and his officers, with victory in sight, lost the Battle of Casas Grandes. During the following month, however, in the northern part of the country there were compensating successes in Sonora, and some gains in Coahuila, Durango, and Sinaloa, while in the south revolt spread in Morelos, Guerrero, Vera Cruz, and Yucatán. Meantime, the main revolutionary body under Madero recouped, and planned an attack on Juárez.[1]

A Liberal–Anti-Reëlectionist clash, reminiscent of the one between Madero and Silva in February, took place during the action in Chihuahua. At the Battle of Casas Grandes, a Liberal force led this time by Lázaro Alanís had, according to the Magonistas, performed a signal service by saving Madero during the retreat after he had been defeated. After that,

91

they were inclined to go off by themselves, because the Anti-Reëlectionist leader would not recognize the validity of the Liberal Party's efforts, but Madero, anxious to hold all rebel forces together for an offensive, successfully pleaded with them to remain as an auxiliary force. However, in April, while the army was encamped at Guzmán, southwest of Juárez, a quarrel arose between Madero and Alanís, during the course of which the latter and several of his officers were disarmed. According to Alanís, Madero, who, because of his small stature and nervous manner, always had difficulty in enforcing his authority, drew himself up and, in a would-be stern and commanding voice, said: "Recognize me as your president and as the head of the revolution." When Alanís and his companions declined to do so, Madero ungratefully had them arrested, and about 150 Magonista soldiers were disarmed.[2] Thus, the third successive possibility of establishing a solid military footing in Chihuahua came to grief, the first one through the leader's death, the other two because of clashes with Madero. In the absence of an Anti-Reëlectionist version of the Guzmán affair, it is difficult to determine the accuracy of the Liberals' account.

Madero, partly because of the influence of his closely-knit, wealthy, and conservative family, which had certain ties with the incumbent government, and partly because of his own characteristic desire to hold loss of life to a minimum, showed a disposition to parley with Díaz while military action was still going on. He probably hoped that the dictator would see the wisdom of resignation. If not, Madero, even with his movement gaining, might have been willing to consider a compromise by which Díaz would have stayed in office at the price of democratizing his administration and making the Anti-Reëlectionists, in effect, the heirs-apparent. On several occasions there were negotiations. In particular, conferences in New York City March 11 to 12, between Madero's brother, Gustavo, who matched Francisco's idealism with an equal measure of realism, and the no-less-shrewd José Yves Limantour, Díaz's most capable cabinet official, led to rumors and speculations. So much willingness to consult, perhaps to compromise, and, conceivably, to be outmaneuvered at the council table, caused great unrest in the rebel army. Nevertheless, in late April, while investing Juárez under apparently favorable circumstances, Madero granted a truce in the course of his personal negotiations with various Díaz officials.[3]

The Junta responded to the various developments of March and April with a lavish, though disorganized, output of energy. In spite of the supercharged atmosphere at their Los Angeles underground headquarters, the audible results were no more than a series of half-muffled explosions.

For a time, two matters especially engaged Flores Magón's attention. One was the American troop movement. This action was prominently reported and loudly denounced by almost all left-wing journals as injurious to the revolutionists and as an ill-concealed prelude to intervention.[4] Flores Magón, who had weighed the possibility of American intervention for a long time,[5] penned the most vigorous of his diatribes, the editorial, "Attila at the Gates of Rome." In the spirit of the closing words of the *Communist Manifesto,* he cried: "The vampires of finance, the boa constrictors of Wall Street open their maws to engulf Mexico. Libertarians of the world, save the Mexican Revolution. Our problem is yours!"[6]

The Junta president, though well aware of the heavy damage done by the troop concentration to the Liberals' cross-border movements, nevertheless probably hoped to reap a minor benefit from the situation. In a curious letter, written in 1908, he made reference to the persistent American appetite for Baja California, and then accurately predicted the frontier situation of 1911. Using exactly the same reasoning as did Foreign Secretary Creel in the dikes negotiations, but hopefully rather than fearfully, Flores Magón anticipated that American troops close to the boundary would be bound to help revolutionary recruitment, since the presence of the troops would presumably engender in the minds of the Mexican people deep resentment toward the impotent Díaz regime.[7] As it turned out, the troop movement may have hurt the Federals and helped the Maderistas, but it did not produce an upswing in Liberal strength within Mexico.

The other problem which particularly concerned the Los

Angeles exile at the time was the ideological feud with Madero. During March and April this rose to fever pitch. Flores Magón's denunciations of Madero's part in the Silva and Alanís incidents were only one aspect. Differing with his rival on many other fundamental questions, political, economic, and personal, the Junta leader aired his opinions in *La Regeneración*. Some of these remonstrations merely reflected his hatred and misunderstanding of Madero, but others showed a keen insight into the shortcomings of the Anti-Reëlectionist movement.

With regard to immediate revolutionary tactics, Flores Magón complained that Madero was willing enough to use the Liberals for military purposes, but did everything possible to stunt their political growth. He also charged that his rival acted without consulting other revolutionary groups, behaving as if the revolution were his personal work alone.[8]

As for the Anti-Reëlectionist–Federal talks, Flores Magón suspected some kind of betrayal in the offing. The Gustavo Madero–Limantour negotations particularly aroused his suspicions. He contended that the "Provisional Clown's" only real aim was to become president: Madero wished to stop the fighting because the rebels (so Flores Magón maintained) were beginning to realize that he was not of sufficient caliber for this high office, and he feared lest the Liberals ultimately supersede him. Referring to the United States troop movement, the exile contended that Madero did not really oppose American intervention; on the contrary, he preferred a neighborly "pacification" that would prepare the way for his own free "election."

Fundamentally, argued Flores Magón, Madero was no friend of the poor. He represented the rich bourgeoisie, desirous only of replacing the Díaz Científico capitalists with his own faction of capitalists. His social consciousness amounted to safeguarding the wealth of his oversized family. Madero was not a true revolutionary: he was the "idol of the idiots."[9]

All of this aroused ill-feeling among American leftists. In pre-Communist days, radicals easily achieved a high level of agreement in attacking finance capitalism, but split into many factions when the opportunity arose to consider their own anticapitalistic program in the light of immediate action. In this instance, Flores Magón, despite his previous editorial of February 25, in which he had roundly denounced Madero as a traitor to the cause of liberty, and his subsequent bitter criticisms, continued to assume that radicals of all stripes would support him as before. However, the Madero question proved to be the catalyst that precipitated a clash of political ideologies: the perennial differences between anarchism and socialism burst into public view. This conflict became manifest when, in mid-April, one of the influential Socialist papers, the *New York Call*, published a long unsigned article which took up the chief question, as well as some corollary ones. This party organ had been backing the Anti-Reëlectionists on the assumption that they would help build a maturing capitalist system in Mexico as the prelude to socialism. Therefore, Flores Magón's anarchist denunciations of Madero shocked the American Socialists. Furthermore, the *Call's* anonymous contributor charged the Magonistas with having broken a tacit agreement binding American radicals, Anti-Reëlectionists, and Liberals to maintain a united front until Díaz should be defeated. Actually, the Junta had given no such guarantee, although perhaps some of their enthusiastic American associates had. The *Call's* article raised another sore point: the striking differences in emphasis between *La Regeneración's* English and Spanish sections. For good measure, the author delivered a personal gibe at the Junta's leader by pointing out that Flores Magón had not "at any time taken part in the fighting in Mexico," but did his "work . . . in perfect security in the office of 'Regeneracion' at Los Angeles on American soil." Finally, the Liberals were warned that if they were "a political organization," they could "hardly expect undivided support from the American Socialist party, which is avowedly political, as long as Ricardo Flores Magón remains its chief spokesman."[10]

For Mexico early in this century, Flores Magón's doctrine of anarchism possibly fitted the actual situation better than the orthodox Marxist argument as propounded by the American Socialists. Their contention that the politically democratic Madero would replace Mexico's feudal economy with a stable, up-to-date capitalism, which, in turn, would be the prerequisite for socialism, appeared a remote hope in that setting.[11] On the other hand, the heirs of Bakunin and Kropotkin hoped to transform feudalism into agrarian anarchism, and, with regard to Mexico's fledgling industries, to utilize the techniques of revolutionary syndicalism.[12] However illusory Flores Magón's hope of abolishing the institution of government might have been, in 1911 his economic program, at least in its agrarian phase, may have been better suited to the needs of the masses of the people than was the Socialists' long-range industrialism. Not only was Mexico an overwhelmingly agricultural nation, but there also existed in the country a tradition of Indian communalism.[13]

The socialist-anarchist disputes contributed to yet another change within the Junta family. About that time, it was announced that, because of her many activities, Mrs. Turner had had to resign her editorship of the English page. Both she and her husband continued to render important, unofficial assistance to the Liberals, but, for John Kenneth Turner at least, the association was no longer as close as it had been. Mrs. Turner's successor was William Owen, an English Anarchist.[14] Thenceforth, no discrepancies existed between the English and the Spanish pages.

Anxious not to lose the major portion of his American support, Flores Magón exerted himself to fend off his attackers. His agent with the *New York Call*, Julius Menke, immediately denied the charges contained in the article of April 12.[15] Meantime, the Junta leader, still seeking as broad support as possible, had made an effort to win the aid of the bourgeois American Federation of Labor by an appeal to Samuel Gompers. Gompers in his reply asked for a positive elucidation of all the Mexican revolutionaries' aims. Flores Magón's response amounted to semi-evasion on the score of the Liberal Party's ultimate objectives. Gompers thereupon dropped the matter, and his reaction in effect amounted to a rejection of the appeal by the American Federation of Labor.[16] The Mexican leader also addressed himself to Eugene Debs in an effort to avert the worst effects of the *Call's* criticisms.[17] This move was partly successful. In a response dated April 15, Debs criticized the break with Madero and called for the renewal of joint action; otherwise, he continued to give his blessing to all Mexican factions.[18]

On this note the controversy died down. Throughout its course, the anarchist and anarcho-syndicalist weeklies gave their unquestioning support to the Junta leader. Flores Magón had succeeded in allaying the dissatisfaction of some of his right-wing critics, but there remained a danger that another incident might alienate the only substantial segment of American support he still enjoyed.

Throughout the month of April, the factional strife did not have an adverse effect on finances, as the Junta's intake from subscriptions and contributions reached its peak. There were three main sources of income. First came the weekly's subscription money. At the time, its readership had reached the 27,000 figure.[19] Second, a minority of subscribers were able to make individual contributions in excess of the cost of the newspaper; some made offerings without bothering with *La Regeneración*. In addition to the usual radicals, there were a number of prosperous American donors, such as people misled by the innocuous-sounding name of the party, ardent sympathizers of obvious underdogs, cloistered radicals, some of whom were well-educated but maladjusted women, and cranks and crackpots. None of these people contributed large sums.[20] As an example, in union meetings among poverty-stricken Italian immigrants of anarchist persuasion, often each member would contribute from ten to fifty cents.[21] The cumulative effect of so many small contributions must have been considerable, however. Later, the office of the United States District Attorney for Southern California estimated that a maximum of $1,000 per month may have been derived from this source.[22]

The third source of revenue was comprised of sometimes substantial amounts coming directly from the field of action. Two springs were tapped. First came taxes and license fees assessed against Mexicali business enterprises, many of which were taverns. There was also an irregular levy on products transported through the Mexicali and Algodones customs houses. All of this may have amounted to $400 to $1,000 per month at the April peak.[23]

Finally, money came from one new and remarkable source. Anarchist doctrine sanctioned the tactics of confiscation of money and property on the ground that such value represented nothing but capitalist expropriation and theft.[24] That Flores Magón was an adherent of this theory is evidenced by his 1908 letter concerning secret Liberal tactics. Thus, after a time, his soldiers did more than issue receipts for borrowed property: whenever feasible, Mexicali property-owners were forced to make contributions which in terms of capitalistic values amounted to tribute, blackmail, and extortion. The result was a small reign of terror directed at Valley property-holders.[25] Several incidents provide illuminating illustration. T. P. Daly, the Cudahy manager, spent a weekend in Los Angeles negotiating with the Junta for non-molestation of ranch property in return for a promise of future contributions to the Liberal exchequer.[26] Doubtless he intended this as a delaying device until the Liberals should be ousted from the peninsula. Lou Little, whose misfortune it was to have his ranch constantly camped upon by both sides, conceded more than Daly, and "upon threat that if he did not pay tribute to the junta its armed force would be turned upon his premises, . . . paid . . . the sum of $500." In another instance, the "junta, . . . for a mere pittance, sold ten thousand acres of land to which a corporation owned by American citizens who have not responded to the demands for tribute" held title.[27] One can imagine the stir that this must have created among the stockholders.

Criticism of such methods has to be tempered in the light of the Federals' willingness to resort to confiscation, though not to tribute.[28] Moreover, in their case, there was no philosophical justification for expropriation. As for the Liberals, paradoxically enough, their archenemies, the capitalists, turned out to be their reluctant contributors. This circumstance, more than any other factor, explains the origin of the myth that American capitalism secretly backed the Magonista revolution in order to turn it into a filibuster.

The amount derived from this source is almost impossible to determine. At a guess it may have reached lump sums of $500 to $1,000 for brief periods.[29] The total income from all sources is likewise difficult to estimate, but may have amounted to $5,000 a month for a time in 1911, and $25,000 for the period from the re-establishment of *La Regeneración* in September, 1910, until June, 1912, according to a very unfriendly but perhaps well-informed source.[30] It would appear that this large sum dribbled through the fingers of the financially incompetent Junta as rapidly as it was received. Even allowing for heavy expenditures on propaganda, and much smaller ones on war materiel, the wastage was fantastic. As party treasurer, Enrique Flores Magón was chiefly responsible.

At Mexicali, the battered little army suffered a brief attack of acute melancholia, induced by Stanley Williams' untimely end. Fortunately, an infallible tonic lay at hand: the election of a new commander. Though Mayol's army still loomed, the vote restored confidence and good cheer: "Tonight the rebels were in high glee. They held an election, and Lieutenant Pryze [*sic*] . . . is in command. . . . They held a regular celebration . . . , and shouted their joy at the top of their voices."[31]

Caryl Ap Rhys Pryce, the newly elected leader, a Welshman in his middle thirties, was an experienced free-lance soldier. His cosmopolitan career had been shaped by the far-flung nature of the British Empire: service in the Boer War, frontier action in India and South Africa, and mounted-police duty in western Canada. While in British Columbia, he had occasion to read Turner's *Barbarous Mexico*. In January, the newspaper accounts of fighting in Mexico not only stimulated his love for adventure, but also roused within him a novel emotion of social consciousness. Consequently, he set forth for Mexico. On his way through Los Angeles he entered the Junta's service without bothering to check into his prospective superiors' political creed. As he had been enrolled at Mexicali before the first battle with Vega, he was a veteran by the time of his election. This born adventurer easily won the confidence of his tattered comrades by associating with them on the basis of social equality. He managed to turn his careful education and the British army tradition of his rather prominent family from a liability into an asset.[32] He soon made evident a dignified demeanor hitherto never associated with the Foreign Legion, thereby opening prospects of improved relations with the population along the border. Since the new chief adhered neither to the Stanley Williams razzle-dazzle school of warfare nor to General Leyva's ultra-Fabianism, a greater elasticity in tactics appeared likely. Though the election system seemed at last to have justified itself on purely military grounds, a wary Junta member—had there ever existed so incongruous a personage!—might have regarded Pryce's previous social and political connections with concern.

Great significance attached to this election. Whereas all previous commanders had been Mexicans, IWW's, or both, for the first time the leader was neither one nor the other. This change coincided with the steady shift in influence within the Magonista army. The bitter quarrels following the organization of the Foreign Legion had hastened the process of dividing Mexicans, IWW's, and soldiers of fortune into sharply distinct groups. During the five months of the revolution, the Mexicans usually retained numerical superiority and continued to strive toward Flores Magón's objective of a nationwide movement. Nevertheless, there were brief intervals, for instance in late April, when they were slightly outnumbered.[33] More important, their influence, which was always stronger at headquarters than in the field, tended to diminish in inverse proportion to that of the aggressive foreigners. Among the latter, the Wobblies, meantime, had developed a somewhat ambiguous goal, reminiscent of the "co-operative commonwealth" mixup. They seemed to think in terms of a utopian community only nominally subject to, or even separate from, Mexico's sovereignty, an area they could use as a base from which to attack American capitalism. Belatedly, the *Industrial Worker* vehemently denied that the IWW's harbored any such intentions.[34] Nevertheless, a characteristically bombastic Wobbly utterance, dated May 24, 1911, and signed not only by three IWW leaders but by the Junta as well, conveys a separatist mood and uses the word "country" in a rather equivocally ringing way:

> We cannot see why you fellows will stand for coffee and in the good "old U.S.A.," while we, your fellow workers[,] are living high and keeping the Red Flag flying here in our country as you see. We have got a Utopia down here. We do not work, and we don't get pulled for vags either.
>
> Now, fellows, this Lower California is a very nice country to have control of. It's not too hot and it is also a very rich country in metals and otherwise, and if you fellow workers back us up with men and money we will surely take this country and will be able in various ways to help organization work in the U.S.A.
>
> Don't believe the Capitalist papers when they tell you there is peace in Mexico because Diaz has resigned. There will be no peace in Mexico until the Red Flag flies over the working man's country and capitalism shall have been overthrown.[35]

From Mexico's standpoint only the third paragraph saves the statement from being outright secessionist. That the Junta sanctioned so ambiguous a declaration is astounding.

Simultaneously, the politically indifferent soldiers of fortune utilized their greater military experience to corner the unit's officer-level positions. With the exception of one Mexican, Adrian López, who served for a time as nominal second-in-command, the new general's close associates, C. W. Hopkins, James Dunn, Paul Schmidt, Captain Leclare, Louis James, and "Shorty" O'Donnell, were veteran adventurers or frontiersmen rather than rebels against society.[36] The IWW's, for a time, offered no objections to their own status as men in the ranks.

Enormous problems confronted the laconic, imperturbable Pryce. It was imperative that he improve discipline in his unpredictable command, increase its size, acquire more ammunition and materiel, improve liaison with the sister force of Mexicans at Mexicali and with the Junta, somehow allay the border population's dissatisfaction, and plan for an offensive that would free the army from its long association with the Valley and perhaps add territory to the Liberal domain.

The leader spent much time on the disciplinary problem. The week before the Battle of Little's Ranch, the more ob- streperous volunteers had again begun shooting at each other.[37] After Pryce took command, an unauthorized group, acting as if the American troops and the boundary were non- existent, raided a ranch on the north side of the border.[38] By curbing the men's homicidal proclivities, and by expelling the border-jumpers, the general improved morale somewhat. At the same time, the incidents warned him that the only sure cure for the soldiers' restlessness lay in taking the field.

By late April, the anti-Liberal clamor in Imperial Valley had risen by many a decible. When, living off the land, Pryce established his base on the hapless Lou Little's ranch, a newspaper reported that the rebels had driven the owner away, and were "having a turkey feast" at his expense.[39] More ominously, the *Calexico Chronicle* noted that the Farmers and Merchants Club, an influential Valley business organiza- tion, had denounced the rebels as predatory marauders, and had twice telegraphed President Taft asking for interven- tion.[40] Doubtless, Flores Magón's tribute policy, as well as the army's occupation methods, helped to embitter the com- plaints.That Pryce knew of the demands for contributions can- not be absolutely proved, though his position as leader made it almost impossible for him to have been unaware of them. In his public remarks, he confined himself to his own occupation procedures, and enjoyed some success in inducing the Ameri- can press to point out, belatedly, that circumstances made the Mexicali ranches the only source of food and supplies avail- able to the Liberals.[41] Peter B. Kyne, the well-known "West- ern" novelist, visited the band at Little's ranch, staying for a tasty dinner at the general's headquarters. To Kyne, Pryce de- fended the army's expropriations on the grounds that this was "a war of the common people" against "these big ran- cheros," who eventually would "have to pay the fiddler." As to the Liberals' methods, the commander queried rhetori- cally: "Suppose we do take a few mules and cows and raid a warehouse? Do they expect us to fight on a slack stomach?"

What had the ranchers to complain of, since all they had done was to acquire "millions of acres . . . for two bits an acre," after which they worked the land "with peons" that they paid "thirty cents a day Mex.?" Pryce also denied to Kyne that this enterprise was in any way an attempt to set up a new socialist nation in Baja California: they were "fighting out of sentiment to help the Mexican peones to get their rights" under the "constitution of 1836 . . . , or 1858 [*sic*]," he was not sure which, but it was an excellent constitution, and a pity that the Díaz regime had not lived up to it.[42]

Some of the ideas expressed by Pryce are identical with those contained in the Liberal manifesto of 1906. It may be safe to conclude that he had been provided with some information relating to that outmoded document. Yet, in discussing the late April armistice between the Díaz and Madero groups, Pryce, in mentioning Baja California's future, suggested a distinctly different emphasis: the reliable *Los Angeles Express* reported that the armistice negotiations would have no effect on the peninsular fighters "if General Francisco Salinas, commander-in-chief of the rebels, and Gen. Rhys Pryce, the Welsh commander of the American contingent of the liberal army, hold to frequently reiterated declarations. . . . While they are fighting for nothing less than the establishment of a socialistic commonwealth in Lower California, they might accept the suzerainty of Mexico as a condition of peace, provided all the rich concessions and great land area now held mostly by Americans are confiscated."[43]

This statement was memorable for more than its content: it is the only instance on record of an agreement on anything between Pryce and Vásquez Salinas. The latter spent most of his time in denouncing the Legion's seizure of ranch property.[44] In response, Pryce kept charging the Mexican, perhaps falsely, with desiring to poison the irrigation water used by the Federals.[45] When more ammunition and weapons were slipped over the line, Pryce appropriated 2,000 rounds, together with all the new rifles, leaving 1,000 rounds and the old guns to his "superior."[46] Soon a newspaper reported that "General Pryce filed with the . . . junta . . . complaint against

Salinas, charging drunkenness and cowardice. Salinas retaliated with a like complaint and as a consequence there is likely to be an entirely new commander-in-chief."[47] Belatedly seeking to avert additional trouble, the Junta dispatched political commissar Antonio de Pío Araujo to arbitrate the differences.[48] Before the latter's arrival, Vásquez Salinas was deposed, and unceremoniously pushed over the boundary by his own men. Since inability to get on with the foreign brigade contributed decisively to his expulsion,[49] it became obvious that the Legion commander exercised the *de facto* supreme authority. It remained for Pío Araujo to confirm Francisco Quijada in the shrinking office of generalissimo.[50]

The Junta agent, in turn, ran into trouble. Returning from the Mexican side, he was arrested in Calexico as a political suspect. After a week, lack of evidence brought his release.[51] Pío Araujo's assurances that property confiscations were a thing of the past[52] must have aroused considerable skepticism. As for the raids, Flores Magón dismissed them as minor incidents in the unfolding of any revolution.[53]

In the midst of these unsettled conditions, Flores Magón addressed a curious, enigmatic letter, dated April 23, to Pryce. After ordering him to collaborate with Vásquez Salinas in attacking Mayol, who had entrenched himself at the Colorado waterworks, the Junta chief continued:

Mr. Thomas Daly, superintendent of the Cudahy ranch, was here. He came to request the Junta's protection so that he may then bring in machinery, equipment for horses and mules, and people, with which to accelerate his agricultural operations. We informed him that if he were amicable with you, that is, if he were disposed to serve you, he had nothing to fear. We did this in order later to obtain a good sum of money from him with which to prosecute the campaign under better conditions. As soon as Mayol is destroyed we shall request a money loan and we are sure that he will loan money on seeing that the Liberal Party dominates the region.

Likewise we have some projects with the Imperial Valley ranchers for the same object, but the complete annihilation of Mayol is necessary first.

Place yourself in accord, then, with General Vásquez Salinas in order to make an immediate attack on Mayol.

Do not molest Daly, as he has offered aid, as I tell you. He made a special trip to request the Junta's protection.

We hope that by now Comrade Berthold's force is there, and if so, the rout of Mayol will be easier.[54]

Three problems arise in relation to this missive. As the message is contained in a very inaccurate account of the events of 1911, the Liberals' defenders have sometimes doubted its authenticity. However, corroborative evidence, as well as the letter's internal consistency, put its genuineness beyond question. A Los Angeles paper reported on April 21 that Daly had arrived in that city to transact some business. Furthermore, Mrs. Turner, in her reminiscences, refers to Daly's visit to Junta headquarters. Finally, an authority friendly to the Liberals has recognized the letter's accuracy.[55]

The import of the epistle is a second source of conflict. Velasco Ceballos, who first printed it, assumes that it furnishes conclusive proof that Flores Magón collaborated with, and received monetary support from, the American ranchers in an attempt to detach the peninsula from Mexico.[56] Actually, the letter simply proves the existence of the tribute policy. Though the ranchers occasionally provided money, and, more often, promises, they obviously did so not out of a desire to co-operate with Flores Magón, but out of grim necessity.

Lastly, did Pryce ever receive the letter? As it turned up in the possession of the Federals, and as the addressee was not careless, it is very unlikely. Nevertheless, it seems highly improbable that, under the prevailing circumstances, Pryce was unacquainted with either Flores Magón's wishes or with the Junta's dealings with the ranchers. During Pío Araujo's visit, and perhaps from other messengers, he must have learned of the Junta's desire for an attack on Mayol. Conversations with the outraged ranch managers surely must have yielded information relating to the forced contributions. At the Junta neutrality laws trial in 1912, for instance, one of the men in the ranks testified that he had acted as messenger in transmitting tribute from the field to headquarters.[57]

Whether the letter itself or merely its import was received, in some way the Berthold group at El Alamo was contacted, with a view to uniting the two forces for an offensive. A new stage in the Liberal Revolution lay ahead.

The Berthold party set off a string of fireworks in its six weeks' southern tour. After parting with Leyva at Laguna Salada on March 15, the heterogeneous collection of Mexicans, unruly Indian scouts, and tough IWW's pounded southward in a generally menacing frame of mind. Perhaps the Wobblies, many of whom had had mining experience, thought of El Alamo as a promising target because of its erstwhile reputation as a booming gold site. Except for a few Indian scouts, Vega had left the area undefended.[58] Some miles short of their destination, the Liberals suffered a stunning blow to their pugnacity: a long-range rifle shot from one of Vega's scouts struck Simon Berthold high in the thigh.[59]

The rebels spent a cold March night or two scouting the area in panic, while the few Federal defenders fled to Ensenada. Thereafter, the Liberals moved into the village.[60] The size of the force varied from fifty-five to one hundred and odd men, depending on the accession of stragglers from Leyva's defeat at Tecate, and desertions or unauthorized scouting forays.[61] By 1911, gold mining at the mine site had become strictly marginal; the outlook for sudden riches was dim. Messengers to and from Mexicali kept the two Magonista groups informed of each other's inactivity, but there was no immediate effort at reunion, despite Berthold's severe injury. With their leader *hors de combat*, the men aimlessly settled down to an extended occupation. The predominantly American-operated ranches in the surrounding countryside proved adequate sources for supplies and food.[62]

As usual, disputes arose. Mexicans and Americans distrusted one another. Several potential deserters aroused suspicion. Individuals shot at each other, and sometimes succeeded in inflicting wounds on their fellows or on themselves, all out of jealousy, spite, or a yearning for noisy recreation.[63]

To the disgust of the foreign element, thirty Mexicans and Indian scouts, led by one Juan Guerrero, departed on a little expedition of their own. On a southward push, they threatened on April 13 to occupy the tiny port of San Quintín, thereby causing a diplomatic incident. Frederick R. Kearny, a minor English official in the Mexican Land and Colonization Company, and an American merchant, Henry Cannon, put in a panicky request for protection. The captain of an English destroyer, the "Shearwater," which happened to anchor in the harbor, landed thirty men to protect the town. Before matters could be settled and the sailors swiftly withdrawn,[64] many Mexicans had jumped to an obvious, if erroneous, conclusion about the significance of an Anglo-Saxon landing of military forces on the peninsula of Baja California.

Back at the village, the residents of El Alamo and the rebels gradually made each other's acquaintance. Aside from numerous poor Mexicans, the population consisted mainly of American and English mine-operators and small shopkeepers. Some of the inhabitants were almost as unusual as their visitors. Among them were Constantin Dubois, a half-witted French Canadian vagabond; John D. Carroll, an American, living under an assumed name, who ran a supply store; Patrick Glennon, an Irish-American shopkeeper; and, surprisingly, an American physician, Allen L. Foster.[65] As sanitation and any comforts of life were entirely lacking, it was even more surprising that two American women resided in El Alamo. One was the doctor's wife, Mrs. Elizabeth Foster, a nurse. The other was Mrs. Nellie Meyers, mining speculator, nurse, palmist, and crystal-gazer. By a remarkable coincidence, she appeared in the village after a long, dangerous trek from Ensenada, almost simultaneously with the rebels. She remained at the mining site only about two weeks.[66] Still another interesting personage was a man named Fuzere, Frenchman by nationality, miner by profession, and Federal spy by avocation.[67]

Instantly, contact created friction. Dr. Foster, worried about the Federals' almost certain reaction, reluctantly attended the stricken Berthold, with the temporary assistance of Mrs. Meyers, whom rumor erroneously reported to be the rebel leader's wife.[68] In gratitude, the rebels constructed a shed for Mrs. Foster's horse, and presented her with Berthold's crimson saddle blanket.[69] For more than one reason, the doctor accepted the payment with a notable lack of enthusiasm. Relations with the shopkeepers Carroll and Glennon cooled as the rebels constantly dunned them for supplies. Seeking to find a suitable occupation for the uninvited guests, Carroll, who had a grudge against another townsman, offered them $100 to arrange his enemy's permanent disappearance. Objecting to plain, unvarnished murder, they clapped their would-be employer into a makeshift jail instead.[70] This sort of behavior provided convincing proof of the visitors' utterly unpredictable toughness. Hence, the party, reputedly 130 to 150 strong, acquired a horrendous reputation among the townfolk, who characterized them as "desperate characters" and as "tough a bunch of cut-throats as ever gathered together." Their especial fondness for dynamite was noted with concern, for having captured fifty-seven boxes of the explosive, they were said to have had "the paths all mined with 3 boxes under Mr. Johnstone's house, 3 under Pat's house, 3 under Mr. Raffi's house, having the whole thing attached with a battery ready to allow the Federals to enter the town without resistance, then blow the thing up and massacre what troops are left."[71] In adopting "dynamite as a means of warfare," the rebels were much helped by the peculiar composition of their force. With "all classes of artisans in their ranks, including miners, electricians, etc.," they would be able to systematize their handling of explosives into a standardized mode of warmaking: "Some of the men are provided with a sack or bag in which is carried lengths of dynamite with short fuses attached, and they propose, when hard pressed, to throw the lighted dynamite in battle. They also have bombs of various kinds." On top of this, they bragged "that each one of them is equal in fighting qualities to four Mexican soldiers."[72]

The common source for these second-hand accounts was Patrick Glennon. Whether such hair-raising preparations actually were made is difficult to prove. Normally, Wobbly bluster far outdistanced performance, but it is undeniable that they sometimes acted upon, or intended to carry out, their wild schemes. Glennon enjoyed the reputation of an honest man,[73] but, living in a tense atmosphere and constantly subject to harassment, he might easily have fallen prey to exaggeration. Probably some embellishments were grafted upon stories that contained some basis of fact.

During this time, Vega, at Ensenada, displayed an inexplicable inactivity. He made no move to drive the Magonistas out of El Alamo, or to provide relief for the frightened people there. Moreover, his continued neglect of the defenses of the capital caused the people there to dislike him even more. In actual fact, a gunboat stationed in the harbor, the "Guerrero," provided considerable protection against a potential invader lacking heavy guns. Nevertheless, the town was short of troops, and the governor did not attempt to train citizen-soldiers or to erect adequate bulwarks against a possible rush attack. Morose, distrustful, and distrusted, Vega sulked in the governor's house.[74]

As the capital could not be besieged from El Alamo, the Liberals decided upon hostilities by remote control. A telephone wire linked the two towns. The critically injured Berthold placed several threatening calls to Vega, demanding surrender. The colonel dared him to attack the improperly defended city.[75] Nothing happened. The "telephone war" ended in a stalemate.

Despite Dr. Foster's ministrations, Berthold's wound became desperately bad. Forced to choose between an agonizing leg amputation without anesthetic, with probable death from shock, or a slower death from gangrene, Berthold decided in favor of the latter alternative. Apparently, he consumed large quantities of liquor in his last days, in an effort to ease the excruciating pain. On April 13, 1911, Simon Berthold, wagon and truck driver, militant IWW, and *ad hoc* general, died and was interred in the forsaken hamlet of El Alamo.[76] Circumstances partly forced upon him an ignoble death, just as lack of opportunities had forced him to live a frustrating life.

Some time before Berthold's demise, it became clear that the army needed an able-bodied leader. Needless to say, the selection of a new chief aroused strife. Briefly, the Mexicans and foreigners uneasily agreed upon a Colonel José L. Valenzuela as the new commander. After a week, the inevitable happened: the non-Mexicans chose their own leader, an American, John R. Mosby.[77]

Jack Mosby, a soldier who was somewhat addicted to emotional histrionics, claimed to be the nephew of the Confederate guerrilla commando, "Speed" Mosby, and the son of a former partner of P. T. Barnum's. He also asserted that he had been a gunrunner in the Cuban revolt against Spain, an officer with the Boers in their war against Great Britain, and a participant in the Panamanian revolt against Colombia. One or more of these feats may have been spurious. That he had joined an IWW local in Oakland, California, seems very probable, and that he was a deserter from the United States Marines is a certainty.[78] As rebel commander, he displayed no particular tactical skills, and he had difficulty controlling the men except through campfire oratory. He appeared to be politically irresponsible, either because of naïveté or from ulterior motives. His chief virtues were a kind heart, and, eventually, a surprising loyalty to Flores Magón.

Whatever the obscure reasons that had orignally drawn the Liberals to El Alamo, the net result was inactivity. Mosby therefore had very little to decide. Nevertheless, his one political effort prior to the army's evacuation of the mining village was startling. In their visits to neighboring farms, the rebels became acquainted with the ranch heads. To one of them, Mosby and his men offhandedly tendered a proposition: "They offered to make Newton House, an American rancher near Alamo, the provisional governor of California. House refused."[79] Doubtless, such an offer, had it been accepted and implemented, would have been tantamount to turning the northern part of the peninsula over to American control. The incident perfectly illustrates how utterly irresponsible and indifferent many of the Wobblies had grown toward even their own objectives, not to mention Flores Magón's.

On April 20, the Liberals marched out of El Alamo, northward bound, probably after an exchange of messages with the Pryce group. Despite the terror in which they had been held, they had inflicted physical injury on nobody, and had ruined very little property except that of the two shopkeepers.[80] Valenzuela led a handful of the Mexicans back to Mexicali. The main body, which included some Mexicans commanded by a man named Francisco Pacheco, headed for Tecate.[81] As Ensenadans jumped to the conclusion that the Liberals were descending upon them, for several days they suffered acute fright. The Mosby men moved leisurely, raiding ranches for large quantities of supplies. On April 30, they camped near Tecate to await the arrival of the Pryce force.[82]

Numerous charges of excesses and atrocities were lodged against the erstwhile occupiers of El Alamo during this last phase of their wanderings. Evidence as to the accuracy of these charges is inconclusive, with most of the allegations coming from strongly anti-Magonista sources. The Federals claimed that there was deliberate and wanton destruction of ranch property, and abuse of women, including the capture of a terror-stricken girl, who was held incommunicado for three days.[83] Near Tecate, on May 2, the Liberals were surprised by a Federal scouting party commanded by Lerdo González, and, in the skirmish that followed, Mosby absorbed a bullet through the chest and lung. His companions transferred him across the boundary, where he began a month's slow recuperation.[84]

According to the most damning accusations, the rebels had tortured, then burnt at the stake, three prisoners who were captured in the fight in which Mosby was injured. Repeated affirmations and denials left the matter very much in doubt. A rebel named Farazon, who was arrested in the United States, reportedly admitted that the atrocities took place, but subsequently repudiated his admission.[85] Except for this doubtful substantiating testimony, the charges were based on hearsay claims. There was more convincing evidence of another misdeed. On April 30, Francisco Pacheco, who, on both sides of the border, had the reputation of a desperado, ordered three Americans under his command to execute the brothers George and Concepción Mason, as well as Plácido Mata. Each of the men had a family; Concepción Mason had six children.[86]

With Mosby incapacitated, still another leader had to be chosen. Again the army took up the ballot and almost obliterated itself in an electoral explosion. After violent arguments, the leadership fell to Captain Sam Wood, another American, until such time as Mosby should recuperate and rejoin the force.[87] At this point, the Pryce party arrived, and the separate existence of the Berthold-Valenzuela-Mosby-Wood unit drew to a close. It was none too soon. Serious violence might have erupted, either on the part of the border population or among the soldiers themselves, had the group continued its erratic antics much longer.

During April there were three foci of diplomatic and political activity: Ensenada, the Imperial Valley, and Washington. The Liberal ups and downs kept United States officialdom busy in a vain effort to determine the import of it all.

In 1911, the State Department maintained only one consular post in the Northern Territory of Baja California. At Ensenada, George B. Schmucker mounted a lonely watch. For the consul, life there contrasted sharply with his earlier environment. Schmucker had spent his formative years as a member of a middle-class family in the tree-shaded, dignified Old Dominion community of Staunton. The State Department had sent the young career Foreign Service officer to Lower California in 1909. During his first two years, the consul occupied himself with routine commercial endeavors and with largely unavailing efforts at controlling the long-standings problem of Chinese-smuggling.[88] A bachelor in his early thirties, Schmucker felt isolated at Ensenada. Nevertheless, he worked hard and displayed noteworthy conscientiousness. On the other hand, his very zealousness, on top of his loneliness, caused him to be overly nervous and prone to excessive worry. Suddenly, the rush of unforeseeable events increased his responsibilities in both weight and number. The rapid exchange of information with the State Department, his contacts with the scattered Americans, and his relations with Governor Vega became crucial.

At the time of the capture of Mexicali, Schmucker, in great excitement, had telegraphed for a warship to be sent from

San Diego to protect Americans at Ensenada. Secretary of State Knox's aides unhesitatingly tabled this request.[89] This urgent cry was typical of the consul's reaction to anything out of the ordinary. After it became evident that the port was in no immediate danger of attack, Schmucker's nervousness subsided for the time being. Never idle, he speculated on the rebels' political aims, for the benefit of the State Department, and provided statistics showing the presence of about two hundred Americans in the northern part of the peninsula, whose property, exclusive of the Mexicali–Imperial Valley irrigation projects, was valued at approximately a million dollars. He also interviewed Harry Dell, the suspicious-acting American arrested in Tijuana in February, whom he reported as probably using an alias.[90]

After the Liberals entrenched themselves in El Alamo, Schmucker's problems multiplied. This sensitive young man was greatly disturbed to read in the California press slighting references to himself in connection with false rumors of injuries to Americans in the peninsula.[91] Simultaneously, his relationship with Colonel Vega deteriorated, as the result of differences concerning the need for more protection for Americans. After Mrs. Meyers' return from her singular journey to El Alamo, the governor became so suspicious that Schmucker was barely able to secure her passage back to San Diego. At one point, the bullying Vega even threatened to force the hard-pressed consul himself to take ship.[92]

Schmucker was in the center of the confusion in the wake of the Magonista evacuation of El Alamo. In fact, his agitated conviction that an attack on Ensenada was imminent spread to the Mexicans, helping to intensify the panic. The excitement diminished only after Patrick Glennon, who came from the village, explained that the rebels were headed north. Since Glennon had had repeated conversations with Mosby and other rebels, Schmucker considered the storekeeper's information worthy of note. He therefore used it as the basis for a significant report to the State Department. According to Glennon, the soldiers were recruited from Canada, the United States, Mexico, and many European countries. They were all IWW's and "militant socialists or anarchists." Of the one hundred at El Alamo, sixty were Americans and other foreigners, and forty were Mexicans who had been residents of the United States. The men had been "promised $600.00 gold and 150 acres of land," and their object was "to form a socialistic or anarchistic republic in Lower California." Schmucker added that he had no reason to doubt the accuracy of these and other statements made by Glennon.[93]

Only three days later, Schmucker sent another apparently important telegram to his superiors:

Confidential. Circumstances seem to indicate that powerful American interests are working through Independent [sic] Workers of the World to establish a republic in Lower California, ultimate object annexation by the United States. . . .[94]

In the Valley, events kept General Bliss nearly as busy, if not as excited, as Schmucker. He was asked to give attention to the merits of the Farmers and Merchants Club's telegrams to Taft, Otis' continued pressure, the Pryce group's raids, the ever-present smuggling problem, and the tendency of military officers to make unauthorized arrests at the boundary. Bliss warned his officers repeatedly not to act as if martial law existed; he felt that any apparent laxness in the surveillance of the rebels' activities was an unavoidable consequence of the loosely drawn neutrality laws. The general described the rebels' behavior as "organized banditism," adding that "the most disagreeable feature is that the only really bad element is the American one."[95]

The last week in April found him especially busy. Bliss reacted negatively to an Otis proposal that his troops establish a three-mile zone of martial law along the border.[96] Then, as a consequence of the ranchers' telegrams, the War Department instructed him to investigate and describe border conditions. Replying on April 26, he stated that roving bands constantly halted canal work, and added that "the temper of the people is such that they may at any time feel compelled to take the law into their own hands."[97] Schmucker's message hinting at American interests backing annexation must have caused a stir in Washington, for the next day Chief of Staff Leonard Wood ordered Bliss to find evidence of any possible American interests behind the rebels.[98] The general replied that he thought the Farmers and Merchants Club, while exaggerating, nevertheless expressed a "well-grounded fear for the future." So far, no violence had been perpetrated by the rebels against the irrigation system. He was of the opinion that no "powerful American interests are supporting movement in Lower California with a view to annexation. . . . They could force immediate intervention by hiring one man to cut water system because 10,000 inhabitants of the Imperial Valley have no other supply whatever. The American interests on Mexican side border are demanding protection from organized bandits and they do not care whether protection comes from Mexican or American Government."[99]

So much turbulence could not fail to attract the attention of the United States Congress. On the floor of the Senate, on April 20, Senators William J. Stone, Democrat from Missouri, Augustus O. Bacon, Democrat from Georgia, and Elihu Root, Republican from New York, held a short debate whether a serious danger existed in the Imperial Valley. While the Democratic pair were inclined to be critical of all Mexican factions during their revolutionary travail, former Secretary of State Root, who usually expressed a friendly interest in Latin American affairs, counseled against hasty decisions with respect to border problems. Stone introduced a resolution asking the Foreign Relations Committee to undertake an investigation on the grounds that Mexico's unrest had led to a menace to American lives, to indiscriminate border shootings, to threats to the Imperial Valley water system, and to potential European interference.[100] Though the resolution was not adopted in this form, the result of the April 20 airing was a study made in 1912 by a subcommittee of the Senate Committee on Foreign Relations, looking into the revolution in Lower California.[101]

The Liberals had likewise made an impression on President Taft. In a private letter, he remarked that anarchy flourished in Lower California.[102] Never did he speak with greater accuracy. Whether understood in the conventional or the theoretical sense, indisputably, anarchy reigned in the peninsula.

CHAPTER VII

Intrigue at Tijuana

Mosby's march to Tecate was the first phase of an attack on Tijuana. Since the Alamo group and the Foreign Legion converged at the border hamlet, it may be assumed that they acted in accord. It is uncertain who conceived the westward plan. Probably it was the work of Pryce and his immediate entourage. Most certainly, it was not Flores Magón's idea.

Repeatedly, the Junta president urged that all Liberal forces join for an attack on Colonel Mayol,[1] who was camping at Bee River, a tributary of the Colorado, in literal fulfilment of his orders to protect Colonel J. A. Ockerson in the completion of his dike work. A defeat of Mayol would eliminate the only sizable regular force to threaten the Liberals. Perhaps Flores Magón also felt that Mayol's defeat would make it easier to link up with revolutionaries on the mainland. Though one can only surmise, it is probable that Pryce, with his considerable military experience, and, perhaps, some embryonic political ideas of his own, preferred a different arrangement. Since Mayol confined himself to guarding dikes, the need for a showdown with him seemed singularly lacking in urgency. Moreover, a move to the east would almost certainly be regarded by the jumpy population of the Valley as a threat to the canals. This, in all likelihood, would precipitate direct American military intervention, with a consequent abrupt end to the Liberal effort. On the other hand, there was much to be said for a march to the west. Capture of Tijuana, only fifteen miles from San Diego, might help recruitment. Also, for launching an attack on Ensenada, it was a much better base than El Alamo had proved to be. Should the capital fall, the Liberal possession of the Mexicali-Tijuana-Ensenada triangle would mean effective control of northern Baja California. Mayol would lapse into complete paralysis, and the Díaz regime would be unable to send reinforcements either by sea or via the west coast of the mainland, because of the desert and revolutionary bands in Sonora.

Accordingly, leaving Commander in Chief Quijada to hold Mexicali, Pryce marched west to the mobilization center at Tecate. As he set forth, the general wrote the Junta to cache 20,000 rounds of ammunition near Tijuana, the better to attack that point and to prepare for the advance on Ensenada.[2] In initiating this action, Pryce disobeyed orders, either explicitly, if he had received Flores Magón's letters,[3] or implicitly, if he had not. As with the tribute policy, he must have known of the Junta president's instructions, from Pío Araujo, from occasional messengers, or from recruits arriving from Los Angeles. In view of subsequent events, Pryce's disobedience is noteworthy. Mosby was guilty of the same offense. Flores Magón was greatly upset by the unruliness of his field commanders. He aired his displeasure in the postscript to a letter written in early May to two members of the erstwhile El Alamo contingent. Stating that Pryce had notified the Junta that he was heading westward, Flores Magón went on:

As he has begun his march already, a messenger that we have dispatched by the Mexicali route did not reach him. You will encounter him when you go along the route to Mexicali. Tell him that the Junta have decided that all the Liberal forces should march toward Mexicali, so that, once reunited, they may attack Mayol. There is no time for delay, comrades. Fly toward Mexicali.[4]

In addition, Flores Magón deplored the disputes that had

rent the El Alamo command. He found it inexcusable that, as a result, Colonel Valenzuela, accompanied by only six men, had marched to Mexicali to rejoin Commander Quijada in anticipation of the stillborn offensive against Mayol, while Mosby, with most of the others, had marched to Tecate.

Finally, after numerous exhortations to order and obedience, the letter made reference to the Liberal efforts in Chihuahua, illustrating Flores Magón's continued interest in his party's activities in other parts of Mexico. The Junta leader's expostulations, however, availed him nothing.

Of the several engagements in this five months' war, the first battle of Tijuana was the most bitterly fought. With weeks and weeks in which to prepare, Colonels Vega and Mayol had failed to take adequate disposition for defense against a lengthy siege, thus greatly increasing the hazards of one. Nevertheless, the leaders, Sub-Prefect José María Larroque, Blanco Silvio, Lerdo González, and Lieutenant Miguel Guerrero, as well as their men, were determined on a last-ditch resistance. Estimates of their numerical strength vary widely, ranging from 70 to 150; the correct figure was probably between 110 and 115.[5] Many were untrained volunteers. As there was ammunition for but a day or two of fighting, their only chance of winning lay in a quick seizure of the initiative. Although they failed to do this, they did put up a remarkable fight under extremely adverse conditions.

On the rebel side, Pryce, seconded by Captain Sam Wood, advanced with about 220 men.[6] The evident ferocity of his aggregation of enthusiastic revolutionaries, soldiers of fortune, tramps, and assorted drifters more than compensated for any divergency in purpose. As the Junta had not cached the 20,000 rounds,[7] the two sides were about even with regard to available ammunition.

After a vain appeal to Larroque to surrender on the ground that defense was hopeless and lives and property could be spared,[8] Pryce began to do battle. It unfolded in three stages. All day on May 8, the Liberals maneuvered into positions surrounding the town. Conserving their ammunition, they fired sparingly. Pryce's tactics earned him the compliments of Captain F. A. Wilcox, head of a company of American soldiers guarding the border, and General Tasker Bliss.[9]

In the second phase, after nightfall, the Federals, led by Guerrero, attempted a counteroffensive, striking from the south in order to simulate the arrival of a relief force from Ensenada. Their sortie penetrated up to Liberal headquarters, resulting in the fall of Captain Wood and Lieutenant Roberts, a Negro. Though it momentarily disconcerted the rebels, it did not, as the defenders hoped, bring about their defeat and withdrawal.[10]

Next, the Liberal commander divided his forces into three parts. Two groups were assigned to hold the approaches to the south and east, to guard against the possible arrival of Federal reinforcements. Pryce led the third company of eighty picked men in an attack at dawn of May 9. In this last phase, the fighting became intense. Without authorization, three buildings were burned when the defenders' stubborn resistance made charges ineffective.[11] The attackers, it was reported, "showed no quarter or mercy. They fought like demons, time and again rushing trenches or strongholds in the face of a veritable rain of lead."[12] By 10 A.M., the Liberals occupied the whole of Tijuana, and the battle was over. The remnant of the defense either took refuge on the American side or retired in disorder southbound toward Ensenada.[13]

On both sides the casualty list was long. The *San Diego Evening Tribune* estimated thirty-two killed, twenty-four wounded.[14] That the Federals lost many more than twenty dead is almost certain.[15] The Liberal general, who listed only nine fatalities in the public announcement, probably underestimated his losses.[16] Wood's death pointed up the unusually high mortality rate from wounds or fatal injury to feelings in the rebel high command. Without a wrangle, C. W. "Melbourne" Hopkins, a close friend of Pryce, was chosen as the general's first assistant.[17] Wood's demise may very well not have been a grievous loss, as it eliminated the possibility of a quarrel over the leadership.

After the battle, Pryce's actions suggested a sense of proportion above average for a soldier of fortune. Amidst the ruins and the burning buildings, he read a brief Episcopalian burial service, and ordered all bodies, Liberal and Federal, buried in a common grave.[18] As an adventurer's gesture toward those whose luck had run out in the midst of a fierce battle, it was fitting, but was it appropriate in a presumably anarchist army? Next, over the soldiers' vigorous objections, he ordered all potable alcohol, except beer and light wines, destroyed, declaring: "There is a time when it is all right to get drunk, but this is not the time."[19] Then, visitors were permitted into Tijuana, and, when reporters interviewed him, Pryce shrewdly hastened to deny that his troops were brigands who went about burning men at the stake: "When we have any fighting to do, we do it, and when we are through fighting we don't go around raising hell as the papers have stated. Of course, war is war, and we must live by what we can find or take."[20]

The final incident in the fall of Tijuana occurred as people clustered into the town and Mexican shops were looted on a large scale. There is general agreement that sight-seers were guilty of vandalism to a much greater extent than the rebels.[21] It was a shameful demonstration at the expense of the citizenry of a friendly neighbor torn by political travail.

Almost simultaneously with the action at Tijuana, another engagement took place. On May 8, Juan Guerrero's group of thirty-odd Indians captured the little port of San Quintín, which they had almost seized in April.[22] This time, no English sailors halted them. In terms of possession of population centers, the twin victories of Tijuana and San Quintín brought the Liberals to their peak.

San Diegans took an intense interest in the little army camped at their doorstep. At news of an impending battle, hundreds had rushed to the border, where, during the daylight hours of May 8 and 9, they had to be held in check by Captain Wilcox, who, consequently, became very unpopular.[23] As the populace had long since become blasé about San Diego's importance as a naval base and a choice site for army maneuvers, this occasion represented the first local display of genuine military activity since the brief excitement of the Spanish-

American War of 1898. In addition, the port city was going through a period of exuberantly aggressive civic expansion. Then, too, the victors' reputation preceded them. People visited the border village with curiosity whetted. They were not disappointed, for the ragamuffin band provided a spectacle to surfeit the most vivid of imaginations.

Men of all shapes, sizes, nationalities, colors, and dress greeted the curious. Some wore parts of khaki uniforms, others looked like cowboys, still others resembled tramps. Many were Spanish-American and Boer War veterans. There was a large proportion of very young men. A number announced that they were college students, though their attire and grammar seemed to belie the claim. Most evaded direct answers concerning their real names or addresses, so much so that some designated them "the army of Smiths." Doubtless, some had no home. Soldiers quit or joined at their pleasure. Though officer designations existed, a rough camaraderie replaced the usual military class distinctions.[24]

A visitor was likely to run into such individuals as "Dynamite Bill," whose sobriquet might merely have been an exercise in bravado, or might actually have been descriptive of his sinister craft: one never knew. If the guest chose to pay a call on the commander, he probably would be escorted by the general's orderly, a gigantic Negro whose appearance terrified friend and foe alike.[25] The essence of the army's style was accurately portrayed by a *San Diego Union* reporter, who glimpsed a German sergeant instructing his men:

"I vant you tam rascals," he said, in addressing the company, "dat ven I calls you, you come. I don't run my tam legs off hunting you, and don't you forget dat. Ven I vant you I vant you, remember. Ve haf no bugle in dis army, but ven I blow dis whizzle, it means you are vanted, and see dat you get here."
A negro at the end of the line called out, smiling:
"Dat whistle done mean Casey Jones, eh, boss!"[26]

Whether this was a circus or an army on display, San Diegans were all for it.

One fact struck everybody: this was supposedly an army of Mexican revolutionaries, yet the Mexicans were hard to find. In fact, during the first days following the capture, the Mexican Magonistas numbered hardly more than 10 per cent of the two hundred and odd men, since most of the Mexicans were with Quijada in Mexicali.[27] So glaring a disproportion could not fail to affect subsequent impressions of Magonism; it has long been a source of embarrassment to Flores Magón's staunchest defenders. In general, they have proferred two explanations. For one thing, they emphasized that the Baja California theatre was only one field of Liberal activity. Spokesmen for the Liberal cause have contended that in relation to the party's strength throughout Mexico, the proportion of foreigners that happened to be fighting in the one region was not excessive.[28] Also, they have stressed that many a fight for freedom has won the allegiance of idealistic foreigners, usually, as in the American War for Independence, enhancing the prestige of the movement. Madero, too, had the assistance of the great Garibaldi's grandson, a well-known liberal soldier of fortune of the day; and at Juárez a number of Americans had joined in the fighting.[29]

The analogies are specious, however. What counts in such situations are proportions and relative influence. While certainly Magonistas did fight in areas other than Lower California, they were submerged by the Maderista tide, so that the disproportion of foreigners in the peninsula was important. As for comparison with the American Revolution or Madero's movement, in neither case were the foreigners a proportionately large group, nor did their influence counterbalance the desires of the native leaders. Nor can the issue be resolved by regarding the IWW's among the Liberals as virtually identical with the Mexicans, for they behaved only intermittently, at best, as if their interests were the same as Flores Magón's. On this question the Liberals' critics have indeed detected a serious flaw in the Magonista explanation of the events of 1911.[30]

How did the two principals respond to the new turn in Liberal fortunes? Unfortunately, very little correspondence between Flores Magón and Pryce, or among other leading participants, exists for the period following the battle. There are only two bases for drawing conclusions: first, their actual behavior, as reported by the newspapers, and, second, various indirect bits of evidence from other sources that help in a reconstruction of their acts.

As events had already made plain, Flores Magón's theoretical mind was not equipped to deal with concrete problems, least of all unforeseen situations. What he should have done after the fall of Tijuana is obvious: it was imperative for him to cross the border, straighten out the tangle, probably dismiss Pryce, and head his followers in the right direction. A leader must *lead,* whatever the risk, or face the consequences. Yet, the exile stayed in Los Angeles. Whether he remained there in seclusion because of physical timidity or doubts regarding his ability to wrest control from the army leaders, his inaction increased the likelihood of still greater trouble to come. The most he did was to send profuse congratulations once or twice to his insubordinate general.[31] After all, the capture of the border town had increased the Liberals' prestige considerably, and anything gained in battle was worth keeping.

Liberal headquarters continued to keep busy with other endeavors. On the propaganda front, the celebrated anarchist Emma Goldman visited Los Angeles in order to exercise her oratorical skill on behalf of the Magonista cause. In an atmosphere of proletarian evangelism, a large crowd listened to IWW's sing workers' songs, and cheered "Splendid Emma" to the echo during and after her vibrant speech. At the rally $113 was collected.[32] From there, she went to San Diego, by coincidence speaking at Germania Hall on the eve of the Battle of Tijuana. She was well received.[33] In that city, the Junta were aided by Kaspar Bauer, a Socialist, and E. E. Kirk, a young liberal lawyer. Both were active in the Anti-Interference League, an organization of progressives and radicals founded some time earlier to oppose any possible United States military intervention in Mexico.[34] Through Bauer's initiative, the local chapter went further: it sponsored meetings such as the one at which Emma Goldman spoke. This sort of agitation must have helped considerably in replenishing the ranks of the Tijuana army.

In the weeks following the May 8–9 action, Flores Magón attempted settling his followers in Baja California. As he came somewhat closer to victory than did most anarchists, the practical implementation, however partial it was, of his equalitarian doctrines is of especial interest. The Junta printed an appeal, entitled "Take the Land." After explaining that the north of the peninsula was rich in resources and possessed a canal, the party leaders invited their readers to colonize. However, the Junta stressed that, as funds were lacking, the settlers had to pay for their transportation and moving costs, a stipulation which to these poor people must have been a severe disappointment. The newly arrived libertarians were to remain armed and alert, lest efforts be made to deprive them of their land. Every person would be allowed to do as he desired; at the same time, it was assumed, all would wish to seek a common goal. While in the past a man had labored long hours on the land for a meager return, communal effort would enable these pioneers to cut the work day to four hours and still reap abundantly. At the same time, there was to be privacy and individualism in family life. People would live in homes and have their own animals, utensils, and personal objects as needed for use.[35]

So much for the ultimate goal. Flores Magón's program for the period of transition resembled the socialists' ideas of society: on May 13, Pío Araujo, representing the Junta, issued a proclamation inviting townsmen to return to Tijuana, where "Security, Liberty, and Justice" were guaranteed: families would be helped, the poor given special consideration, and there would be no customs levy on the exchange of provisions or clothing.[36] Twelve days later, on May 25, E. E. Kirk issued a statement enumerating the rebels' accomplishments to date. Among other things, refugees had again been invited to return; the San Diego and Arizona Railway had been ordered to pay a minimum wage of $1.50 per hour and to guarantee a maximum eight-hour working day; and the civil authority, which controlled the military, was exercised by Mexicans, who acted on behalf of everybody, not just one class. Simultaneously, a Junta directive explained that, as soon as the Liberals were in complete control, the rich foreigners' lands would be expropriated on behalf of the Indians in Lower California, and, as Magonista fortunes prospered, in the rest of Mexico as well.[37]

Judging by the evidence, then, Flores Magón conceived of anarchism as unfolding in three stages: an initial period, comparable to what the moderate socialists had in mind for their ultimate goal, an intermediary stage of expropriation and consolidation, and, finally, anarchic equalitarianism by means of communism in production and small-scale individualism in consumption. In regard to the problems of production and consumption, there is some resemblance to the nineteenth-century utopian socialists' aims.[38] Otherwise, the approach calls to mind Marx's and Engels' plans, as elucidated in the *Anti-Dühring* and in the *Critique of the Gotha Program*,[39] except that, like Bakunin, Flores Magón wished to eliminate institutions as rapidly as possible during the transitory phase from the old society to the new. The Marxists' experience in inducing the state to "wither away" does little to encourage the belief that he would have enjoyed any greater success along these lines than they did.

Meantime, Pryce found himself in a state of suspended animation. His opportunistic march to Tijuana left him groping aimlessly for his next move. Reach where he would, there was nothing firm to grasp. At the time he enlisted, he had committed himself to the advancement of Liberal interests. But events in the Imperial Valley had not inspired his confidence in the Junta, and he had just provided a reinterpretation of their interests on his own hook. Surely the move to Tijuana would force headquarters to follow his plans for a move on Ensenada, or else compel the Junta to decide on a new policy. As his previous and subsequent military record suggests a man loyal to his commitments,[40] it seems probable that if the Junta had followed his lead, or, alternatively, provided him with the means to carry out their own freshly clarified plans, his allegiance to that body would have been re-established. But it neither denounced him nor sent the ammunition he had requested. The receipt of irrelevant rhetorical congratulations did not increase his respect for his superiors.

Within this context, Pryce began to cast about on his own, partly to elicit a commitment from the Junta, partly to prospect for new opportunities. True, he announced an early advance on Ensenada, where, as he put it, a "stable government," under a leader whom he did not care to name, would be established.[41] He knew, however, that many recruits and larger weapons were needed before a siege of the capital, guarded as it was by a heavily armed gunboat, would be possible. The recent victory, coupled with the radical agitation in San Diego, portended a speedy solution to the recruitment problem. Nevertheless, it would take time and artifice to smuggle ammunition across, and especially to obtain artillery.

As Pryce pondered, he had the opportunity to mull over the contents of two editorials appearing simultaneously in the San Diego press, the first of which was entitled, "May Cause Complications." The editorial writer first described at some length the efforts of the nineteenth-century filibusters to wrest the peninsula from Mexico, and stressed the deep-seated resentment that these encroachments had engendered. The Washington government had had to go out of its way to persuade Mexico that it had "no design upon Lower California" and that it would "sternly repress filibustering expeditions." Then he went on to say that it appeared "that a band of American filibusters, calling themselves 'insurrectos' and ostensibly taking part in the general movement against the Díaz government," were attempting once more to achieve what other Americans had planned previously: "In other words, the so-called 'revolution' in Lower California is simply another effort by dare-devil citizens of the United States to wrest that territory from Mexico." Looking ahead, he predicted a good chance for the success of the scheme, in which case, "the United States will have at its door a filibuster 'republic' or 'commonwealth'—whatever name may be given it—governed by a body of adventurers and fellows who have the best reason for remaining on the south side of the boundary line." He concluded by suggesting that this would "be embarrassing" to the United States, for it would give Mexico the firmest possible grounds for complaints based on the old fears arising from the numerous attempts made in the past by Americans against Baja California.[42]

The other editorial, written in the same vein and entitled, "The Future of Lower California," claimed that it was general knowledge that the Pryce force, which was about to move on Ensenada, was "largely composed of lusty young Americans." Assessing the group's objectives, it speculated that, "their motive is a mixed one. They are moved by the spirit of adventure. . . . But that is not all. They have read 'Barbarous Mexico'; their eyes are alight with the fire of revolution; they believe something of value to humanity will come of the struggle that is rocking the whole of Mexico today." Concerning the future of the adjacent peninsula, the San Diego paper worked up to a crescendo of civic parochialism: "Texas was conquered by Americans. It is American yet. . . . If Lower California should wake up some morning to find the stars and stripes floating over it, San Diego would suddenly become more than ever a City of Destiny."[43]

At Mexicali, Pryce had displayed a faintly equivocal attitude. It is likely that the editorials, as well as the general atmosphere in the San Diego–Tijuana area, stimulated his latent seditious thoughts. Here was a man familiar with South Africa in the wake of the notorious Jameson coup. To him, the situation in the Californias must have presented an obvious rough analogy. To an adventurer, the fact that Jameson failed would be less significant than the fact that he had made a sporting try. His British Empire background made it easy for the Welshman to view relations between well-established powers and economically dependent areas from the popular contemporary standpoint of Kiplingesque paternalism. As the *Union* editorial implicitly showed, service in the Magonista army provided a potential filibuster with an ideal revolutionary disguise. Nothing that had happened in the Imperial Valley could have encouraged him to believe that the United States government would smile upon a coup, nor did the *Union* editorial offer encouragement on this important point. Yet, rumors of the imminence of the event might help to change official attitudes, or, at least, open the way to new support. Why not take a few soundings to find out if a filibuster were feasible? At worst, the resultant mystery would create a public furor; at best, something might really develop. Accordingly, Pryce made himself available for interviews. A strikingly enigmatic note crept into the conversation of the usually laconic Britisher.

Shortly after the Battle of Tijuana, a man named Daggett, manager of San Diego's Brewster Hotel, asked Pryce what protection the occupiers would provide for his peninsular properties. The reply was inconsistent with the fulfilment of Liberal objectives: "Gen. Pryce laughed and said quietly, 'You'll be a whole lot better off.' "[44]

A few days later, the *Union* gave feature treatment to the commander's mysterious goals and curious political theories. While his general purpose, Pryce claimed, was "to free the peons," and "his views . . . [were] those of the Liberal Party," he nevertheless did "not deny" the possibility "that vast changes in Lower California's mode of government, even from what might be established by the rebels in Mexico proper, might be made." Again, as he had done when interviewed by Peter B. Kyne at Little's Ranch in late April, he advocated that the Mexican constitution be strictly interpreted and blandly asserted that this "would suit all wings of the rebel movement." Concerning Lower California, he considered "the idea of making . . . [it] a republic with which the United States will be glad to deal as a valuable addition commercially and in republican form of government." Specifically, "the government to be established . . . must be of the making of the Liberal party and an ideal form of republic, where white men, as well as Mexicans, can secure justice."[45]

This certainly was an astonishing potpourri of Flores Magón's, the IWW's, and his own political concepts. That Americans and Englishmen, who owned almost all of the valu-

Richardo and Enrique Flores Magón, 1916.

Mosby and Staff at Tijuana, 1911.

Both photographs courtesy of the Historical Collection, Union Title Insurance Company, San Diego, California.

Rhys Pryce, 1911.

Jack Mosby, 1911.

Both photographs courtesy of the Historical Collection, Union Title Insurance Company, San Diego, California.

The Red Flag at Tijuana, May, 1911.

Dick Ferris, 1908.
From the *Los Angeles Examiner*.

Rebels crossing the line after the surrender.

Courtesy of the Historical Collection, Union Title Insurance Company, San Diego, California.

able land in the upper peninsula, were deprived of justice had not hitherto been suspected; the announcement that the new regime would provide it was news indeed.

The following day, the headline of the same newspaper blazed: "American Flag Is Floated by Rebels. General Pryce Does Not Deny Desire to Give Peninsula to United States." The article thereunder recounted that Pryce, with a reporter present, "intimated . . . again . . . his fondness for the United States." This intimation was offered "in a significant way," because the topic of conversation was "the American flag flying over a building in Tijuana with the red flag of the rebels above it." In fact, according to the paper, there were "at least four places in Tijuana" flying the stars and stripes and only one place—the edifice across the way from the commander's headquarters—where the revolutionary flag flew above the American emblem. A rebel, standing in front of Pryce's headquarters and contemplating the double emblem across the street, reportedly said, noting the red flag above the American colors: "It seems a shame to see them that way, doesn't it?" Back came the reply, "I'll gamble that it won't be three months till the stars and stripes float there alone—and in the rest of Lower California too." As Pryce was within earshot, the reporter asked the commander to comment on the prediction, whereupon the Welshman answered without hesitation: "It sounds good to me."[46]

A day later, Pryce deftly retreated within the confines of orthodox Liberal doctrine. Complaining that the "popular conception" of their purpose was "vastly wrong," he distributed copies of a Liberal brochure which emphasized their aims: the defeat of Díaz, and land reform throughout Mexico.[47] In addition, the American pennants disappeared. Actually, the colors incident meant little, as most of the flag-wavers were American civilians with possessions in Tijuana who hoped to gain the protection that their flag usually afforded.[48] Nevertheless, as might be expected, the newspapers continued to buzz with filibuster rumors, and public interest reached a high pitch of intensity.[49]

From his headquarters, Flores Magón did his best to counteract the pernicious rumors. Under the caption, "Tijuana," he denounced stories that the American flags flew and that the Liberals intended to join the area to the United States as malicious lies designed to ruin the Magonista movement. Moreover, he reiterated with great vehemence what he had repeatedly stated on earlier occasions: "No, lackeys of Porfirio Díaz and Madero, the Liberals do not intend to separate Baja California from Mexico. . . . Baja California will be the principal base of our operations to carry the Social Revolution to the whole of Mexico and to the whole world."[50]

An administrator, Antonio de Pío Araujo, was dispatched to handle civilian affairs[51] and to make future announcements concerning Liberal goals. The authorized statement issued a few days later, on May 25, by E. E. Kirk denied that the Tijuana army was engaged in a "soldier of fortune campaign," or "filibustering expedition," and affirmed that the civil authority, managed by Mexicans, was in "complete control of the movement of the military," in whose ranks served "a large number of American volunteers."[52] These measures helped a little, no doubt. However, Flores Magón, by failing to dismiss Pryce, once more missed the opportunity to cut out a critical cancer.

A valuable week slipped by before Pío Araujo reached Tijuana. In the interval, Pryce undertook to initiate some important civil measures on his own. With no money and little ammunition, he decided to tap the tourist trade for revenue. Beginning May 15, all visitors were charged twenty-five cents for admission. More significantly, Tijuana was thrown open to all "good spenders," with faro and poker games as the featured pastimes. Southern California gamblers were to provide their own venture capital, and the army of occupation would collect a 25 per cent tax on receipts.[53] Plainly, Tijuana as a frontier Monte Carlo was much closer to the popular image of a filibuster republic than to the picture of the first stage in the evolution of a utopian society embracing all of Mexico. At any rate, business soon provided the army with an income running to hundreds of dollars. On two occasions, Pryce sent messengers north carrying sums of $313 and $150.[54] The emissaries were to inform the Junta to use the money to buy and send ammunition as quickly as possible; one of them was to supervise the completion and purchase of a piece of heavy artillery under construction in the backyard of a Socialist printer in Los Angeles.[55]

During these Tijuana days, a familiar but long absent figure swaggered onto the stage: the redoubtable "Daredevil Dick" Ferris, archintriguer. Since the episode of Miss Russell and the "Republic of Díaz and Equal Suffrage," the actor had kept an unaccustomed silence concerning peninsular affairs. His work in connection with a San Francisco Native Sons Fiesta had kept him from indulging in his favorite pastime of minding other people's business. In early May, Ferris began work on his assignment as manager of San Diego's Pan-Pacific exhibit groundbreaking festivities, scheduled to begin July 19.[56] He had committed himself to beat all his previous records as a purveyor of publicity. Just before he was to start on the humdrum preliminaries, the Liberal army conveniently swept into Tijuana. As a result of his February antics, Ferris' reputation as an organizer of phantom filibuster forces and a conjurer of cockeyed schemes for conquest in Mexico was secure. The Tijuana situation obviated the need to concoct any new gimmicks. There was no necessity for letters of introduction to get acquainted with the tatterdemalion army, and association with that aggregation could not fail to furnish all the publicity mileage any promoter craved.

On a visit to the frontier town shortly after the battle, Ferris got a *San Diego Union* reporter to introduce him to General Pryce. Incidentally, circumstances strongly suggest that this newspaper, or its reporter, consciously encouraged Ferris in his publicity schemes by providing him with unusually extensive coverage and by exaggerating his exploits. Ferris asked Pryce several leading questions. The promoter wanted to know whether the general was "working on his own initiative," or "in harmony with [the] junta." When Pryce replied that he was working with the Junta, Ferris opined that he was "too nice a fellow to be mixed up with that kind of bunch."[57] Pryce's answer indicated that, despite his trial balloons, he still felt some attachment to the Junta, or that he did not then feel able to sever connections with that body. The actor-adventurer and the soldier-adventurer became good friends. Possibly, it was Ferris who suggested installation of gambling at Tijuana, since in February he had advocated a peninsular "sporting republic." One wonders, also, whether he might not have had a hand in Pryce's "ideal republic" proposals. That Lower California was peculiarly destined for the "white man" was one of the impresario's favorite notions. Ferris visited the army camp quite frequently. As he described it, there were a "lot of very decent fellows . . . ; also a lot of cutthroats and outlaws, the most heterogeneous mass that could be assembled."[58]

By mid-May, it was known that Díaz was weakening rapidly and that Madero might win out in the very near future. No ammunition had arrived, nor were there instructions from the Junta. The military leaders had learned that John Kenneth Turner, who consistently maintained close contact with the non-Mexicans in the army, would soon visit San Diego. On May 17, Pryce, accompanied by his adjutant, Hopkins, was driven to the port city by Dr. James Jackson, a physician who had become friendly with the rebels while representing the Red Cross.[59] With Madero likely to win, Pryce and Hopkins decided to discuss with Turner the question whether or not they should discontinue the Liberal fight and disband the army. While in San Diego, they also called at the hospitals where the wounded from both sides were recuperating.

Dressed in mufti, Pryce registered at the U. S. Grant Hotel as "Mr. Graham," an English gentleman. Nevertheless, since the "hero of Tijuana" had become a local celebrity, he attracted a great deal of attention. In the lobby of the hotel, he was introduced to scores of prominent persons, including Louis J. Wilde, one of the city's most respected leaders. Mrs. Dick Ferris gave him the pleasure of her company for most of the evening.

The next day, before meeting Turner, Pryce and Hopkins were informed that they stood in imminent danger of arrest by the United States Army. Their subsequent flight toward the border was intercepted. They were apprehended, sent off to Fort Rosecrans, and at first held without charge. General Bliss had ordered the arrest in conformance with an April 18 directive of the War Department instructing him to take into custody all prominent rebels or Federals found on the American side of the boundary.[60] At first, it had been erroneously reported that J. Díaz Prieto, Mexican consul in San Diego, had obtained the arrest. While in custody, the two were well treated. Dick Ferris engaged a motorcyclist to roar out to the Fort with a change of clothes for the two distinguished exponents of libertarianism. Turner visited, and privately urged cessation of fighting, as the Liberals could not possibly oppose both Federals and Maderistas.[61] He also seems to have felt that Madero deserved a chance at governing Mexico.[62] The Junta, with whom Turner was in contact, did not see things in this light. Though unenthusiastic about continuing, Pryce and Hopkins rejected Turner's private proposal.

In Tijuana, consternation reigned after the leaders' arrest. Some of the men began to carouse heavily. After Pryce managed to smuggle out a message telling his soldiers to "stand pat," their apprehension was allayed, and the army's version of order was restored.

The legal ramifications of the Pryce-Hopkins detainment proved to be exceedingly interesting. Public sentiment in the area was strongly in favor of the defendants and against military arbitrariness. As with earlier arrests, the absence of martial law along the border made the army's case tenuous. The Junta and the Anti-Interference League employed E. E. Kirk to defend the two men. In addition, Ferris provided them with his own counsel, E. H. Lamme. He was doing so, he claimed, because of his continued hope to have Baja California the "white man's land" of Mexico, adding that Pryce was "a fit man to carry out such project, if the Liberal party would ever agree to such a proposition."[63]

When the case came up in Superior Court before Judge W. A. Sloane, Kirk turned in an excellent performance as defense attorney. He and John Kenneth Turner feared that the Mexican government might seize the occasion to seek Pryce's indefinite detention on the ground of violation of the neutrality laws, or, in popular parlance, "filibustering." When this did not come to pass, Kirk found it comparatively easy to induce Judge Sloane to grant his application for habeas corpus proceedings. Thus, the United States Army was ordered immediately to produce evidence to warrant the further detention of the defendants.

Late on May 20, General Bliss ordered the two released. After repeatedly telegraphing the War Department, the future chief of staff received a message on that day stating that in regard to "detention of Mexican prisoners, after consultation with state department and department of justice, secretary of war directs . . . you release the prisoners referred. . . ."[64] Interpreting the order literally, he freed not only Pryce and Hopkins, but all other war prisoners, Federal and rebel, including Lieutenant Miguel Guerrero, Jack Mosby, and Francisco Pacheco. Subsequently, the Washington government was annoyed with Bliss for his understanding of the ambiguous message.[65]

The early release of the rebel high command turned into a contretemps for Dick Ferris. His plan had been to dash to the boundary ahead of Pryce, then stage an elaborate demonstration for the general. Instead, Pryce and Hopkins were driven back by Dr. Jackson, arriving before Ferris.[66] All the manipulator could produce were a few anticlimactic "Vivas." The *Union* helped Ferris by reporting the incident as if it had gone off as planned: "About fifty of the rebels, mounted, met their commander and Hopkins at the line and almost at the same time recognized Dick Ferris. The rebels fired their rifles and revolvers in a welcoming volley and shouted 'Viva Libertad,' 'Viva Pryce' and 'Viva Ferris.' "[67] The *Sun,* on the other hand, insisted on the actual facts, stating that the party arrived "after midnight and just 10 minutes before the opera bouffe crowd came. At headquarters there was a quiet, earnest demonstration of welcome, no noise, no shooting, no reading of any comic opera manifesto. . . ."[68]

And what was Flores Magón's reaction? For the third time he failed to dismiss Pryce, though the San Diego press had given much space to the commander's amicable association with prominent members of the bourgeoisie, including the notorious Dick Ferris. In fact, though the latter's harlequinades had loomed as a serious potential threat to the Junta for several months and were becoming an outright danger to the Liberals since the fall of Tijuana, *La Regeneración* did not feel impelled to make a single reference to him in its issues of May 20, 27, or June 3.

Meanwhile, at long last the Federals swung into effective action. No credit, however, is due those two stalwarts of the ancien régime, Colonels Vega and Mayol. After the battle of Tijuana, near-panic again reigned in the capital, for the governor was no more helpful than was his wont. Amidst conditions of martial law, most Americans and other foreigners, as well as many Mexican women and children, took ship for San Diego. When the rebels failed to appear immediately, more normal conditions returned. Vega continued to lag in preparing defenses.[69] Over on the other side of the peninsula, Mayol, who was handicapped by a small army of refugees, cautiously made preparations to return to Ensenada without attacking Tijuana.[70]

By contrast, Federal sympathizers in southern California were very active. Many border Mexicans became convinced that the territorial integrity of the country was endangered. From the beginning, this had been Vega's claim, but the ill-tempered and unsubstantiated contentions of the dictatorial governor had impressed very few. But after publication of many photos showing Tijuana occupied by heavily armed, rough-looking, obviously foreign types, no Mexican could be blamed for feeling uneasy. Now it was Flores Magón's turn to find it hard to convince peninsulars, as his finespun theories concerning the aid he obtained from ideologically reliable foreigners seemed to collapse before the hard facts of life across the border.

Among those active in organizing the anti-Liberal drive were Dr. Horacio E. López, Carlos Mendoza, and Consul J. Díaz Prieto of San Diego, and, in Los Angeles, Consuls Antonio Lozano and Arturo M. Elías.[71] The Federal activists, though they often charged the Magonistas with bad faith and dubious conduct, did not trouble themselves any more about fine distinctions than did their rebel opponents. For instance, the consuls clearly exceeded their authority by recruiting men. A letter found on sub-Prefect Larroque's body after the Battle of Tijuana indicated that Consul Díaz Prieto was busy recruiting, and had even sought financial aid from wealthy Americans.[72] As a device to arouse Mexican workers in Los Angeles against Flores Magón, an assistant in the consular office, using an assumed name, published an ungrammatical open letter, purportedly from a laborer, accusing the exile of being the clandestine driving force behind vandalistic filibustering in Baja California.[73]

In San Diego, Dr. López was instrumental in organizing a society, the "Defenders of the National Integrity." Since this group had access to people with comfortable or sizable incomes, it far outdistanced the Magonistas in the speedy collection of funds, in spite of its very recent origin. For example, in just two meetings at Germania Hall $1,000 was donated.[74] On May 22, the Integrity committee announced it had received $10,000 in contributions.[75] As spokesman, Dr. López offered, for the friendly *Evening Tribune*, a psychological explanation of the career of Flores Magón. He held that at one time the Los Angeles revolutionary had been the victim of unjust persecution, but, deserted recently by numerous friends and adherents, he had become a cynical hypocrite, and, embittered by the cruelties he had suffered, was taking out his spite on the entire nation: "This man Flores Magón is a dreamer, but a dreamer of evil dreams. He is doing more to harm his country than its worst enemies have ever done. . . . In theory, his program sounds all right, but in attempting to carry it out he has succeeded in attaining exactly the opposite results to what he claims his party will do."[76]

The San Diego Federals issued a widely distributed circular, making the following charges: The Liberal army consisted of foreigners who intended to deprive Mexico of the northern part of her peninsula. In Tijuana, a hard-working merchant's house had been turned over to a gambler. "Wide open" towns were the only result of their "Eutopian [*sic*] campaign." Criminals had taken refuge in their ranks. If Lower California remained in the Liberals' hands, the area would be no more than a center of crime, immorality, and vice.[77] That some of these charges hurt, and hurt badly, may be gathered from Kirk's statement of May 25 and Flores Magón's outburst in the May 20 issue of *Regeneración*.[78]

The Integrity people notified Governor Vega of their work,[79] and began to ship volunteers to Ensenada. In doing so, they resorted to wholesale violation of the United States' neutrality laws, the very offense which had aroused Federal ire against the Magonistas and the United States government. Since they hardly attempted concealment, they were readily detected. Pryce, Kirk, and Pío Araujo reminded the authorities of their duty, and, on May 25, the leaders, including López and Mendoza, were arrested at the San Diego docks, as a band blared out the Mexican national anthem, and a ship prepared to lift anchor.[80] The incident outraged the Mexican government. Anxious to mollify it, the Washington authorities ordered the release of the men on May 31. Most of them subsequently made it to Ensenada.[81]

By the month's end, about 150 volunteers had reached the capital.[82] Vega did not seem to appreciate them. He was detected in an attempt to deprive them fraudulently of part of their pay. A secret report, dated June 1, to the Ministry of Justice detailed his misdeeds, and virtually recommended his dismissal.[83] In spite of the governor's ineptitude, the Federal resistance had gained greatly in terms of numbers and stiffened morale, while the Magonista army underwent a corresponding psychological decline.

While Baja California witnessed such stirring events, much had been taking place in mainland Mexico as well. The April conference with Díaz officials, undertaken by Madero while he was investing Juárez, had bogged down after two weeks of negotiation.[84] As a result, the battle-and-bargain period of the Anti-Reëlectionist revolution came to an end.

A climactic phase, lasting less than three weeks and ending triumphantly for the Maderistas, thereupon opened. It commenced unexpectedly when Madero ordered a withdrawal from Juárez lest fighting result in shooting into El Paso, only to have his army, impatient after so much parleying, defiantly launch an attack on the border city. In the ensuing fighting, the Maderistas captured Juárez at the same time as Pryce took Tijuana. As many people, including the Tijuana army leaders, had anticipated, Madero's triumph proved decisive. In the following fortnight, the rebel forces routed the government armies all over Mexico. The old dictator had to admit defeat. On May 21, his representatives reached a peace accord with Madero at Juárez. Four days later, Díaz resigned, and departed for exile in Europe.[85]

The postlude was curious. More anxious to end fighting than to press for a complete victory, Madero naïvely gave away half of the rebels' well-earned fruits of victory by permitting Francisco de la Barra, Díaz's last foreign minister, to act as interim president, pending free elections.[86] In the weeks that followed, this arrangement made the restoration of normal conditions difficult. The victor had reduced himself to the function of mere adviser and go-between, influential but lacking the sanction of public office. On the other hand, the conservative de la Barra occupied the executive seat, but, because of Madero's popularity and his own identification with the repudiated regime, lacked the prestige and perhaps the desire to perform effectively.

The Liberal Junta reacted vigorously. The outcome had confirmed Flores Magón's suspicions concerning Madero's negotiations. After the failure of the conference preceding the Battle of Juárez, he insinuated that Madero had been trying to arrange with Díaz a liquidation of the revolution in return for 20,000,000 pesos. The great movement would continue if the army would only compel Madero to return to the United States.[87] The Junta's response to the end of the fighting and the designation of de la Barra as temporary president was a policy statement announcing that, regardless of what others might do, the Liberals would continue their fight to carry out an economic revolution. They would do this with the armed forces they claimed to have doing battle throughout Mexico.[88] Despite this display of defiance, within a month's time the peace brought about by Madero fatally undermined the Liberals. After Díaz had gone into exile, most people did not look beyond the formal political victory achieved, so that it was difficult to engender much enthusiasm for a continued fight.

Upon his return to Tijuana, Pryce, once again heading the army, watched it grow numerically, notwithstanding the recent discouraging events. The tourist traffic made it very easy for men to join. There was a steady influx of IWW's, who, after drifting into San Diego, would cross the line.[89] One colorful personage who entered the rebel ranks during this time was the famous Wobbly troubadour, Joe Hill.[90] On May 28, after their return from San Quintín, Guerrero's forty Indians came in. Simultaneously, thirty Mexicans from Juárez and about fifty Italian anarchists from the Northwest arrived.[91] Possibly, also, Ferris, who had a knack for staying barely within the limits of the law, caught the spirit, and verbally encouraged stray adventurers to join the army.[92] Pryce followed a laissez faire policy, accepting all comers, whether social radicals or soldiers of fortune. At the close of May, the army reached the peak of three hundred to five hundred men. Mexicans still made up far less than half of the total. The adventurer element outnumbered the IWW's.[93]

The newspapers repeatedly charged the army with harboring a choice collection of California criminals and desperados. Specifically, there were stories that Marshall Brooks, cattle rustler from Campo, California; Henry Hall, trunk-looter, who with Brooks had effected a sensational escape from the San Diego jail several years before; "Mojave Red," charged, among other things, with beating a man's brains out; Sam Barron, a train robber; and James Dunham, famed Los Gatos axe-murderer of his wife and several in-laws, were in the troops at Tijuana. Kirk's statement sharply denied the rumors. The soldiers explained that they had rejected "Mojave Red's" offer of his services, shoving him back across the line. It is possible that Brooks and Hall were at Tijuana, since many visitors reported talking to them.[94] As for the others, it would be impossible to determine.

Too often, individual soldiers belied the leaders' claims of a law-abiding army. The army was constantly plagued by the

personnel's "carelessness." On the night of Pryce's return, Otto
Sontag, a German, was killed on sentry duty by another sentry.[95] Ten days later, a more serious incident occurred. Francisco Pacheco, who had returned to service, and another Mexican, Tony Vegas, quarrelled over the management of a tavern.
Vegas challenged Pacheco to a duel. When the latter refused,
Vegas shot him anyway. Pacheco fell dead. The affair occurred
at a time when tension between Mexicans and non-Mexicans
had once again grown rife. The Mexicans liked Pacheco, the
others, Vegas. After deploring the violence, Pryce, at the Mexicans' insistence, reluctantly ordered Vegas court-martialled
and shot at dawn of May 31.[96]

Only once, in late May, did the possibility of a new major
battle arise, at the time when Mayol returned to Ensenada.
That the troops had lost none of their zeal was plain from the
soldiers' attitude. Because everybody demanded to fight, those
designated to be left behind to guard Tijuana proved poor
sports, and almost started a civil war with the ones lucky
enough to go on the Mayol hunt.[97] But it made no difference,
for the colonel slipped through to Ensenada because of the
shortage of amunition.

After his return, Pryce again found it impossible to act.
His temporary arrest made it plain that American officials
were not interested in encouraging a potential filibuster. The
Junta's thought processes continued to be unfathomable to
him. Just after the armistice at Juárez, he made the specious
declaration that he "always stood with the junta, still supports
and will continue to be governed by its views."[98] Then came
the Junta's policy statement on continuing the revolution,
about which he learned only by reading the newspapers. The
statement was not implemented by any specific orders.[99] In
effect, the Junta asked the army to fight on, but without instructions and without ammunition. As for the other possibilities, there was a potential value in Ferris as a free publicity
agent who might attract new sponsors, unless his comic-opera
pranks should reduce everything to absurdity. However, no
matter how useful he might prove, the promoter could not
possibly solve the weapons problem.

Though he was thinking of quitting,[100] the general desultorily resumed his filibuster sparring. According to a *Chicago Daily Socialist* report, "Pryce speaks modestly, but the dream of empire is in his eyes. It is empire for the common man, as he tells it. He stands on the revolutionary manifesto of Ricardo Magón. . . ." A strong military government would "be followed by a model state with the most advanced institutions. Such a state could live under a liberal regime in Mexico, or as a separate republic, or as part of the United States."[101] The *San Francisco Chronicle's* account was slightly different; it speculated that the general "might effect an arrangement either with the provisional government to establish a socialistic regime in Baja California, or with the United States Government for the admission of the peninsula as a state under the same status as Texas when it came into the Union." The northern California daily also knew from hearsay that Pryce had "declared his intention of hoisting the United States flag if he could receive assurance that Washington would look upon such an act with favor."[102]

Of greater practical significance, after his release Pryce and his officers talked over the possibility of disbanding the army. On May 30, he made up his mind to have a conference with Flores Magón and, if possible, John Kenneth Turner. He had about decided to quit, or, possibly, to continue if the confusion and uncertainty could be resolved to his own satisfaction.[103] Dick and Mrs. Ferris drove Pryce and his friend, Hopkins, to the San Diego railway depot, travelling the fifteen miles on a flat tire. Because he left in secrecy to forestall the possibility of a second arrest on the American side, his men were dismayed when they discovered that he was gone. The story spread that he and Hopkins had absconded with the rebel's war chest of $8,000. A check of the records by an army committee showed the rumor to be baseless[104]—actually, only about a tenth of that amount had been collected at Tijuana.[105] Pryce carried about $20 in expense money with him.[106] After midnight, the two boarded the Los Angeles–bound "Owl," determined upon a showdown with Flores Magón.

CHAPTER VIII

The Ferris Filibuster

Several pressing issues stood in dire need of clarification as Pryce, accompanied by his second-in-command, boarded the "Owl." The money that he had sent north had been meant as a prepayment for supplies and ammunition, and he was anxious to find out why nothing had been delivered.[1] As he could not conceive of a policy of continued fighting without specific orders, he intended to ascertain what these were.[2] According to the *San Diego Union*,[3] he planned to submit three alternative proposals for the Junta's consideration: First, the Liberals should recognize the de la Barra regime as the legal government, provided the latter, in turn, gave fair recognition to the rebels' services, "and fair representation [to them] in the government of Baja California." (Actually, at the end of May, arrangements on this basis might have been possible, had Madero been the intermediary. Had that happened, the Magonista soldiers would have received some kind of recompense for their services.) Second, defy de la Barra and Madero, secure the support of Figueroa's army in south Mexico, and fight the Maderistas on all fronts. At this time, the Junta leaders deluded themselves into believing that Madero's sometime ally, General Ambrosio Figueroa, was a prospective Magonista. With or without Figueroa, this plan would have required more weapons, ammunition, and men than the Liberals had ever disposed of. Third, disband the troops at Tijuana and elsewhere. In general, the officers felt that the impact of recent political events on the mainland of Mexico would almost force them to choose this third path.

A few stray comments by Pryce comprise the only information extant concerning the Los Angeles meeting. As his remarks are not inconsistent with other information, it may be assumed that he spoke accurately, if very incompletely. The confrontation in the dark offices on the second floor at 519½ East Fourth Street must have been unusual in the extreme. Two men more different it would be hard to imagine. The hunted theoretician and the enigmatic soldier of fortune, separated by nationality, language, occupation, values, and aims, met to discuss matters of mutual interest! There were none, and neither man had the slightest comprehension of what the other was thinking.

One object of the general's trip was to get the Junta to send some of their members south to observe the unsatisfactory conditions. Apparently, he thought that an investigating committee or commission would verify his analysis of the situation, and probably order an end to the fighting. He was confident, in any case, that the soldiers would quit, should he not rejoin them.[4] Actually, when the commission did go down, it helped to arrange a continuation of the military effort. This unexpected development came about partly because Pryce had overestimated the extent of the soldiers' allegiance to him, and partly because the commission arrived in the midst of some startling events which made many of the men willing to continue the struggle. As for himself, Pryce made it plain that he would not go back until the commission had investigated and reported.[5]

In view of earlier events, Flores Magón should have been only too anxious to encourage this troublesome adventurer in his desire to quit. Instead, he urged him to resume his command at Tijuana. Moreover, the exile described Madero as "worse than Díaz," a statement that amazed the Britisher.[6]

According to Pryce, his connection with Flores Magón and

the Junta came to an end as the general asked again what they proposed to do for the army: " 'We cannot do anything,' they said, 'we have no money.' 'Then good-by,' said I."[7]

At this time, Hopkins, using his *nom de guerre,* "Melbourne," wrote a letter to his friend James Dunn, who had been wounded in the Battle of Tijuana. As it turned out, Dunn had rejoined the army before Hopkins mailed the letter advising him not to do so. Evidently, federal authorities intercepted it. This document is valuable for several reasons. It sheds light on many of the events of May, reveals the feelings of the officers concerning the Junta, and refers to some of the Tijuana army's internal troubles. In addition, there are a few obscure references, the meaning of which can only be surmised. The letter largely explains Pryce's frame of mind, as his second-in-command reflected the general's thinking except on the matter of leaving: Hopkins was more determined than Pryce to quit. Finally, in the two-day interval between the date that Hopkins wrote the main portion and the time that he added his postscript, a great deal happened at Tijuana:

LOS ANGELES, June 1, 1911

JAMES DUNN, POINT LOMA

DEAR FRIEND:

I am writing you . . . to give you the facts of my case. . . . Pryce and I left . . . to confer with the junta. The officers all knew that Pryce was coming up. We did not think it advisable to tell the boys. Neither of us took a cent from the funds. . . . On account of the junta not assisting us, we have had a hard time to get ammunition, etc. We raked in about $850 from license fees, etc., and were holding it with the intention of getting field pieces and machine guns, expecting the junta to come through with rs. and amm. They have been receiving contributions right along and never came through with a gun or a cartridge. But that was not the worst. They did not send anyone down to transact the official business of the town, excepting toward the last they sent one down to handle the customs. All they ever did was to write letters of congratulation. Mayol got away from us on account of lack of ammunition. When we marched from Little's ranch Pryce sent a letter to the junta asking that 20,000 rounds be sent to Tijuana to be ready for us when we arrived. They did not do this, nor did they even reply to the letter. If this had been sent we could have

marched directly on Ensenada before Mayol could have started
from Bee River. . . . It disgusted us so much that we decided to
quit. Even after Madero had won out and declared . . . us to be
filibusters, etc., the junta did not visit us. Only through the
papers we learned of their intentions. J. K. T. [John Kenneth
Turner] visited us while at the fort and said that we could not
fight the feds. and the Maderists, as the junta wanted us to do.
We had a meeting of the officers after we got back and practically decided to throw it up. We were leary of the Mexicans and
did not know how to go about it for the best. We were afraid
that on account of the junta still ordering us to continue the
fight that if we had a meeting of the boys and declared it all off
the Mexs. would call all filibusters, etc., and start a young civil
war among us. On the other hand, we figured that if Pryce blew,
the bunch would disappear.

Your gun was stolen by some one. It was in Schmidt's company, and I showed him your letter, but he did not appear to be
very eager to return it; next I heard it was gone. He was out of
town when I left or I would have seen him about Nolan, though
he would not have moved in the matter, I know. He was all for
B company. He caused lots of ill feeling among the boys. If a
saddle or horse was stolen, B company had it. Pryce had already
sent $10 up to you when I spoke to him about your letter. I
wanted to send you another 20, but it was too late.

MELBOURNE

June 3

Just saw James; he tells me he saw you down there. . . . I was
hoping that this letter would reach you in time to prevent you
from going down. As far as I can see, the game is up—that is, the
financial end of it—and I do not feel like risking my life for nothing. . . . My next move will be either South America or the South
Seas. James says you are all right except for the bullet in the
shoulder. Hope you get it out soon.

If you wished to keep in touch with me, address me care of
Dick Ferris; he is a good fellow and can be trusted.

Address: C. W. Hopkins, care of Dick Ferris, U. S. Grant Hotel, San Diego.

P.S. When you have read this, burn it.

P.P.S. Will write further when I receive an answer from you.
Am working on the "Pearl proposition."[8]

Numerous details in the letter are verifiable. It is accurate as
far as it goes.

The soldiers at Tijuana had not been given advance intelligence concerning Pryce's mission to Los Angeles, nor had they been informed of its purpose. As a result, his sudden departure produced chaos. The order of things had already been undermined by uncertainty about the future and by bickering of long standing, climaxed by the Vegas-Pacheco tragedy. Now, the rebels split once more into three factions: adventurers, IWW's, and Mexicans. Within each of these factions there were dissident movements, thus compounding confusion. Not many troops were left in the bedlam-ridden town; some had deserted when they heard the rumor that Pryce would not return, and others were out on patrol duty.[9]

Thursday, June 1, was hectic. An old problem reasserted itself. Pryce had left the camp in charge of Acting General Tamlyn. On a few previous occasions, during the temporary absence or elimination of a regular leader, the rebels had relied on an acting commander. This time matters varied somewhat: should the duly elected general really have quit, it was necessary to choose a new one. Among the candidates were Tamlyn, Captain Paul Schmidt, who had filled in briefly as leader after Williams' death and during Pryce's incarceration, and a Captain Curtiss. A fourth aspirant turned up in the person of Jack Mosby, who, having partially recovered from his wounds, crossed over to Tijuana, spoke to the men on behalf of his own candidacy, and was well received by his audience. However, Tamlyn was elected commander, pending clarification of Pryce's status and intentions, and with the added, potentially contradictory, proviso that Mosby, after his full recuperation, would be installed as general. These agreements were highly tentative, because of the absence or desertion of many men and the friction among the several factions. Simultaneously, in San Diego, the Anti-Interference League, led by Kirk, was trying to keep in touch with the Junta and Pryce concerning their plans.[10] Lastly, a Los Angeles news item, carried by the *San Diego Union* on June 2, quoted Pryce as saying "that members of the junta, probably headed by the president, Ricardo Flores Magón, are due to arrive in San Diego on the Owl train this morning"—that is, on Friday.

Friday dawned, marking the third day without Pryce and

the third day without any action by the Junta. Moving slug-
gishly, the dazed Liberal leaders had dispatched their commission, which arrived in Tijuana just too late, on that Friday,
to avert a catastrophe. The vacuum had been filled by the
ubiquitous Dick Ferris.

The mystifying events of June 2 to 5, and especially the peculiar incidents of June 2, constitute the eye of a veritable
hurricane of disputation which to this day, whenever the issue
happens to arise, works havoc among interpreters of the Baja
California situation. The evidence available consists of Ferris'
sworn testimony before a United States Senate Foreign Relations Subcommittee, newspaper reports, explanations of the
Mexican Liberals and their defenders, the accounts of their
allies, the IWW's, and other radical participants, and the versions of the Mexican Federals and their defenders. Pieced together, these provide a fairly clear picture, though some details
are left in the shadows.

During his several visits to Tijuana, Ferris had made the
acquaintance of Louis James, a particularly irresponsible
member of Pryce's entourage.[11] Choosing to disregard Ferris'
clowning, James approached the actor as if he were an important new force in peninsular affairs. Whether this was James's
own idea, or whether Ferris had deliberately encouraged an
approach, was never made clear. The two were brought together by divergent purposes that harmonized for just an instant. Ferris, for his part, saw that the Liberal army was breaking up and decided that he would salvage James as an instru-
ment with which to perpetrate a comic-opera hoax. James, for
his part, was still anxious to fight and wanted to use the promoter to obtain aid for the army. With Pryce away, then, the
amiable actor stepped forward as advisor and counsellor
for the soldier-of-fortune faction. According to Ferris, that element sent him "a man named Louis James, who claimed to be
a West Point graduate. He was one of the nicest fellows over
there." He recounted the situation to the impresario: "that
Madero had practically forsaken them; that he had it from
authoritative sources that the country was soon to be divided
up into a number of republics anyway," which would leave the

Baja California rebels "alone over there." The rebels, however, were impeded, as they lacked supplies, ammunition,
and financial sponsorship. Ferris asserted that he did not en-
ter into a serious discussion of the matter with James, but
crossed the border with him; then James wanted to know "why
I [Ferris] could not, with the force he had over there, put
through the same idea that I had outlined to President Díaz."[12]

The impresario explained that a venture of the kind would
require plenty of money, as well as consultation with the important interests then dominant in Lower California. James
responded, "The biggest interest I know of right now is the
Spreckels interest."[13]

At that point, Ferris suddenly evinced a concern for legal
technicalities, stating that he himself would not go to see Mr.
Spreckels, that he did "not care to do anything to violate the
law," yet added enticingly, "but you are at liberty to do so."[14]

Later, Ferris learned in a roundabout way that the headstrong James actually had had nerve enough to call upon J. D.
Spreckels. When the adventurer "forgot himself and made
some threats about what it was possible for [the rebels] to do,"
the businessman ended the conversation. Needless to say,
the James-Spreckels conference came to naught.[15]

Ferris visited Tijuana again, either on Thursday afternoon or early Friday morning,[16] more likely the former. When
the rebels asked him what they should do, the promoter
launched into a political oration: "You have got to haul down
this red flag. While that might be the symbol of the Liberal
Party, so called, in Mexico, it means anarchy in America, and
you have got that out in sight of every American who passes
this border. You have got to cut out your socialism, your
anarchism, and every other ism that you have got into, and
form a new government if you hope to do anything right." The
ad hoc political theorist went on to predict that, pursuant to
the establishment of a proper government, they would be likely
to succeed with an "appeal to the young blood of America,"
as well as to her press, in which case there would be "no trouble" in getting American sympathy and money. They might
even persuade "the better class of Mexicans to join" them.[17]

Following this exhortation, Ferris returned to his Exposition offices in San Diego. On the morning of June 2, one of the many meetings among the soldiers took place, with James presiding. He claimed that the entire army, then consisting of only 150 soldiers, was present.[18] As there were 300 to 500 men the day before and the day after,[19] many must have been out scouting or were otherwise missing. With a representative assortment of the army's unattached adventurers, malcontents, derelicts, and hangers-on gathered about him, James delivered a speech. He urged that those preparing to quit stay until Pryce returned.[20] He declared that, though they had been deprived of the fruits of victory, they were the same group they had always been: "soldiers-of-fortune, Socialists, IWW's."[21] The time had come to inform the world of their cause. Without their effective diversionary efforts, Madero would have had to oppose another 2,000 Federals in Chihuahua. Therefore, a new republic ought to be proclaimed, on behalf of the "white men" who had shed their blood in Baja California. They ought to lower the anarchist flag, and replace it with a more fitting one. Applause greeted the speech, and the flags were lowered.[22]

This was the James version of the remarks, as subsequently recounted by their author to Ferris. It is possible that some magnification took place, either by James in the telling, or by Ferris, who made his living by exaggerating.

After the speech, the assemblage held the most memorable of the numerous Liberal army elections. At that particular moment, anybody could have been elected to anything. James recommended the sagacious Ferris. The promoter described the scene on the basis of the account that James gave him: "They decided that they would form a new government, without any idea of what they were going to do. . . . .They had no more idea than a rabbit what they were going to do. They held an election and unanimously elected me president of their republic, without having a constitution, and without knowing what they were going to do."[23]

James rushed up to San Diego and Ferris' office: "Come to Tijuana right now," he pleaded. "They are waiting for you.

They have elected you president, and they want you to put in force the new government." "I am very busy," was the actor's anticlimactic reply, "besides you have gone off half-cock." James was not easily shunted aside: "They have cut down the red flags, and they want you to give them a new flag." Ferris grabbed paper and pencil and sketched two horizontal bars across a field of blue with a white star at the center. Motioning to a costume tailor in his employ, he asked him to execute a flag according to the specifications. "I'll have it ready for you tomorrow morning," promised the theatrical tailor.[24]

On his own, Ferris made announcements to the press, conveying the impression that he was giving serious consideration to the offer. The new state, he said, would be known as the "Republic of Madero." Resuming his old game of name-dropping, the promoter claimed that a Los Angeles manufacturer would subscribe $12,000 to keep the peninsular campaign going, adding that others would follow suit.[25] Arrangements would be made to notify Madero of the newborn state, whose independence he would have to accept. In compensation, the entrepreneur said, he would "agree to provide $15,000,000 bond to cover the cost to the Mexican Government of the revolution in Lower California."[26]

With reference to the Junta's commission, which had arrived in the area late on Friday, Ferris explained that the rebels were severing all ties with the Liberal organization. In addition, he volunteered information concerning Pryce. The latter had not come south with the commission, because he had told the Junta he would discontinue his services to them "if they had nothing better to offer his men." Instead, he would remain in Los Angeles until the commission "returned with the decision of the insurrectos and he knew well what that decision would be." He, Ferris, however, would attempt to engage him as generalissimo, because the Welshman still enjoyed the troops' loyalty.[27]

Having provided his farce with the trappings of authenticity, Ferris entrained for Los Angeles. Meantime, the impetuous James tried to steer his fragile craft of state. According to a *Union* report, James, Mrs. Ferris, and a woman friend drove to Tijuana and succeeded in smuggling across quite a bit of ammunition packed in cases of soda water.[28] Ferris later denied this tale, asserting that the "only ammunition he had ever smuggled in was one bottle of beer."[29] James also prepared to confer with the Junta's commission,[30] presumably to inform them that their services were no longer required. But by this time, to his dismay, the army's political preferences were undergoing yet another shift. Leaving Tijuana again, James rushed to confer with his chief-of-state-designate. This memorable day ended with the president-maker of the "Republic of Madero" aboard one Los Angeles–bound train, and the product of his statecraft ahead of him on another.[31]

Even as the Ferris-James plot unfolded, the political weather vane had begun veering back in the direction of the Liberal Junta. On Friday afternoon, the commission addressed the discontented soldiers. So did Mosby, who for the second straight day was cheered, and then collapsed from overexertion. In the *Sun's* opinion: "Many of the rebels seem to believe that the junta has not acted in the best of faith."[32] However, Ferris' maneuver infuriated the Wobblies, even though they had previously shown no visible concern over the growing signs that some sort of coup, comic opera or otherwise, might be attempted. Before the afternoon was over, the Junta's defenders managed to push through courts-martial *in absentia,* without announcing charges, against Pryce and Hopkins.[33] Later, one of the members of the commission simply stated that the former, in comparison with the rest of the army, was "not so radical."[34] Thus, as James sped north, the Liberals had nearly re-established their shaky control. In the following three days, the Magonistas strengthened their grip. During the successive absences of Pryce, Ferris, and James, Captain Paul Schmidt, an unscrupulous and opportunistic free-lancer also known as Paul Smith and P. Silent, became field leader of their faction. Schmidt was Mosby's opponent in an election held June 3 to select a new regular general. Couriers were dispatched to the most distant outposts to collect the ballots in this crucial vote. If the *Union's* information was correct, Mosby beat Schmidt by a mere 20 votes,[35] a narrow margin indicative of the strength of the anti-Magonista element even after many desertions from their ranks. After his defeat, Schmidt quit, and immediately was arrested on the American side, charged with trying to smuggle his horse across the border.[36] Also eliminated was Captain Curtiss, whose novel anti-Junta, anti-Ferris, pro-Pryce position[37] was difficult to classify: evidently, he favored non-farcical filibustering. With Schmidt and Curtiss out of the picture, many of the soldiers of fortune deserted, thus further ensuring Liberal control.[38]

June 3, then, marked the first day of the Magonistas' triumph over the counterrevolutionaries. It was then proclaimed without reservation that Mosby was the new general. He and the civil commission made several important announcements for the press. The general and his adjutant, Bert Laflin, stated:

Dick Ferris has absolutely nothing to do with the revolutionary movement and his presence in Tijuana is not desired.

The fight is not being waged in the interest of Dick Ferris and the American capitalists, but solely in the interests of the working class.

Lower California will not be separated from the rest of Mexico, but the revolution will be carried on in all the states of Mexico until the Mexican people are freed from the present military despotism and slavery, peonage abolished and the lands returned to the people, which have been stolen from them by Mexican and foreign capitalists.[39]

This statement was clear enough. The denunciation of Ferris and the reassurance concerning Baja California would have been much more effective, however, had it been placed before the public in such unequivocal terms weeks earlier.

In the same vein, Pío Araujo declared that "all reports to the effect that a new republic will be established in Baja California are absolutely false." In addition, he reiterated a policy statement made in May that, regardless of who commanded the army, the commission would administer civil affairs systematically and possess ultimate control in all respects.[40] With the exception of a translator, that body was made up of

Mexicans: Pío Araujo, president; Guyton, treasurer; Lirma [*sic*], customs commissioner; Flores, postmaster; and Peterson, an IWW member, translator.[41] With these policies and institutions set up, the Liberals awaited the counterthrust from the Ferris faction.

In Los Angeles, Ferris prepared to observe from a safe distance the results of his practical joke, before deciding to add more fancy frills to it or to abandon it as unproductive of further laughter. As James was to pick up the completed flag in San Diego, he would not have to bother with that zealous and unpredictable pest for several days. Great was his surprise, then, when the adventurer descended upon him shortly after his own arrival: "These men are getting desperate down there. They do not understand why you do not come back there and talk to them."

At this point, Ferris hastened to disentangle himself from his Mexican meddling and told "this man James" that he "refused to accept the election they had held there."[42] The impresario added: "Look here James, I can not . . . violate the neutrality laws. . . . So far I have not done so. I have not engaged a man, nor have I sent anything over there, nor have I contributed, and I do not propose to lay myself liable."[43]

Nonetheless, Ferris' friends held an all-day banquet for him at the Alexandria Hotel on Saturday, June 3, to celebrate his elevation to the "Provisional Presidency." At the dinner, "his eyes grew bright as he spoke" rejecting the tender: "There is no use . . . , it is a forlorn hope—this idea of establishing a republic in Lower California, and . . . I shall tell the boys Monday that there is nothing doing."[44]

For his San Diego audience, the promoter chose to proceed in a slightly different manner. Amidst the news of the Liberal resurgence at Tijuana, the *Union* published his statement datelined Los Angeles, June 3: "My election to the presidency of the provisional government of Lower California was without my solicitation or consent, and I have not been officially notified of the fact."[45]

This was not quite a repudiation. Along the border, he

wanted to keep the show going as long as it could be made to go. In saying that he had not been "officially notified," Ferris implicitly repudiated James's repeated notifications, thus recognizing that the latter did not represent the army's official viewpoint—a fact obvious from the very beginning.

James stayed in Los Angeles over the weekend, partly to try to induce Pryce to return, and partly in a desperate and fruitless search for arms and a new sponsor. Meantime, Ferris had prepared a flowery letter of resignation. He believed that James could still be useful as a performer in the last act of his comedy. Accordingly, he gave him the letter, together with a "note to Kabierski, the man who was making the flag."[46] Then James departed for the border, while Ferris found it convenient to remain where he was for a few days. The "red, white, and blue letter" became very famous throughout the region for a time. Dated Los Angeles, June 4, it reads in part:

SOLDIERS AND CITIZENS
OF THE REPUBLIC OF LOWER CALIFORNIA:

I keenly and sincerely appreciate the great honor you have conferred upon me in electing me your first President, and sincerely do I regret my inability to be with you at this moment to address you in person, but I am detained here on private business of the greatest importance.

I hope that each and every one of you will allow nothing but the highest patriotic motives to lead in your future military and governmental actions; that you will forget the different classes that originally constituted your ranks and henceforth become a unit in ideas, hopes, actions, and ambitions. Let your sober second thoughts prevail at all times so that your every step be recognized, approved, and applauded by every liberty-loving nation of the world.

It affords me great pleasure to present to you the new flag of the Republic. The red stripes represent the blood that has been spilled for countless ages in the cause of liberty; the white stripes, the purity of your motives, the blue fold, the stanchness of your purpose; and the white star in a dual capacity represents not only the new Republic in the firmament of nations, but like the famous Star of Bethlehem, your constant guide to victory.

May God bless you all, give you strength and courage, and be with you constantly as he always is on the side of right.[47]

As James detrained from the return "Owl," early on Monday morning, he was ready with a series of reckless and unfounded statements timed for the benefit of the afternoon editions. This was his story: with Schmidt having just quit, he would run against Mosby in yet another election for general, and, after the latter's deposition, the Ferris flag would be raised, and the "Provisional President's" letter of resignation read. At that very moment, reinforcements in the form of 200 soldiers, 20,000 rounds of ammunition, and some field pieces, were en route to Tijuana. The soldiers would be informed that the Junta had completely repudiated them. They would then accept the guidance of the influential men who were backing Pryce. The latter, having turned political broker, was at that moment on his way to Washington for a conference with President Taft. James further claimed that on his person he had a telegram from Taft, but, significantly, failed to produce it.[48] Since James, unlike Ferris, was not an adept in the fine art of plausible deception, his preposterous yarn appealed only to the *Tribune,* which, as the afternoon cousin of the *Union,* may have been short of copy.

Then James set out for Tijuana to implement his plans, which in any case were pointless, in view of Ferris' withdrawal. In an effort to emulate the West Coast Thespian's flare for the melodramatic, James attached the Ferris flag to the front of his chauffeur-driven automobile, sped through customs, and on into Tijuana, where he found the troops "in a riotous state."[49]

The Mosby men were waiting for him. Before James could descend from his auto, he was seized, and the standard was torn off. The Liberals burned the captured flag, destroying the only specimen of that celebrated emblem. Many of them demanded James's immediate execution. Remnants of his following intervened, however, and, after further argument and some scuffling, it was decided to expel him from Tijuana under threat of instantaneous death should he ever return. The discomfited James slunk back to San Diego, there to spread tales of his persecution in Mexico.[50]

Thereafter, the customary claims and counterclaims were

filed, causing the exasperated *Union* to comment: "It's too bad Sam Lloyd died—even at a ripe old age. Lloyd was the champion puzzle-maker of the United States. Maybe—just maybe—if he were alive now he could solve the puzzle of what is what and which is which, in the insurrecto situation, across the line at Tijuana."[51]

Despite the *Union*'s confusion, the Liberals' explanation this time carried a clear ring of authority. With reference to Ferris' alleged letter of resignation, a Junta spokesman pointed out that, since the actor "was never legally elected to anything," there could be no declination.[52] This statement was correct, although on the morning of June 2 it would have been difficult to distinguish anything as clear-cut as a coherent or "legitimate" army viewpoint. Fernando Palomárez, who had recently been sent by the Junta to serve with the civil commission, explained the events of Monday, the fifth: "We are trying to prevent any race prejudice from becoming a factor in the revolution in Lower California. The flag sent by Dick Ferris was publicly burnt in the streets of Tijuana this afternoon. . . . Some in the command—Indians—thought it was the U.S. flag or the Lone Star flag."[53]

In an interview Palomares again denied the independent republic stories and concluded: "Ferris seems to have been trying to make a joke out of the movement. . . . We don't look with favor upon any effort to make a comic opera out of the war."[54]

During this hectic week every important leader connected with the Tijuana army, save one, changed his locale: Flores Magón held forth in his Fourth Street offices at the end, as he had at the beginning. After a costly miniature civil war, the Liberals had regained complete control of their movement.

The fast-expiring filibuster faction had yet to undergo its death rattle. In Los Angeles, the leader, ex-general Pryce, though bound to Ferris by ties of friendship, kept a discreet and noncommittal silence during the *opéra bouffe* phase. He probably realized that involvement in the Ferris farce would ring the death knell on any slight chance of continuing, either under Junta auspices or independently. With the actor's withdrawal, Pryce's interest in Lower California momentarily revived. It is hard to see why: He had lost control of the army, was in some danger of arrest, could not disentangle himself from James's extravagance or Ferris' fopperies, and had no access to new supplies. Perhaps he regretted missing so much excitement at Tijuana, and hoped that if he returned it might still be going on. During the weekend, he had been waited upon by various followers, such as Steve O'Donnell, Captain Curtiss, and James,[55] who urged him to return; perhaps, like Walker and Raousset, once his imagination had been fired by the romance of filibuster, he found it impossible to blot out the grandiose vision. In an interview on June 5, he announced that he was returning to Tijuana, and he reiterated his intention to set up a republic in the peninsula. Incredible as it sounds, he said that he had wired Madero, "asking for his acquiescence and support," for without that, his force would be in for a hard struggle. Possibly, he conceded, Tijuana might have to be abandoned, as it was a strategically poor site from the defender's point of view, but there were other towns in Baja California which could be fortified and made virtually impregnable. Hitting a more realistic basis for his optimism, he concluded: "At present it appears that the Mexican forces are united, but it is my firm opinion that they will be divided among themselves in the next three months."[56]

This was the wistful gesture of a fading would-be filibuster. Pryce never did go near Tijuana again. Privately well-aware that "the jig was up," as he expressed it, he "wrote back to the boys . . . and advised them to disband."[57] He sought help from Dick Ferris, for he was in dire straits: "My clothes were in rags, and I was penniless, and I called on Dick Ferris, who was very kind to me. He bought me this suit of clothes I am wearing now."[58]

A few days later, a dispatch from San Francisco reported the erstwhile popular Liberal commander in that city, seeking employment. His only profession, he said, was soldiering, and, in the absence of military openings, he was looking for any job that would "furnish excitement."[59]

The Ferris filibuster caused an enormous stir in California's

Southland. Here, at last, was an episode reminiscent of the fabled adventures of the nineteenth century. It mattered little that garish headlines about the incident inflicted severe wounds on Mexico's national pride or that the heroic deeds and frightful sufferings of the Walker invasion were now re-enacted in the form of a tawdry *commedia dell'arte*. The events seemed to show Marx's amendment of Hegel to the effect that everything in history happens twice, the first time as tragedy, the second time as farce, to be correct.

As far as dynamic Dick personally was concerned, he reaped the greatest publicity bonanza of his colorful career. Almost every California newspaper capitalized on the Ferris story. For days, there were jokes about the new president's program and his actress-wife's plans for her First Inaugural gown and Inaugural ball. Under a heading, "Viva Ferris!" the *San Diego Sun* featured a series of "news specials," purportedly from capitals all over the world, congratulating the impresario on his role as father of a new country.[60] Among the tongue-in-cheek accounts, the *Los Angeles Herald*'s was the most amusing. Under the promising headline, "Viva Dick Ferris! Rebels Elect Him. Leaderless Insurrectos Choose Promoter as President of Republic of Lower California. Incorporated Man Accepts. Angeleno Very Modestly Agrees to Steer Destinies of Newly Acquired Countrymen," it recounted that, as a result of the favorable vote of June 2 and the severance of ties between the Tijuana rebels and the Junta, the promoter was henceforth to be known to one and all as "Dick Ferris, president of the republic of Lower California." The story went on to explain that in the recent past the fledgling chief executive had been but a "self-styled capitalist. Then he incorporated himself for $10,000 and became 'Dick Ferris, Inc.' His wife took $100 stock in him. Now she's to become the 'first lady of the land' in Lower California."

The *Herald*'s account went on to explain that after his incorporation Ferris branched out into the business of promoting intrigues south of the border, such as the Lower California purchase plan and the Russell stunt. After these early schemes, "the presidential bee had . . . got in its work," and as soon as Díaz had stepped out, "Ferris thought the time had come for him to go to the aid of his newly acquired countrymen." Accordingly, upon having congratulated the Tijuana troops "on their splendid work in the cause of freedom," he called to their attention "his great philanthropic scheme of forming a new republic wherein all men would be equal and start in the race for fame and fortune from the same toe-mark." The leaderless rebels responded to the stimulus by creating a new state "on the instant." As they were searching for a chief executive, they "spied Ferris. He had remained modestly in the background, but a patriot was needed and Ferris was equal to the occasion. . . . He stepped forward and in tremulous tones thanked his compatriots . . . , gave of his wisdom on how to guide the ship of state freely;" and then Ferris and the rebels set forth on the task of writing a constitution and designing a flag: "It is understood the latter will have red for its motif, as a touching tribute to the hirsute adornment of the new republic's first president." Meantime, the statesman was supposed to be busy preparing his inaugural address.[61]

Ferris once mentioned that, despite the transparency of his practical joke, everybody persistently insisted on being taken in by it.[62] There was no reason for Americans to misconstrue his activities, although many did so, but when he failed to realize that Mexicans would interpret them very literally, he exhibited a lack of sensitivity to their feelings, characteristic of his antics throughout 1911. In Baja California, partly as a result of the extensive newspaper coverage and publicity, misunderstandings exist to this day regarding Ferris' precise role.[63]

Those Mexicans who have been convinced that their territorial integrity really was threatened have bracketed Ferris and Flores Magón as the twin betrayers of 1911. The historian Velasco Ceballos, after denouncing the Mexican exile throughout most of his book, labelled Ferris as the chief financial backer of the Magonista filibuster, and Pryce as the actor's military proxy, thus, by implication, linking the three. It was his conviction that the filibuster failed only because of rivalries and misunderstandings among Pryce, James, and Ferris.[64]

In the same general pattern, the Tijuana *Imparcial*'s commemorative "Gloriosa defensa de Baja California" held that the "multimillionaire" Ferris and Flores Magón were from the beginning collaborators in trying to set up a socialist republic. Flores Magón's function was to draw Mexican support. On January 29, the promoter's lieutenants, Leyva and Berthold, captured Mexicali. After several battles, Tijuana fell, and from May 10 until June 22, the date of the final battle, the Ferris "Republic of Lower California" existed.[65]

These theories and legends are without foundation. Conclusive evidence presented to investigators of the Senate Foreign Relations Subcommittee showed that Ferris was not a wealthy man, and that there had been no contacts between him and the Junta. To be sure, there were links between Pryce and the Junta, and between Pryce and Ferris, but none between Ferris and the Liberal Party. A rumor that Ferris had given Pryce a check for $2,000 for supplies and ammunition proved groundless.[66] If a slight danger to the integrity of Mexico ever existed, it came from Pryce, the adventurer, and not from Ferris, the clown.

In reverse, the Liberals as well, together with their defenders, fell victim to the myth of Ferris' wealth and connections. At the time, the IWW's were convinced that the promoter was a rich capitalist. The Wobbly correspondent, who subscribed himself "Chili Con Carne," recounted Dick's doings in the light of Wobbly understanding:

During this time a dirty capitalist politician named Dick Ferris began to send a lot of cutthroats to join Pryce's Liberals in an effort to get control of the outfit and start a filibustering expedition for the purpose of capturing Lower California and annexing it to the United States. . . . The Ferris outfit . . . tried to put their man Schmidt in command and Ferris was so sure of having captured the outfit that he sent down a new flag for "the republic of Lower California." . . . However, he had not reckoned with his host, for the I.W.W. men and the Socialists and anarchists would not stand for a deal like that and Ferris was told that he would be shot if he showed his face in Tijuana again and his flag was burned. . . . After this the Ferris outfit seeing they were goners, stole all the good horses and all the good guns and went to the United States, where some of them are now in jail charged with smuggling and here's hoping they get sixty years for it. Dick Ferris was arrested, but being a capitalist, nothing will be done to him.[67]

Similarly, Flores Magón referred to the actor's intervention as an act of calumniation by the "millionaire Ferris."[68]

More recently, two studies have maintained that Ferris, directly or indirectly, acted as agent for Otis and Chandler, both of whom desired a filibuster to preserve their land holdings in the Mexicali Valley.[69] Even on the incorrect assumption that Otis wanted a filibuster, it is inconceivable that the hard-bitten publisher would engage a clown to minister to his interests. Most important, the Senate subcommittee turned up no particle of evidence showing that Ferris in any way knew this influential father- and son-in-law. It is a striking fact that in 1911 the humorless editor of the *Los Angeles Times* viewed Ferris' antics with Olympian disdain, according him no attention whatever.

The important peninsular historian Pablo L. Martínez holds two interesting theories. He maintains that the unfriendly reportage on the Magonista movement often to be found in the Hearst, Spreckels, and Otis papers can be explained in terms of the owners' fear of the effect of the Liberals' economic doctrines on their Mexican land holdings. In particular, he attributes the Ferris agitation largely to the *San Diego Union*.[70] It should be pointed out, however, that the *San Diego Sun, Los Angeles Express,* and *Calexico Chronicle,* liberal-minded as they were, tried to give the Magonistas the benefit of the doubt when considering the rebels' intentions. At the same time, these three papers, none of whose owners was financially interested in Mexico, reported almost the same factual news as the conservative press. This consideration definitely weakens Martínez' thesis.

Secondly, Martínez maintains that the Ferris election in Tijuana, June 2, never took place. Since the promoter only wished to play a joke, he arranged the "election" in his San

Diego exposition office, using his hireling, James, to give the tale the pretense of a Tijuana setting. In support, Señor Martínez writes that James's name appeared suddenly in connection with Liberal affairs only at this particular moment, and that all the Ferris filibuster stories are based on the *San Diego Union*'s account of June 3, with others appearing only subsequently.[71]

On the whole, the evidence does not seem to bear this out. Two newspapers, the *Sun* and the *Evening Tribune*, carried the Ferris story the afternoon before the *Union* did. Two others, the *Los Angeles Herald* and the *Examiner*, printed it at the same time as the *Union*. Furthermore, James had been reported as a member of the Liberal army more than two months prior to June 2.[72]

Though James and Ferris were not reliable persons, their account is not implausible against the background of events leading up to June 2. Finally, there is indirect confirmation of the Ferris filibuster in the reaction of the Italian anarchists in the Magonista ranks: all quit at a time when the adventurer element was in control. A little later, some returned, after the Junta's policy of "prudence until the minority should become a majority" had won out.[73]

In the United States there were rumors that, aside from what Ferris allegedly did or did not do, various California interests had lent the revolutionists a hand. Again, the stories were proved incorrect. It was thought that Los Angeles gun shops and ammunition firms had helped the rebels. There was no evidence of this. Nor had any large economic interests, including the Otis-Chandler empire, aided them. In view of the proximity of the rebels to the San Diego and Arizona Railway construction, there were tales that the railroad had helped them. A check of the Sherer Company, the contractors employed by the Spreckels interest to build the line, revealed that neither management nor employees had encouraged the Magonistas—on the contrary, the rebels had threatened the railroad. The voluntary financial contributions the Liberal Junta received came, it has been firmly established, exclusively from a large number of small contributors and sympathizers.[74]

CHAPTER IX

The End of an Upheaval

Somber events at Ensenada and El Alamo were partially overshadowed by the bizarre developments at Tijuana. In the region to the south, the months of Liberal-Federal strife saw much that was of an unexpected, mysterious, and suspicious nature. The culmination of it all was the mental collapse of one individual, the brutal murder of four others, and the death in battle of eleven more.

At the time the Mosby army marched to Tecate, mounting responsibilities caused Consul George B. Schmucker to show signs of severe strain. Ensenada's isolation oppressed him. He grew ever more sensitive to the charge, levelled at him by the California press, of neglect of the besieged Americans at El Alamo. American settlers living near the border inundated him with complaints of injuries inflicted on their property by the rebels. His alternately friendly and unfriendly relations with Governor Vega made him uneasy.[1]

Schmucker succumbed to panic. For a second time, he telegraphed for a warship. Secretary of State Knox wired Ambassador Henry Lane Wilson to sound out the Mexican government on the possibility of requesting the United States to send a naval vessel.[2] Mexico proved unwilling, and nothing came of it. Simultaneously, the consul, under the impression that American interests were backing the rebels, lent his help

163

to Colonel Vega in preparing a list of the companies allegedly conspiring. As a result, on May 23, the governor wrote a significant letter to Foreign Secretary de la Barra. Foreign interests, he said, had been helping the rebels from the beginning. Their investments would greatly appreciate, were the filibusters to win. American annexation would not be long in coming. As chief offenders he cited the Mexican Company of Terrain and Colonization, the Colorado River Land Company, and the Cudahy interests.[3] Ironically, this letter, which did much to confirm the Mexican Foreign Office in the conviction that the United States was covertly promoting a filibuster, was prepared with the assistance of a disturbed American official.

For Schmucker, panic gave way to complete collapse. Though the State Department would have welcomed a responsible analysis of the peculiar situation at Tijuana, Washington received only a series of mystifying, contradictory, and, eventually, completely incoherent messages:

May 1. . . . Governor and the highest loyal officials . . . believe that American capitalists are responsible for the insurrection.

May 1. Confidential. Leader of seceded free masons in Mexico probably pro-revolutionary.

May 1. Confidential. Church of Rome in Mexico probably bitterly pro-revolutionary. Threatened attack on Ensenada probably for effect in order to encourage military intervention. Mexican church women are not concerned.

May 2. Confidential. I am morally certain of the allegation in my recent telegrams. Action should be taken before May fifth. Loyal citizens and officials are trusting you and the President of the United States to save Mexico. Telegraph line cut.

May 7. Confidential. I am morally certain that head of institution mentioned in my May 1 . . . is primarily responsible for disturbances in Mexico, Portugal, Spain, France, and Morocco. Capitalists in America and socialists of Europe and America undoubtedly mere tools. Representatives of capitalists and insurrectionists here believe me in sympathy with them.

May 12. Conspirators believe that next Mexican President will be in sympathy with them. In Lower California conspirators had planned to hire new force to exterminate original insurgents. Residents preparing to depart for the United States excepting the Americans and others in confidence of conspirators.

Please order . . . my transfer to unimportant post.[4]

On May 23, Schmucker again requested that he be replaced, declaring that his position was "becoming known."[5] The plea prompted a distracted State Department official to write a colleague: "The first part of this—'Send my Successor'—is the most sensible thing he has sent recently."[6] On May 26, the Department received its Ensenada man's final confidential "information" in two messages: "To comprehend political and social conditions at present moment, study and apply latter part of the Book of Revelation, Holy Bible," and "I have a plan that will result in bettering civilization everywhere and in preventing my own assassination. Answer."[7]

On the same day word came from F. R. Sawday, the emergency deputy consul at Ensenada: "Geo. B. Schmucker [had a] complete mental breakdown." Separately, two resident physicians sent an affidavit stating that he was "suffering an acute, dangerous form of insanity." Washington instructed Sawday to provide the stricken consul with an attendant, and to send him home at once.[8]

An acquaintance of Schmucker's described his symptoms: he "was abnormally suspicious, . . . feared attempts upon his life," and talked of "certain alleged incidents as if convinced that they actually occurred."[9] Since he had formed an image of powerful American interests helping the revolutionists, his disordered mind drew the logical conclusion that representatives of these interests were seeking to kill him in order to destroy the invaluable secret information that he possessed. As a result of these delusions, Schmucker behaved in extraordinary fashion in dealing with his fellow Americans. Vega arrested several foreign Ensenadans on the basis of the young man's imaginings.[10] In particular, he had a Dr. Chamberlain and a Mr. Taylor unceremoniously apprehended and jailed at one o'clock in the morning on the charge of attempting to chloroform the consul.[11] An incident that took place June 2, as Schmucker was about to be helped aboard the San Diego–bound steamer, well illustrates his helplessness: momentarily left alone, the pathetic ex-consul plunged neck deep into water before he could be rescued.[12]

Simultaneously, a tragedy unfolded at El Alamo. A circuitous chain of circumstances linked the events at the mining site and the consul's breakdown. After the rebels had left the village, Mexican authorities gave no more attention to its population than they had previously. The month of May passed uneventfully. However, for some time rumors concerning the friendliness of resident foreigners toward the rebels had been rife in Ensenada. When storekeeper Glennon visited the capital in late April to fetch supplies for the villagers, Vega suspected him of planning to give them in reality to the revolutionists.[13] According to Fuzere, the governor's agent in the village, several Americans had collaborated with the occupiers.[14] Perhaps worse, the insane Schmucker "denounced various Americans" and especially "denounced Doctor Foster as a rebel, and possibly also Glennon, Carroll and others."[15]

At long last, when late May came about, Vega had galvanized himself into action. By this time, however, he was absolutely convinced that Americans were at the root of all his troubles. He detailed a vigilante unit to scour the countryside for "filibusters."[16] Three members of the expeditionary force stood out. The commander was Lerdo González, an experienced, vigorous, and brave Federal soldier, who, moreover, had the reputation of being violently anti-American. There was a warrant out for his arrest in California.[17] Another leader was Juan Riviera, an outlaw in both countries, who, with several of his men, had raped to death a twelve-year-old Indian girl.[18] Third was Juan Moore, a Chilean, informer, and ill-reputed hanger-on at El Alamo.[19] Fuzere, who kept in contact with the governor, said that a list of rebel sympathizers had been prepared, and that these individuals were to be shot by the González squadron.[20]

On June 4 came the first warning. After the rebels' departure, Glennon, in an effort to protect his shop from both sides, had raised the American flag over it. Riviera and his men tore down the emblem and shot Glennon's dog,[21] the lonely bachelor's sole companion.

June 10, the González group encountered a number of Indians believed to be allied with the revolutionaries. They were engaged, and eleven were killed,[22] without any effort having been made to determine whether they were or were not rebels.

At noon the following day, a beautiful Sunday, June 11, Lerdo González and forty or fifty of his men rode into El Alamo. Dr. Foster, Glennon, Carroll, and the half-witted French Canadian petty thief, Dubois, were arrested without warrant. The soldiers badly frightened Mrs. Foster, as they threatened the doctor, and helped themselves to cuff links, a gold nugget, and her wristwatch. The four men were marched to the outskirts of the village. When Carroll tried to flee in panic, all were shot down, one after another, and the bodies thrown into placer holes.[23] Moore took $187 in cash from Glennon's body, and $18 from Foster's.[24] Then the vigilante squadron rode off.

For days, the residents huddled in unrelieved terror. People were afraid to visit the frantic Mrs. Foster, for fear for their own lives. At last, after several days, in a state of nervous collapse, she was accompanied to Ensenada, and thence to California.[25] Three Americans, Charles L. Myers, Carl Carlson, and D. W. Church, a man over eighty, who thought their names were on the execution list, fled. Travelling night and day, and avoiding trails, they finally reached San Diego totally exhausted. There Church told their story.[26]

González turned in a false report to the governor, explaining that the "filibusters" had been killed while defending themselves in a fortified house. Vega did not question this version.[27] Foster was killed because he had tended the wounded Berthold, Glennon because of the flag and because he had been in too close contact with the rebels, Carroll because he too was said to have consorted with the occupiers and because he had been generally disliked, and Dubois just for having been a minor nuisance.[28] Actually, all had been neutral, or actively anti-rebel. Of Glennon, this was especially true: though he had once offered the opinion that Madero had the "right principles," he had also referred to Mosby as a "big liar at the head of a gang of cutthroats."[29]

Doubtless, at the bottom of this misapplication of the *ley de fuga* lay the Mexicans' anti-Americanism, kindled anew by the sight of so many Yankees in the rebel ranks. Flores Magón had written in 1908, at a time when Americans displayed an undue interest in Baja California, that "at these moments there is a tremendous anti-Gringo agitation."[30] Three years later, his own American followers were to provide validation for his observation! As the sad fate of the eleven Indians proved, the tragic incidents were more than a demonstration of anti-Americanism.

The grimness of the drama was accentuated by the tangled relations laid bare by its sweep. Glennon had relatives in Chicago and Indianapolis, who bickered over the inheritance of the little shop. The brother of the other shopkeeper revealed that Carroll's real name was Sprankle and that he was a fugitive from American justice as a result of a shady business transaction long in the past. Dr. Foster turned out to be a bigamist. He and his second wife had fled, penniless, to Ensenada and then El Alamo; his first wife had sworn out a warrant for desertion against him in California. He had abandoned her and two daughters after years of strife.[31] The two women blamed each other for Foster's death and argued over possessions. And finally, for years, the Mexican and American governments fenced inconclusively in an effort to fix ultimate responsibility for the tragedy.[32] As for the Indian victims of the vigilantes, since they had no relatives who were citizens of a powerful nation ready to lodge a protest on their behalf, nothing is known concerning the justice or injustice of their fate. Probably they should be included among the long line of Indians who were mistreated by the representatives of the Díaz regime.

As long as there was military activity in the peninsula, the two national governments continued to argue fine points of diplomacy. One question solved itself in anticlimactic fashion. As action moved westward soon after Colonel Mayol reached the Colorado, his protection for Colonel J. A. Ockerson proved largely superfluous. On May 10, the United States Army engineer notified Mayol that after the fourteenth his services would no longer be needed, since the dike work was nearly completed for the year. Knox thanked the Mexican Foreign Office, closing the matter.[33] Incidentally, Colonel Ockerson did not succeed, despite confident early assertions,[34] in ending all danger of future floods.

Two or three interesting points in international law were taken up in the course of the latter part of the long debate over the Liberal Party's activities. On May 24, the new Mexican ambassador, M. de Zamacona, asked Knox why the Justice Department, which had sufficient evidence, did not institute proceedings against "Flores Magón and his confederates, principals in the many scandalous filibustering attempts organized against . . . Lower California." Another message informed the United States that Mexico would not assume any obligation for damages wrought by them.[35] These dispatches greatly annoyed the irritable Knox. In a reply June 6, he stated that the United States had not permitted "scandalous filibustering attempts," but, on the contrary, had carefully guarded the boundary, while there was a "conspicuous absence of similar measures upon the part of the Government of Mexico upon its own territory."[36] The next day, he pointed out that, since there were only about five hundred rebels under arms, vigorous action by Mexico would solve the problem. With reference to a Mexican contention that the United States should draw distinctions among the different groups in that country, Knox maintained that it was not the northern nation's duty to distinguish between "organized insurrections" and "filibusters whose objects and principles are not approved by the Mexican Government." The United States expected Mexico to assume responsibility for damage done to any foreign property or persons by rebels of whatever stripe, as the international law covering this issue was clear.[37] Finally, with regard to the entire question whether or not the Liberals were filibusters, the Secretary of State held,

that the movement in Lower California appears to be the result of the activities of a Mexican political party; that it is reported that the avowed object of this Mexican political party is the throwing off of Mexican authority and the establishment of a

socialistic republic in Lower California; and finally that the sub-
version of one form of government and the establishment of another has, upon this hemisphere, been uniformly regarded as a
political movement irrespective of the propriety or justice of the
cause espoused.[38]

As far as the United States government was concerned, these
exchanges wound up the discussion of the principles so long at
issue in connection with the Liberal movement.

Meantime, the Justice Department, as the Mexican government had been eagerly expecting, undertook preparations for
action against the Liberal leaders. On March 1, Wickersham
had written the United States District Attorney for the Southern District of California to proceed cautiously because he
feared the "disastrous effects of a possible defeat." Accordingly, the federal prosecutor's office and the Bureau of Investigation agents had moved circumspectly in an effort to accumulate enough solid evidence with which to file a neutrality
violation charge. After not quite three months, McCormick
wrote Wickersham that he was ready to prosecute, if the Attorney General so desired.[39] The next week, Wickersham informed Knox that he had wired McCormick to institute grand
jury proceedings, with a view to indicting the Junta and any
others active in violating the neutrality laws.[40] Interestingly,
on June 2 a Bureau of Investigation agent consulted Madero
in El Paso to learn his thoughts on the pending action. The
recent victor replied confidentially that he would be delighted
were it to be consummated.[41]

Thenceforth, matters moved swiftly. Grand jury proceedings were held in Los Angeles early in the second week of
June.[42] The four leading Junta members, Ricardo and Enrique Flores Magón, Librado Rivera, and Anselmo Figueroa,
were indicted, and so were Richard Ferris and Caryl Ap Rhys
Pryce. On successive days, June 14, 15, and 16, the Junta
leaders, Ferris, and Pryce were arrested. Bail for the latter two
was set at $2,500, and for the Junta president, at $5,000. In
addition, Pryce was separately charged by the Mexican government with murder and arson in connection with the Battle of Tijuana. For him, there was to be no possibility of re-

lease from jail, bail or no bail, until settlement of the question of extradition.[43] Flores Magón's arrest, despite prompt release on bail, further damaged his movement in Mexico, as Madero no doubt hoped it would.

The three leading figures reacted variously. Pryce was matter-of-fact. He said that, since he had gone to Mexico voluntarily and had not actively recruited men, he had not violated the neutrality laws, and also that, since a state of war existed at Tijuana on May 9, he was confident that he would not be extradited on the charges of murder and arson.[44]

Ferris really was surprised. Though they pretended unconcern, both he and Mrs. Ferris were dismayed to find that his joke had boomeranged.[45] Because a flood of criticism poured down on him, the promoter felt constrained to resign his position as manager of the Panama-Pacific groundbreaking festivities. His self-justificatory statement reflected his usual style. He pointed out that he had accepted the managership of the groundbreaking fiesta "without promise of remuneration," living at the U. S. Grant Hotel on a ten-dollar-per-diem expense account, not only providing for his wife, but also "supporting an auto," and, simultaneously, "keeping the dignity of the office, as well as working night and day, all for this amount. I also have paid all our railroad fares, and anybody who knows anything can figure that I am out considerable money." Furthermore, Ferris explained, he had a vast backlog of experience in garnering publicity, so that, when a timely opportunity presented itself, he seized upon it "even to the extent of making a buffoon of myself to advertise the celebration," and that "it was only ignorance of appreciation and rural judgment that offered criticism instead of praise."[46] However, the actor brightened, announcing that he was inclined "to adopt Mrs. Ferris' suggestion that the two of them take advantage of the limelight immediately by returning to the stage and playing 'The Man from Mexico.' "[47]

Flores Magón in his reaction was as true to form as the self-possessed Britisher or the breezy impresario: he penned a vitriolic editorial denouncing Taft. The Junta's arrest, he claimed, was discriminatory, or else Madero should have been apprehended on the same charge.[48] In so arguing, he again forgot that the easiest way for him to have avoided neutrality law trouble would have been to go to Mexico and to throw himself into the revolution, as his rival had.

At the time of the arrests and the attendant disintegration, two clues emerged, providing a partial answer to the mystery of what had become of the money the Junta had been collecting so assiduously. The party did not have funds sufficient to post the $5,000 bail for the leader's temporary release. Fortunately for him, prosperous well-wishers in Los Angeles came to the financial rescue.[49] At that time, Flores Magón remarked, in an interview, that the Junta had always received money in small amounts, "so small that little can be done with it."[50] Evidently, then, they spent the heaping piles of dimes and quarters, and often dollars, as they were received, rather than saving for specific objectives. Apparently, also, at least one of the faithful lost his faith, because Flores Magón denounced Rosalío Bustamante, an old adherent who had turned Maderist, for absconding with thousands of the party's pesos.[51]

Plainly, the Liberals' days were numbered. In the summer of 1911, however, there was a brief upsurge in their military activity outside Lower California, coincidental with the near-cessation of fighting following Madero's victory. The Magonistas were particularly in evidence in Nuevo León, Chihuahua, and Sonora.[52] In Chihuahua, Prisciliano Silva and his sons, assisted by Jesús Rangel, sought to renew their drive, and briefly, in late June, the Magonistas did succeed in recapturing Casas Grandes.[53] In Sonora, a group of them were captured in the Altar district, the traditional trouble center of that state. Twenty-eight were executed, including José Cardoza, the leader who had left Mexicali during the factional strife in March.[54]

In the Imperial-Mexicali Valley, the revolution was threatened with death from boredom. Summer came to the Valley with temperatures between 95 and 105 degrees by mid-May. At the time the Pryce army moved, the thought of marching up to the cool western plateau must have aroused many a soldier's enthusiasm. A searing lassitude overcame those who remained with Quijada.

For a time, Calexico, more than Mexicali, was the center of interest. Almost the only influential person still friendly to the Liberals was Otis B. Tout, editor of the *Calexico Chronicle*. Since arguments concerning the rebels had gone on for months, he arranged a postcard poll to determine the state of public sympathy. His ballot asked for approval of the revolution and of the *Chronicle*'s support of the rebels, or disapproval, which meant that the voter believed that the revolution "'should be quashed and the old order of things restored in Baja California.'"[55] Tout sent out about four hundred postcards, but received only ninety-five answers, ninety of which indicated approval.[56] A violent dispute ensued. The Farmers and Merchants Club began to withdraw advertising from the paper. The editor was charged with unfair posing of the question, as his poll did not make provision for approval of the Maderista revolution as an alternative to the Liberal one. Tout got back his advertising revenue only after openly admitting his error and apologizing for it.[57] It is interesting to note that Tout favored the peninsular revolutionists so strongly because he felt that their victory would ultimately turn Baja California into a Texas: "Americans conquered Texas, made it independent, applied for admission to the Union. . . . Americans are carrying on the war in good part in Baja California. Let them succeed, make it independent, and then ask for admission to the Union, as they should. The effect along the border would be magic. Calexico would become immediately the very center of the whole Imperial Valley and would in time leap to the front . . . ; the Mexicans themselves would be better off; the owners of the large estates would be better off; foreign capital would be better off"— there would be an all-round improvement.[58] An editorial in the rival *Imperial Valley Press* indicated that its author held an identical view.[59]

By late May, the Mexicali army had about one hundred members, consisting of thirty-five Mexicans, thirty Cocopah Indians, and thirty-five American IWW's. The current talk of future possibilities was largely irrelevant because the army was barely able to exist. When Mayol marched past, no battle took place. The rebels were too weak, and this time the literal-minded colonel was following orders to march to Ensenada.[60]

In the absence of other activity, a hassle developed between the army and local business interests. For some time, the army's electric bills at Mexicali had remained unpaid. The town's power was supplied by W. F. Holt's Holton Electric Company. When the company ordered the switches pulled, darkness suddenly shrouded the strategists at rebel headquarters. The insurgents countered with a threat to blow up the company's power canal, upon which the entire Valley depended for electricity. In this crisis, both utility capitalism and anarchism held firm, the loser being the petty bourgeoisie, as several of Mexicali's small shopkeepers agreed to pay the bills. The lights flashed back on.[61]

A more serious dispute arose over alleged damage to crops and the harvesting of the sugar beets. General Otis had moved to the Willard Hotel in Washington, partly in order to lobby for more federal funds for flood control,[62] partly to bring his own personal influence to bear on President Taft to resolve the dangers threatening his California-Mexico Land and Cattle Company holdings. There, Otis received various telegrams from Harry Chandler. One of these said that the rebels had destroyed $40,000 worth of property in three days and had threatened to blow up the main canal works unless paid a large sum of money. Another claimed that the company's losses amounted to $325,000 up to June 1.[63] Otis' influence could be potent: he telephoned the President personally to lodge his complaint and filed the telegrams with the President's secretary.[64] However, Taft gave no sign of willingness to send American troops into Mexico on behalf of a wealthy particular interest.

In addition, the Imperial Sugar Beet Company, controlled by the Cudahy organization, wanted to harvest its crop. Two bridges on the Inter-California Railway had to be rebuilt to provide the necessary transportation facilities. General Quijada asked for a payment of $5,000, to be used for ammunition and supplies, before the bridges could be rebuilt. A stalemate followed. When Quijada lowered his figure to $550, it looked as if there might be an agreement.[65] However, new developments made this arrangement unnecessary.

The Mexicali Liberals were on the brink of extinction. Madero seems to have envisioned a three-pronged policy aimed at silencing the Magonistas. He hoped that the United States Department of Justice would deal them the fatal blow. He also repeatedly threatened to send an army to Lower California to crush them.[66] Or, if he could induce them to give up through negotiation, force would not be necessary. However, his own anomalous position during the de la Barra interregnum made it difficult for him to carry out any plans.

After several weeks of hesitation and palaver, Madero made up his mind to send troops into the peninsula. The Otis-Chandler partnership may have been one of several influences that caused him to take this decision, for Chandler telegraphed Madero on May 24 that President Taft would permit Mexican troops to be transported to Lower California over American territory, if he and de la Barra requested it.[67] On June 6, Mexico made the request, and the next day, Knox granted permission, specifying merely that the troops were to travel unarmed.[68] As their arms were stacked in the baggage cars, the distinction was meaningful only to the diplomats.[69] On this occasion, as on many earlier ones in the Baja California revolution, a clear-cut decision, arrived at after much soul-searching, was of little avail: events had virtually run their natural course by the time the troops arrived.[70]

In Mexicali, Magonism was dissolved by diplomacy. In relation to the small size of the group, the number of negotiators was large and the transaction intricate. In addition to General Quijada and his men, participants included Rodolfo Gallegos, an ex-Liberal who had just organized a vigilante force whose members were drawn in part from the Magonista army; Benigno Barreiro, a Spanish merchant in Mexicali; Antonio Lozano, Mexican consul in Los Angeles; Alberto Andrade of the Southern Pacific Railway; Aurelio Sándoval, a wealthy peninsular merchant; Carlos Bernstein, a young Maderista, newly arrived from Sonora; and—in addition—former General Leyva, just in from Juárez, and clad in the mantle of pacificator! Chiefly through the efforts of Sándoval, who put up $600, Bernstein, and Leyva and his travelling companion, Jesús González Monroy, the rebels surrendered on June 17. Each man received ten dollars. The Mexicans dispersed as best they could. The Americans were fed their first full meal in several days at a Chinese restaurant in Calexico, then were taken to the railroad tracks and told to scatter by the time they reached El Centro.[71]

After five uneasy months, the pillars of respectability stood erect on both sides of the border. Regular Mexican troops were to occupy Mexicali, the crops were to be harvested, and General Otis' property was secure. Undismayed, the Wobblies, with the scorching summer sun beating down on them, and with ten dollars in their pockets, jauntily shuffled down the tracks, looking out for the freight on whose break-beam they were to ride gratis into the next trouble.

At Tijuana, as well, the Liberal army had fallen upon evil days. It never really recovered from the Ferris stunt. Nevertheless, General Mosby, in an effort to establish a more orderly camp, instituted a clean-up campaign, abolishing gambling and inaugurating an era of prohibition. As a matter of principle, soldiers of fortune were to be eliminated from the ranks. To put an end to the multitude of unauthorized and often compromising announcements, intentional or accidental, the civil commission set up a press bureau, which thenceforth was to issue official statements of policy.[72]

Ghosts reared up out of the past to vitiate Mosby's laudable effort. Over the course of time, the army had come to adopt a style all its own. How was it to switch from the sensational to the sensible over night? The recruiting of IWW's increased appreciably, but the soldiers of fortune were never quite eliminated, and, indeed, hardly could be when the commander himself was partly one. The new press bureau did not function well, because, coincidentally with the Junta's arrest, Pío Araujo vanished. Once again, there were unexplained shootings in camp, and tension between Mexicans and foreigners:[73] "There was fighting at Tijuana last night among the rebels, and it resulted in the separation of the races. The Mexican soldiers quarreled with the Americans, the result of a long-suppressed ill-feeling. The quarrel terminated in bullets and the departure of the Mexicans."[74]

Ferrisism gave a last flicker. Notwithstanding the threat to her husband's life should he ever reappear in town, the adventurous Mrs. Ferris, accompanied by three friends, paid an unannounced call. The party was immediately surrounded by aroused Mexicans; and, told by Mosby to hasten back across the border, they returned to San Diego in a state of high agitation.[75] More ominously, the newspapers reported that the pesky James was busy drilling recruits in preparation for an attempted coup to regain control of the Tijuana army.[76] But by a remarkable coincidence, he too vanished, never to be seen again, at the very moment that Ferris appeared in answer to the summons of the Los Angeles grand jury.

Finally, the old ammunition-supply headache remained. Still unable to get enough help from the Junta, the rebels resorted to holding a Sunday Wild West show, and auctioned off many curios. Much to their sorrow, they did not realize a large return from the tame venture.[77]

The Tijuana army, like its Mexicali twin, managed to unsettle some powerful interests along the border while it was in its death throes. Apprized of the Madero army's imminent arrival on American railways, the rebels took great fright lest they be caught in a pincer between Vega to the south and the Madero men to the north. Previously they had merely helped themselves to supplies and had frightened employees, but now they were desperate, and they threatened the railroad ownership and management. Consequently, on June 13, a letter signed by Mosby and his adjutant, Bert Laflin, was addressed to the "Transportation Department, Spreckels Bros. Commercial Co." After stating that the Liberals had read in the papers that the railroad would transport Mexican troops, the communication continued in a style of conventional politeness that sharply contrasted with its unusual contents:

"If you have made any arrangements for the consummation of these plans, we hereby advise you to issue an order of nullification, else we shall take such steps as are consistent with our self-preservation to abrogate your system in this territory." In closing, the correspondents indicated that, "we shall anticipate an immediate reply . . . and we trust you will see the advisability of negating the reports of the press relative to the subject we mention therein."[78]

Though the message was chiefly aimed at the San Diego Southern and the San Diego and Arizona, the two Spreckels lines, copies were sent to the Southern Pacific and the Santa Fe as well.[79] The last part of the last sentence did not appear in the public print, and, instead, there were subsequent denials on the part of the rebels that the letter had ever been sent.[80] The consensus was that the phrase "to abrogate your system" meant to blow it up.

San Diego buzzed with excitement, while the Spreckels interests hastened to exert their political influence. Evidently, they were not quite as well-connected as Otis, for they worked through regular War and State Department channels. John D. Spreckels wired California's aged United States Senator George C. Perkins, who promptly transmitted the message to the War Department, that the current "threat of destruction is practically threat against these interests for carrying out the law of the United States controlling railroads and is an indirect threat against our Government. Gen. Bliss under instructions can protect my property and the lives of people working on it if directed by Government. . . . Also important retain fleet here protect people on border from these desperadoes."[81]

The War Department asked Bliss to verify the alleged danger. The general replied that Spreckels exaggerated, that there was little evidence that the rebels were preparing to blow up the railroad except in utter desperation, and that their threat was largely bluff.[82] However, because of the fear of the Liberals, local military authorities envisaged the readiness of five large cruisers, a fleet of auxiliary vessels, a "strong" detachment of marines, and two regiments of infantry to protect the population and the twenty-five miles of railroads under construction "from the terrible brigand Mosby and his band of 150 (or 200) desperadoes."[83]

At the same time, Harry L. Titus, secretary of the Spreckels companies, wrote Bliss to complain about the continuing danger. He emphasized that "there is a general feeling throughout the community that these filibusters in the last few days of their control will endeavor to destroy our property." To illustrate the peril inherent in the situation across the border, Titus explained that, "yesterday the conductor of our train operating from San Diego to the end of the line in Lower California went over to Tia Juana on business, and while there one of the Filibusters assaulted him and pointed a pistol at him and snapped it twice before he could be disarmed, and afterwards endeavored to strike the Conductor with a sword." In conclusion, Titus suggested that Bliss send two hundred of his men to be deployed along the lines of the road and stay there until the arrival of the Mexican troops so that "these bandits will not destroy the property."[84]

Bliss flatly rejected the request for troops. He explained that he had very definite orders regarding his lack of authority in regard to "protecting property or other interests lying outside of the territory of the United States." Ever since the rebels had taken Mexicali, on January 29, his instructions had strictly prohibited "any American troops from crossing the international boundary in the absence of specific orders . . . from the Government in Washington." The request submitted by the Spreckels interests that two hundred troops be sent to guard the railroad until the arrival of Mexican troops ran "directly contrary" to Washington's "positive instructions."[85]

Probably Mosby's gesture was but a ruse. In the Magonista army, however, there was always a distinct possibility that some of the troops might translate a general's tactical bluster into a *fait accompli*. In any case, no explosion went off. Perhaps Mosby chose this means to forestall the arrival of the Maderista forces, the better to engage in peace parleys.

Again, involved armistice negotiations had been set in motion. This time they fell short of success. Mosby, who felt that it would be sensible to give up on the best terms obtainable, sent an emissary to try to induce Flores Magón to agree,[86] but received no response. In the meantime, Leyva and González Monroy, continuing their peace mission, arrived from Mexicali. Also involved were Consuls J. Díaz Prieto and Arturo Elías. The difficulty of negotiating was aggravated because many of the men were spoiling for yet another fight and because General Leyva ranked second only to Dick Ferris on their black list. Moreover, Leyva temporarily misplaced his credentials, and Consul J. Díaz Prieto understood him to be expressing Flores Magón's approval of negotiations. When it was learned that he represented only an aide to Madero, Abraham González, the provisional governor of Chihuahua, matters became further complicated. In this inauspicious setting, Mosby put forth a stiff set of demands: his men should receive a $100 bonus, the dollar-a-day pay promised the Liberal fighters at the outset, and 160 acres of land each. In addition, they should be permitted to retain their equipment, and all of E. E. Kirk's legal fees should be taken care of. Leyva replied that he was authorized to treat for $10 per man, and nothing more.[87] Before matters could go any further, another battle broke out.

At Ensenada, Governor Vega had completed preparations for the showdown. At the time of the Madero armistice, he had notified Mexico City that in his district the peace would not be put into effect.[88] With Flores Magón also rejecting the armistice, the Liberals and the peninsular Federals came out even, that is, both outside the general law. The colonel put together a well-equipped and effective army of 560 men, composed of some of Mayol's fighters, his own troops, and the Integrity volunteers. Leaving Mayol (who seemed to specialize in guarding unthreatened places) to hold Ensenada, Vega bore down on Tijuana, confident, determined, and vengeful.[89]

The famed Magonista Foreign Legion, living up to its bellicose tradition, did not back out of the fight. On June 22, 155 foreign Wobblies and adventurers, most of whom were Americans, and 75 Mexicans and Indians made ready for the second Battle of Tijuana. Commandeering a five-car work train, they got up steam with difficulty, and rolled out to meet Vega, with the infantry atop the cars and the cavalry riding alongside. Far inferior in equipment and manpower, Mosby also found himself badly outgeneraled by Vega, with the result that the battle, though hard-fought, ended in a rout after only three hours. The Mexicans fled into the countryside to the east, and hoped for the best. Mosby, overcome with emotion and "weeping like a child," and 106 of the non-Mexicans threw down their arms and crossed the boundary as political refugees.[90] Another contingent, probably including the notorious outlaws, if they ever actually served, refused to cross, saying that they were going to go down "with their boots on."[91]

Vega admitted to no more than four dead and three wounded, probably an underestimation. Upwards of thirty rebels were killed, among them James Dunn, erstwhile boon companion of Pryce and Hopkins. Twelve deserters from the United States Army and Navy, including Mosby, a Marine private, were counted amidst the refugees. According to the *Union,* the interior of Tijuana buildings bore evidence of the rebels' vandalism. On the other hand, as their attorney, Kirk, pointed out, none of those held briefly on the American side before being sent on their carefree way was identified as one of the famous criminals. Vega, for his part, refused to permit the Red Cross to visit the battlefield, and was charged by the press with disposing of stray wounded.[92]

After a no-holds-barred war, the Liberals were finished. With public opinion along the border strongly against them at the end, the *Union* contemptuously dismissed the rebels as a "wretched band of outlaws," and even the *Sun* expressed the feeling that the "Liberal army, with its generals, Berthold, Leyva, Pryce, Stanley, Smith and Mosby, has gone down in history with the band of William Walker, that terrorized the peninsula 50 years ago."[93]

As a result of the many years of torment, suffering, and exile, Flores Magón had developed a monumental persecution complex. At the moment when his world came crumbling down, the symptoms of this complex asserted themselves. His reaction to the Ferris incident was typical. While denouncing the "swindler" Ferris as one who "calumniated" the Liberal movement, he simultaneously reproached the bourgeois press bitterly for extending the impresario ample coverage, and for failing at the same time to report the resounding rebuff administered Ferris and his faction by the Magonistas.[94] For the Los Angeles press this accusation had some validity, but for the San Diego papers, all of which fully reported on the Liberal resurgence, it was untrue. Moreover, there was doubt whether the defeat administered Ferris and James was as effective as it had been decisive.

Even more symptomatic was Flores Magón's reaction to Madero's efforts at obtaining a surrender. On the theory that a direct appeal to Flores Magón should have the greatest chance of success, the Anti-Reëlectionist leader sent two emissaries to Los Angeles at the same time as Leyva went to Mexicali. These were the oldest of the Flores Magón brothers, Jesús, and Juan Sarabia, just released from prison and a recent convert to Maderism. In a conference June 13, their hope of convincing Ricardo came to nothing; he emphatically rejected all arguments on the subject of quitting. On the next day, the Junta were arrested. This disaster, argued the rebel leader, was the fault of the unwelcome visitors. Sarabia, he continued, had told him that he was going to do him as much harm as possible, should he fail to give up.[95]

He responded in much the same way to other matters crowding in during these eventful last days. Pryce had left without turning in party funds. The military reverses in Baja California and the transportation of Mexican troops on American trains were the fruits of the betrayal of Rodolfo Gallegos and the machinations of the "land pirates" Otis and Bliss.[96] Furthermore, the misconception that the Liberals wished to detach Baja California from Mexico was the work of the bourgeois press, the wicked capitalists, and Madero. Every week now, in anguish, he wrote about the peninsula, begging, ordering, exhorting, *commanding* his readers to understand that their enemies had conspired to perpetrate this fraud.[97]

The harsh truth was that by this time every group, with

the exception of the anarchists, had turned against him. As other elements had been growing increasingly hostile, he had come to count more and more on his tenuous alliance with the Socialists. However, the course of events, particularly Madero's victory, loosened this bond to the severance point. For a second time, Juan Sarabia appealed to Flores Magón to surrender. By means of an "Open Letter," he stated the reasons why the small group of Mexican Socialists favored the discontinuance of the Magonista crusade. Pointing out that Flores Magón's "anarchistic movement" did not have "the sympathy of the people," and that the "patriotic sentiments of our people which are still uncontrolled and show very little logic, view with disgust the large number of foreigners in Lower California," Sarabia stressed that the "sympathy and admiration . . . that surrounded your name is fast disappearing and is changing to hatred toward you. . . . Brother Ricardo, it is time that this fighting and violence should stop; there should be no more human bloodshed. Do not keep so many fellow beings in a desperate struggle with no good result in sight. Change your methods of fighting, put down your arms, . . . and accept what the actual circumstances will allow."[98]

The American Socialists had similar feelings. Congressman Victor Berger of Wisconsin, through his secretary, W. J. Ghent, issued a statement repudiating the peninsular rebels on the question of revolutionary reliability. Whereas Comrade Berger himself most certainly was a Socialist and emphatically adhered to the principles of the Second International, he was convinced that the Magonista rebels not only were not Socialists, "but in the main . . . opposed to Socialism." Far from being an essentially Mexican movement, they were a movement with roots in the United States, whose "promoters and followers are a mixture of men of every creed except Socialism. Some of them are merely vague utopians. Some of them are so-called 'direct actionists.' Others are avowedly anarchists. Still others are revolutionaries by temperament and would as readily revolt against a Socialist administration as against a capitalist administration." In fine, American Socialists could not afford to have any connections with the

Magonistas, who appeared to be too revolutionary for them.[99]

The *Appeal to Reason,* America's most widely read Socialist organ, also spoke against them. Although it expressed "both sympathy and admiration for the handful of patriots . . . engaged in an independent armed rebellion in Lower California," it nevertheless felt that Flores Magón, from "the security of his office" on American soil, was "pushing them to inevitable disaster." The *Appeal* took especial issue with the Junta president's "utterly impractical" contention that if both Madero and the United States would only keep a hands-off policy, the Liberals would win. Madero could not possibly keep his hands off, the paper maintained, just as Lincoln could not, when faced with secession, and just as Flores Magón, were he ever to be president, could "do nothing but force it [Lower California] to remain"; and for exactly "these reasons the Mexican government will be forced to interfere with the armed rebellion in Lower California. If it does not, then the United States will have legitimate excuse for intervention. Magón's 'direct action' is for the first time in the course of the insurrection really endangering the independence of Mexico."[100]

In addition, Eugene Debs, whose support Flores Magón had done his utmost to retain, became skeptical of the Liberal Party's program on the grounds that it was anarchist, that it did not plainly state this fact, and that, in view of the backward economic state of the Mexican proletariat, it was bound to come to nought.[101]

La Regeneración's response to its Socialist critics was bitter: Juan Sarabia was a Judas, the Socialists had swallowed the capitalists' propaganda, and Madero's money had bought off the Socialist press, together with Debs, Berger, and others.[102]

All was not entirely serene even within the anarchist family circle. Though no official split ever materialized, three subjects generated much ill-feeling: the mystery of what had become of the Junta's income, the importance of Baja California in the Liberal revolution as a whole, and Flores Magón's failure to participate personally in the fighting.

The Italian anarchists in the United States and the IWW's,

after a fashion, had been Flores Magón's most faithful allies. Italian workers again and again made contributions out of their hard-earned wages. Afterwards, some difference of opinion arose among the rank and file, though not within the leadership, as to whether funds had been misused. *L'Era Nuova,* which backed the Liberals to the bitter end, refused to publish a "calumnious" communication hinting at Magonista financial irresponsibility. Another Italian journal, the *Lavoratore Italiano* of Pittsburg, Kansas, had printed the message, which described the Mexican revolution as having, in addition to its socio-economic aspect, a "sumptuously remunerative aspect for its revolutionaries of the gambling table."[103] The IWW grumbles were louder. Apropos the government's arrest of Mosby and other Wobblies, an IWW organizer complained that the Junta were contributing nothing to their defense, and that during the fighting they "never saw any of the money they sent in to that bunch."[104] Burdened with a host of problems after their arrest, the Liberal leaders met these criticisms with silence.

In their interpretation of peninsular events for the benefit of the confused reader, Flores Magón and William Owen stressed that soldiers fighting in Baja California acted in but one portion of the larger Liberal theater. One week, Owen, on the English page, dwelling on this theme, casually remarked that "nothing . . . could have shown more complete ignorance than the centering of attention on the exceedingly subsidiary movement in Lower California."[105] When the Wobblies read this cavalier dismissal of their military exploits, they exploded:

Many deserving men went down there, and *who* sent them there? Who? I do not like to ask this question, but it is one the Revolutionary Junta Should be Forced to answer. Just because men proclaim themselves Revolutionists is no reason why they should not be forced to answer for what, to me, on their own admission, savors of a crime against the International Proletariat. Force the Junta to answer and to give some explanation better than an anarchistic shriek at a lot of socialistic politicians.[106]

No matter how loudly the IWW's roared, their outcries did not change the conviction of the Junta, with their sights fixed on a distant horizon, that the Liberals were fighting effectively on a number of fronts throughout the whole land of Mexico.

During the campaign in Baja California, and for some time thereafter, many radicals severely criticized Flores Magón for restricting his role to editing a weekly newspaper, instead of going to Mexico to act as field leader. In response, Owen pointed out that the exile was an intellectual, a theoretician, and a propagandist, interested in a long-range economic and social movement, and therefore could not be expected to participate in a brief, passing phase of the ever-unfolding revolution.[107] Nevertheless, this aspect and others came up for scrutiny by the leaders of international anarchism. In Paris, *Les Temps Nouveaux,* perhaps the most influential Anarchist journal, took Flores Magón to task for failing to participate in his own revolution. It also blamed the Junta for using money contributed by people in many lands to foment personal factionalism in Mexico. Lastly, and interestingly, it censured the Liberals for operating during the revolution under their program of July 1, 1906, which, as the journal pointed out, was not an anarchist one. Only in September, 1911, after all was over, did the Junta drop the reformist program of 1906 in favor of an openly anarchist one and officially replace the slogan "Reform, Liberty, and Justice," with "Land and Liberty." The party leadership managed to survive these criticisms partly because Peter Kropotkin, oracle of world anarchism, came to their defense. He pointed out, without displaying a keen perception of the particular case at issue, that there was much more to anarchism than fighting on the barricades.[108]

Defying everything and everybody, Flores Magón struggled on. By now completely blind to facts, he could not see that his revolution was over: although guerrilla bands occasionally caused trouble here and there, never again did the Liberals field an army, capture important towns, or try to administer an area. Hunched over his desk, the rebel against political tyranny, against Mexico's economic domination by Americans, against entrenched wealth, against religion, against law, against society itself, wrote on:

Law is a farce, a chain to tie down the poor. . . . Law is a prosti-
tute who lends herself to those who have money and turns her
back on those who do not.

.   .   .   .

I do not doubt that some day my poor skin will serve . . . as a
footrest, because with money anything is possible . . . ; but the
idea is immortal. Man is worth nothing; the idea is everything.

.   .   .   .

Death to Authority, Death to the Rich!

.   .   .   .

We know that we are destined to absorb a dagger in our flesh or
to die of consumption in some prison. We accept our destiny with
pleasure, satisfied with having accomplished something on behalf
of the slaves.

.   .   .   .

Mexico's revolutionary spark is the beginning of the purifying
fire that from one moment to another will envelope every country in the world.[109]

CHAPTER X

Aftermath

In the epilogue to the Liberal revolution two interesting legal proceedings played a part: the Pryce extradition hearing of September, 1911, and the Junta's trial in June, 1912, for violation of the neutrality laws.

The period during which the two actions were brought up was one of great social strife in California. It was the time of the tense McNamara trial in Los Angeles[1] and the noisy Free Speech riots in San Diego.[2] The Magonistas' legal difficulties were part of this mood.

Though Pryce and the Junta had repudiated each other, his extradition hearing was of great importance to both. To the Welshman personally, the outcome may have been a matter of life and death, since it was generally believed that, if handed over to the Mexican authorities, he surely would be executed. There was a broader question involved as well: had he been the leader of a regularly organized revolutionary group aiming at political ends, or had he simply been at the head of a gang of looters and pillagers? If the former, he was entitled to the protection of political refuge; if the latter, he was subject to extradition as a bandit and murderer. For the Liberals, the issue was vital, because on it hinged the question whether the United States government was willing to recognize them as a revolutionary group, rather than to expose them all to extradition as thieves and assassins.

The hearing, which took a week and had all the elements of a trial, attracted wide attention and aroused strong feelings. Pryce gave a good account of himself. He had the adventurer's knack for dramatizing his situation in a light highly favorable to himself and for gathering about him an unlikely assortment of friends and defenders. Individuals representing all the factions in the Liberal army testified on his behalf. At the diplomatic level, Great Britain's scholar-ambassador, Lord Bryce, wrote urgent letters to the State Department concerning the case. On the personal level, the public learned with some surprise that the soldier of fortune had a fiancée, a Miss Hattie Biggs of Vancouver, British Columbia, who appealed to President Taft to prevent his extradition.[3]

The case was decided strictly on the basis of legal merits. The United States commissioner held that the evidence clearly showed that Pryce had been the leader of a revolutionary army, and therefore was not subject to removal to Mexico. There still remained the neutrality violation count. Army friends helped to scrape up bail money, and he was released.[4] For the Liberals, the outcome was gratifying: their movement was recognized as a political one, and it was plainly futile for the Mexican government to pursue extradition proceedings against anyone else.

The Junta's trial was a radically different matter. It was as if the whole Liberal movement, army and all, had literally moved into the courtroom: misunderstandings abounded, charges and countercharges whirled through the air, and new hatreds were grafted onto the old. So much suspicion and bitterness was created that, somehow, all official transcripts of the proceedings have disappared from public depositaries.[5] The only sources are newspaper accounts.

Assistant United States District Attorney Dudley Robinson, later to become a well-known Los Angeles attorney, handled the case for the federal government. The Junta had employed Job Harriman in the pretrial stage, but lost him, which may have been unfortunate for them. His successor was Willedd Andrews, a young and inexperienced lawyer, who proved unable to present a convincing case for the defense. On both sides, the preparations and the courtroom procedures left much to be desired. As in the cases of Haywood-Moyer-Pettibone and the McNamaras, there were many signs of wholesale perjury and suborning of witnesses. Individuals made statements, unshaken by cross-examination, that were patently in contradiction to known facts as reported in the newspapers at the time of the campaign in Lower California. More significantly, after the trial, a flood of affidavits poured in, repudiating, reaffirming, and re-repudiating testimony.[6]

The prosecution found the roving habits of potential witnesses a severe handicap in attempting to prove its key contention that the Junta had recruited their army on American soil for service in Mexico.[7] Two who so served the government were Paul Schmidt or Paul Smith or P. Silent and Peter Martin or Pedro Martínez. Afterwards, they either repudiated their testimony or threatened to do so, although on the witness stand neither had displayed the slightest trace of doubt or hesitation in detailing his information. Schmidt claimed that he had decided to serve as witness for the prosecution on promise of exemption from sentence on a smuggling offense. Moreover, he had been promised employment, he further stated, in rounding up testifiers at a wage of ten dollars per day and ten cents per mile for travel expenses. He turned in travel vouchers for long distances, although the witnesses came to Los Angeles from nearby points. No doubt there was some truth in Schmidt's account of his association with the government. However, as confirmation of the truth of it, he gave the impression that he had not served a sentence on the smuggling conviction, whereas actually he had.[8] Peter Martin, who at one point had found himself detained on suspicion of having fed poisoned candy to a little girl, also testified on the subject of illegal recruiting. Under threat, he started to repudiate his testimony; under counterthreat, he did not do so. Later, he claimed his original evidence was accurate.[9] These men were two of the prosecution's chief witnesses.

On the other side, the defense resorted to threats against

witnesses. The IWW's demonstrated against witnesses from their seats in the courtroom; others were menaced while in jail; and, after Peter Martin's testimony, Lucile Norman Guidera, Ricardo Flores Magón's stepdaughter, called the witness a traitor and struck him in the face.[10] Furthermore, the defense's arguments were weak. When testimony from the Pryce hearing was admitted in evidence, their contention that no connection existed between the Junta in Los Angeles and the army in Baja California appeared absurd, since the Liberals had depended heavily on the earlier case to prove that the existence of their army showed that they were operating a political organization and were not a band of marauders.

After two weeks, a verdict was reached. On June 22, a year to the day and hour after the final battle in Lower California, the Junta leaders were found guilty of violation of the neutrality laws. Three days later, they were given the maximum sentence under the law, that is, one year and eleven months in federal prison at McNeill Island in the state of Washington. The end of the trial was in keeping with everything else connected with the Liberal movement. Lucile Norman Guidera, "with eyes flashing scorn, lips trembling with anger and calling out the word 'cowards' . . . precipitated one of the wildest riots ever witnessed in the streets of Los Angeles."[11] Order was restored in the city that had been the Magonista headquarters, and the condemned were hastened on their way to the penitentiary.

Some of the Junta's friends, who harbored doubts concerning the fairness of the trial, appealed to the Department of Justice to pardon the prisoners. Their go-between was United States Representative John P. Nolan, Democrat of California. A memorial to President Wilson, newly installed in office, was prepared, calling upon him as a scholar and historian to study the case, and, after convincing himself of its many injustices, to liberate the prisoners. Wilson and his Attorney General, James C. McReynolds, gave the case a fresh examination. On July 22, 1913, the Chief Executive wrote Congressman Nolan: "I took up and examined very thoroughly the case of Ricardo Flores Magón . . . , and am sorry to say that, after looking into the case as fully as possible, I am convinced that it would not be wise or right to grant a pardon."[12] This, then, was the verdict of the scholar-president.

Thus closed the final chapter of the Liberal revolution of 1911. Circumstances had confined the movement largely to one part of Mexico, where it aborted. The history of the area militated against it. Its enemies, Mexican and American, spared no pains to establish it in the public mind as illegitimate. The soldiers' insouciance and their leaders' naïveté enabled adventurers to meddle at the heavy expense of the sponsors. Finally, the Liberal Junta helped to encompass their own ruin through devious methods, clumsiness, and inability to attract people in sufficiently large numbers. The insurrection was fraught with elements of such implausibility that many Baja Californians to this day remain convinced that it was a filibuster that boomeranged.[13] This was not true, except insofar as the Ferris stunt was a farcical echo of the former menace. The transfer of territory by means of a filibuster from one national sovereignty to another was the last thing that the anarchist Flores Magón, the enemy of all states, aimed for. Nor, contrary to rumor, in the absence of United States acquiescence and American capitalist support could others, using or abusing his name, have done so. The most that can be said is that Flores Magón, because of his ineptitude, permitted a filibuster *potential* of sizable proportions to develop at Tijuana in May and June. The Baja California movement of 1911 was an attempted *anarchist* revolution. When this is understood, acrimonious disputes over its manifestations become unnecessary.

The peninsular strife graphically illustrates most of the Liberal Party's weaknesses. However, there are three other shortcomings of Flores Magón and his organization that help to explain, in a context broader than that supplied by the events of the California war, why the leader and his organization were unable to achieve more than limited and temporary success.

First, it is significant that an unusually large number of people defected from the Liberal movement. Among others,

Francisco I. Madero, Antonio Villarreal, Lázaro Gutiérrez de Lara, Juan Sarabia, Antonio de Pío Araujo, Rosalío Bustamante, and Caryl Ap Rhys Pryce quit in disillusionment, disappointment, anger, or indifference.[14] Furthermore, there were serious quarrels involving Praxedis Guerrero, José María Leyva, and John Kenneth Turner. Some of these men were mere drifters and hangers-on, others were sincere idealists. The Liberal Party attracted too many drifters and proved unable to retain the allegiance of many idealists. This failing not only limited the movement's success but also detracted from the stature of the leader.

Second, Flores Magón, for one whose creed was predicated upon a belief in the essential goodness of man, expended enormous energy in denouncing others, and, particularly, in stigmatizing erstwhile followers. The majority of revolutionary extremists have indulged in this practice, but Flores Magón did so with unhealthy zeal. Torrents of abuse descended upon former adherents; their motives were self-evidently low; his alone were high-minded. Madero, who paid with his life for attempting to give Mexico too much freedom too fast, was a "traitor to the cause of liberty" and a "tyrant worse than Díaz." Villarreal, his companion of many years' standing, was labelled a "homosexual" and an "assassin." Juan Sarabia, who, in the service of the Liberal cause, nearly went blind in Díaz's worst prison, became a "Judas" the instant he joined Madero.[15] Such denunciations were bound to discourage potential followers. Yet, strangely, there was a lapse in Flores Magón's vindictiveness. Surely, the two men who did the most damage to his movement were Pryce and Ferris. In Pryce's case, he contented himself with a hint, in a private communication to a third party, that the Welshman had made off with party funds.[16] As for Ferris, after denouncing him a few times,[17] Flores Magón omitted further references to the comic. In striking contrast, he bitterly castigated Villarreal for many weeks in the pages of *La Regeneración*.[18] This inconsistency of Flores Magón's may be capable of psychological explanation. Possibly, a seasoned adventurer like Pryce intimidated him slightly, while Ferris may have induced in him a certain feeling of guilt for having failed to denounce that meddler weeks before he saw fit to do so. In any case, his selective vindictiveness further diminished his standing as a leader.

Finally, at the core of Flores Magón's Liberal movement lay a fundamental, unposed question. Can deceit and deception, advanced to the level of systematic policy, ever open the way to a desired end? The thought is an intriguing one. Is it possible to achieve an end while continuously denying that that goal is the objective? Unless all participants understand and accept the underlying deception, the method is necessarily self-defeating. However, in that event, the technique itself is unnecessary. While at times all movements will deceive, out of expediency or convenience, it appears to be humanly and logically impossible to succeed with deception as the foundation of policy. For Flores Magón, the technique led straight into the web of misunderstanding that linked the two Californias in 1911. There was something deficient in an enterprise that had to be pursued with such complete lack of candor.

What happened to the leading figures of 1911? For several, participation in the ill-starred revolution seemed to have cast a shadow over the rest of their lives. None subsequently achieved greater fame or happiness. With many, it was quite the contrary.

A possible happy exception was General José María Leyva. The Fabian associated himself with the Maderistas, and, later, with other moderate elements during Mexico's long revolution. He entered the regular army, rose in rank, and eventually retired as a brigadier general.[19] Though long harassed for his part in Baja California events, he lived in Mexico City in reasonable comfort until his recent death.

Colonel Vega went on to participate in the notorious Huerta–Féliz Díaz sham civil war in Mexico City during February, 1913,[20] which brought about the forcible displacement of Madero as president of Mexico. The reputation of no one, except possibly Madero, was enhanced by involvement in that affair.

Former Consul Schmucker found that his collapse was the

ruin of his career in the consular service. He recovered his faculties after a rest, and was transferred to the immigration service. In 1917, he sought reinstatement in his former agency, but the State Department preferred not to grant his wish.[21]

General Jack Mosby came to a mysterious end. After having controversially testified in the Junta's neutrality trial, he was sentenced to the penitentiary for desertion from the marines. En route to jail, he was killed while trying to escape.[22] Though American history is dotted with instances of the use of extralegal means for the elimination of unpopular individuals, the use of the Mexican *ley de fuga* is uncommon. Could the headstrong and unhappy Mosby really have attempted a rash escape?

As for the Wobblies, a few found work in and around San Diego on a day-to-day basis. At one stage, a car dealer paid a group of them to crowd into an automobile to advertise his latest roomy model. Another enterprising businessman sought to attract prospective customers by engaging a dozen Wobblies to lounge in his show window and play cards. Others among them looked for jobs with the proposed Wild West show at the Ferris-less Pan-Pacific groundbreaking festivities.[23] The majority drifted on, as had their brethren at Mexicali.

The three foremost principals of the events of 1911 continued to lead lives as diverse as their philosophies. For a time, Dick Ferris rode high. Since the government could not manage to accumulate enough incriminating evidence, it dismissed the neutrality law violation charge against him.[24] He made a successful comeback behind the footlights. Because of the ample publicity he had manufactured for himself in connection with peninsular events, he and Mrs. Ferris played before packed houses up and down the West Coast in "The Man from Mexico." To Ferris the Mexican struggle for freedom was a circumstance to be exploited on the farcical level of a play whose punch lines were "Mexico is nothing but a cell," and, "There are bars all around me but I can't get a drink."[25]

Thereafter, the Ferris luck was not quite so steady, and he captured the headlines much less frequently. In 1913, Mrs. Ferris divorced him, returning to the stage under her for-

mer name of Florence Stone. The two had been closely associated in the public's mind, and, operating on his own, Dick
seemed to have lost some of his verve. By 1920, his name did
not appear in the Los Angeles City Directory. In 1921, becoming active again, he helped organize the city's Yellow Taxi
Cab service. His interest in aviation reawakened, and the later
twenties found him actively engaged in promoting transcon-
tinental air service to the West Coast. Another old interest
aroused him. In collaboration with movie and sports figures,
he managed to lease 14,000 acres of land between Tijuana and
Endenada in 1926, for the purpose of developing a luxury resort, to be known as the Paradise Beach Club. This news, if
they read it, must have embittered his old, and now battered
and weary, foes of the 1911 revolution. By the 1930's, Dick
had retired. An adolescent to the end, he created his own
Fountain of Youth by proclaiming on each birthday that he
had just turned thirty-eight. In 1933, Ferris died.[26]

Dick Ferris was a remarkably versatile promoter, actor, and
buffoon. By his antics he earned at least a small place in history. Dick Ferris, unlike the old-time filibusters, who revelled
in danger and hardship, will be remembered as the only
known filibuster-clown. In Mexico, his name evokes scorn to
this very day. Dick, who lived his life on the surface, would
have regarded contempt as a small price for fame.

For Pryce, adventure was life. After his release from the Los
Angeles County jail, a fling at the new profession of movie acting earned him some money. He played the part of a cowboy
hero.[27] In view of the subsequent success of movie cowboys, he
might have done well to stick with that career. In July, 1913,
the neutrality law violation charge against him was finally
dismissed, as the Justice Department came to the conclusion
that his contention was correct: he had gone to Mexico without solicitation, and had not recruited soldiers while on
United States soil.[28] When World War I broke out, Pryce,
who had in the meantime returned to Canada, immediately
joined the Canadian army, later transferring to the English
army. He managed to survive four years of trench warfare on
the western front, was wounded in action, won the 1914–15

Star, the British War and Victory Medals, and received appointment as a Companion of the Distinguished Service Order. In 1919, he resigned at the rank of major. He corresponded with the British army records office until 1925;[29] after that time, nothing more is known of him.

Without a doubt, the Welshman turned into a would-be filibuster, not so much because of a deep-seated personal ambition as because of the Junta's inaction and preoccupation with radical ideology. This was his undoing: as a filibuster he lacked, not ability, energy, or courage, but the iron will of a William Walker. In addition, as he found out, the times were inauspicious for a successful coup d'état. When Walker and Raousset could not consummate a successful filibuster under relatively propitious circumstances, there was scant chance of doing so in 1911. In the Age of Discovery, when adventurous imperialism was not only applauded but encouraged, Pryce would have done well. In the twentieth century, his love of adventure and intrigue needed a political outlet, but the times did not provide a legitimate means. Consequently, with occasional pangs of conscience, he took up the role of latter-day filibuster, only to find that his efforts could not get beyond the verbal stage, and his intrigues gave way to a buffoon's comic-opera stunt. As one who hesitantly ventured along the well-worn and perilous path marked out by Burr, Walker, and Raousset-Boulbon, Pryce will rank behind these notorious figures in Latin American history. Like Ferris, his name is hated in Mexico. Unlike his Thespian friend, Pryce would be a little disturbed if he knew it.

As for Flores Magón, after the failure in Baja California, he was never able to regain his once great influence on the Mexican political scene. In contrast to other ideological leaders of his generation, such as Antonio Díaz Soto y Gama, Antonio Villarreal, and Francisco Madero, who achieved fame in the wake of Díaz's downfall, the exile became nearly forgotten. His fame declined partly because his revolutionary ideal represented too thoroughgoing a cure for the ills of Mexican society, or for any other society. Thus, as those in control of events dispensed strong, but palatable, medicine, Flores

Magón, who prescribed a remedy that would have entirely transformed the body politic, found that time and circumstances had passed him by. Another reason for the eclipse of the Liberal leader lay in his unhappy facility for disappearing behind prison walls, indefinitely removed from the public gaze.

In January, 1914, the long-time revolutionary completed serving his 1912 sentence for violation of the neutrality laws. As persistent as ever, he resumed the editorship of *La Regeneración*.[30] By then, however, the Liberal movement was all but defunct. Emiliano Zapata, though he never considered himself an anarchist, had popularized much of Ricardo Flores Magón's economic program, as well as his slogan, "Land and Liberty," and was fighting for them. The Junta leader himself was confined almost entirely to propaganda as his means of exerting influence.

It took Flores Magón two years to fall afoul of the law again. A vehement attack on Carranza, whom the United States meantime had decided to recognize, led to his arrest in February, 1916, and to a year's prison sentence. He managed to gain his freedom while his appeal was pending, and promptly ran into trouble with the law once more. Consequently he came to serve the February, 1916, sentence concurrently with its successor and final sentence.[31]

By the early part of 1918, the fourth year of World War I was approaching, and the Russian Revolution had taken place. After the United States had entered the war a year earlier, Congress passed an Espionage Act, whose chief effect was the prosecution of radicals for obstruction of the war effort. Flores Magón violated this law.

The circumstances of his apprehension were unusual. After the Espionage Act had been passed, the editor was forced to use some measure of circumspection in writing in his weekly, lest he be instantly embroiled with the law. Trouble befell him in March, 1918. Partly inspired by the Russian Revolution, Flores Magón and Librado Rivera, speaking on behalf of the Junta, published an appeal to anarchists and workers of all lands. The manifesto, whose phraseology was somewhat ambiguous, predicted the imminent downfall of bourgeois, capitalist society and the coming of the revolution, not upon the initiative of particular human beings, but in response to long-standing, overwhelming injustice. For the time being, the role of intellectuals should be to prepare the masses for the great occasion. The appeal made no direct reference to the United States or to her war effort, and its only suggestion of force was in a slightly obscure passage to the effect that the long oppression was causing the fists of the downtrodden to contract and their hearts to beat violently, preparing for the moment when they would drop their tools to "seize the rifle which nervously awaits the caress of the hero." Then followed the striking words: "The moment is solemn; it is the moment preceding the greatest political and social catastrophe that History will register: the insurrection of the poor everywhere against existing conditions."[32]

For writing thus in a foreign-language periodical with limited circulation, Flores Magón and Rivera were arrested as violators of the Espionage Act. As on previous occasions, the government's case lacked solidity, not because Flores Magón was not an advocate of violence, but because in this particular piece of writing there was very little stress on the direct use of force. In an effort to add substance to its case, at the trial the prosecution submitted information not within the terms of the indictment, in order to corroborate the contention that Flores Magón had for many years believed in anarchism and advocated force. The government made reference to a speech delivered as late as May 27, 1917, just before the passage of the Espionage Act of June 15, 1917. In that address the rebel leader had said, among other things, that Right, as personified by the workers, "roars its vengeance in dynamite, and belches lead from the barricade." Flores Magón and Rivera were found guilty of violation of the Espionage Act. Flores Magón was sentenced to twenty years in prison.[33]

With the benefit of hindsight, it seems plain that the verdict was based mainly on ex post facto considerations. Flores Magón was condemned, not for a clear violation of the law of June 15, 1917, but for all that he had done prior to its passage.

Ironically, the manifesto of March 16, 1918, was far less violent than some of the tracts penned during the period from 1910 to 1912. This time, by meting out drastic punishment, the government compensated for its previous inability to obtain anything more severe than two-year convictions.[34]

The sentence caused a great deal of misunderstanding. On the one hand, the government, as well as conservative Americans in general, greatly overestimated the effect of Flores Magón's ideas within the United States. In the era of the first "Red Scare," the A. Mitchell Palmer raids, and the subsequent Harding administration, conservatives denounced efforts at either a reduction of the sentence or a pardon. On the other hand, American liberals tended, as on earlier occasions, to sentimentalize Flores Magón's intentions. Noting, correctly, that the government had got a conviction on contrived evidence, in an atmosphere of wartime hysteria, not for the commission of deeds but for words spoken and written, they addressed themselves to the tradition of free speech. At the time, public meetings in favor of the broadest possible definition of this constitutional principle, including its extension to the country's radicals of the Flores Magón stamp, occasionally were held. Liberals who were directly interested in Flores Magón's case usually understood little of what his tenets up to his conviction of 1918 had been. Consequently, after his death, they depicted him as an incipient pacifist, a follower of Tolstoy, a "philosophical anarchist," and a believer in a "world ruled by good will, coöperation and brotherhood."[35] This is palpably misleading. Possibly, during his last few years, which he spent hidden from the public behind prison bars, his outlook on the use of force changed. However, there cannot be any doubt that up until his final arrest he was a violent anarchist, though on occasions he found it convenient to conceal this fact.

After his last conviction, Flores Magón was never to be a free man again. Existence in the penitentiary not only oppressed him spiritually but also caused a steady deterioration in his precarious health. At the same time, the onetime fierce polemicist mellowed considerably. Letters to friends now contained a large measure of tolerance and forbearance in his judgments on individuals and rival political movements, while the prose he used to give expression to his libertarian creed was unusually lofty and moving:

If there were not injustice on earth, I should not be a rebel, but as long as there are tears, sadness, and anguish . . . , my soul cannot be at peace.

. . . .

The dreamer is the designer of tomorrow. Practical men . . . can laugh at him; they do not know that he is the true dynamic force that pushes the world forward. Suppress him, and the world will deteriorate toward barbarism. Despised, impoverished, he leads the way . . . , sowing, sowing, sowing, the seeds that will be harvested, not by him, but by the practical men of tomorrow, who will at the same time laugh at another indefatigable dreamer busy seeding, seeding, seeding.

. . . .

I affirm that if the human species is some time able to taste true fraternity, liberty, and social justice, it will be through the medium of anarchism. . . . When I die, my friends will perhaps inscribe on my tomb, "Here lies a dreamer," and my enemies, "Here lies a madman," but no one will be able to stamp the inscription, "Here lies a coward and traitor to his ideas."[36]

Interestingly, his views on the Communist experiment in Russia altered rapidly. At first, like most radicals, he had hailed Lenin and Trotsky as the heralds of a new golden age of human liberty. However, very soon, he grew suspicious of the all-powerful Communist state. As early as 1921, he wrote that the "so-called transition necessary between Tyranny and Liberty has proved really to be a transition between an abortive revolution and normality; it is Czarism, with a new dress in order to satisfy the frivolity of the masses. . . . The dictatorship of the proletariat is in reality the dictatorship of Lenin and Trotsky over the proletariat. I have been observing day after day the . . . murder of the revolutionary principles in Russia."[37]

After 1920, unsuccessful efforts were made at obtaining the old rebel's release, or, failing that, at lightening the burden of his sentence. In Mexico, early in the Obregón administration, Congress offered pensions to Flores Magón and Librado Rivera, with the intention of easing their imprisonment by providing them with some small funds. After thanking the Mexican Chamber for its generosity, Flores Magón, true to his tenets, refused the help:

> I do not believe in the State. . . . I fight for the universal brotherhood of man. I consider the State an institution created by capitalism to guarantee the exploitation and subjugation of the masses. Consequently, all money derived from the State represents the sweat, anguish, and sacrifice of the workers. Were the money to come directly from the workers, I should accept it with pleasure and pride, because they are my brothers. But coming by intervention of the State . . . , it is money that would burn my hands and fill my heart with remorse.[38]

Had the prisoner only been willing to request pardon from the Justice Department, the liberal intelligentsia would probably have been able to mobilize sufficient pressure to have his liberty restored. His response to the dilemma of swallowing his convictions as the price for freedom, or, alternatively, consigning himself to a living death in prison, was striking. He preferred death to the odium of having to ask a favor from a government: "This seals my fate. I shall go blind, putrify, and die within these horrendous walls that separate me from the rest of the world because I am not going to request pardon. I shall not do it! In my twenty-nine years of fighting for liberty I have lost everything . . . I have consumed many years of my life in prison; I have experienced the feeling of the vagabond and the pariah; . . . I have lost all . . . except my honor as a fighter."[39]

Flores Magón's body was found, November 21, 1922, on the threshold of his cell in Leavenworth.[40] The day before, he had been in poor spirits, yet able to move about by himself. Was he murdered by an enemy, or did he die as the result of a coronary or consumptive attack? His friend Rivera was quite sure it had been murder.[41] On the other hand, his cell neighbor, the well-known Wobbly Ralph Chaplin, believed that a sudden physical breakdown ended his life.[42] In either case, Flores Magón's death prophesy of 1911 was fulfilled. The remains were transported to Mexico for burial under the auspices of the railway workers union. To the poor people of the nation, the name of the old warrior against Porfirio Díaz had, in the meantime, become a legend. The passage of the funeral train brought forth expressions of admiration and reverence.[43] Though he had been *persona non grata* in his own country throughout most of his life and certainly up to 1920, Mexico's Congress memorialized him upon his death. During the course of a debate on whether or not his remains were to be transported under government sponsorship so that they might "rest in the soil of his country," one of a group of friendly deputies gave expression to the belief that this would be a fitting "posthumous homage to the great Mexican revolutionary, Ricardo Flores Magón, martyr and apostle of libertarian ideas, who died poor and blind in the cold cell of a Yankee prison."[44] Flores Magón would have appreciated the last, more than the first, part of this laudation. Completely to his taste would have been the tribute of Antonio Díaz Soto y Gama, the great orator, Zapatista ideologue, and his long-time personal friend, who said, addressing the deputies: "Instead of asking for an expression of sadness—black crepe or mourning—I request that the Mexican revolutionaries, brothers of Flores Magón, applaud enthusiastically in honor of that great rebel, profoundly troubled spirit, and great man of untarnished and undeviating character called Ricardo Flores Magón."[45]

Thus spoke the rebel's countrymen at the moment of his death. To be sure, Flores Magón's standing in history will not be based upon funeral orations. What will his niche be?

Flores Magón occupies two places: primarily, he was an ideologue active during the modern political liberation of his country, and less important, he was a revolutionist of international repute identified with late nineteenth-century and early twentieth-century anarchism. As he himself regarded revolution in Mexico as but the first step in a greater transformation of mankind, he would have assigned equal importance to both his roles. But for the first he achieved greater renown.

In Mexico, Flores Magón's reputation is assured. With a half-century elapsed, his countrymen remember him chiefly as an actor who spoke the lines of the prologue to their revolutionary drama, rather than as the author of his own unsuccessful radical play. His name lives on as the Great Precursor: without a Flores Magón to prepare the way, the deeds of Madero and Zapata, of Carranza and Villa, would not have been possible.

In his other role, the Mexican revolutionist, like many other extremists of the era, is more difficult to judge. The man who was to some a peerless rebel was to others a renegade and a traitor. In one way or another, Flores Magón resembled such European revolutionaries as Marx, Bakunin, Blanqui, and Mazzini. As a journalist and a theoretician, he approached, and at times achieved, greatness. On the other hand, as a leader of men, his incompetence was truly breathtaking. However, as several other well-known extremists had the same defect, albeit usually in a lesser degree, this alone would not have disqualified him from lasting fame as a major international revolutionary figure. Yet, the excessive caution that he displayed with regard to his person, and his inveterate resort to deception, strongly suggest that something was lacking. The nineteenth-century giants of revolution were indifferent to their own fate, and found it unnecessary to dissimulate their aims.

In life, unhappiness and suffering pursued Flores Magón and all whose fate it was to cross his path. In death, he was finally rewarded: on May 1, 1945, his remains were interred in the Rotunda of Illustrious Men in Mexico City.[46] The Mexican state gave its blessing to the man who had cursed the existence of the State. It was a generous but ironic compliment. Would Flores Magón have felt that his country had done him justice, or would he have rebelled against this form of encomium?

REFERENCE MATTER

NOTES

Throughout the notes, Flores Magón's newspaper, *La Regeneración*, published in Los Angeles, is cited as *LR*, and the National Archives of the United States as NA.

CHAPTER I

1 *People's Paper* (Los Angeles), August 13, 1910.
2 Pedro María Anaya Ibarra, *Precursores de la revolución mexicana* (Mexico City, 1955), pp. 11–19; Guillermo Medina Amor, *No fué filibusterismo la revolución magonista en la Baja California* (Mexicali, 1956), pp. 1–2; Jenaro Amézcua, *¿Quién es Flores Magón y cuál su obra?* (Mexico City, 1943), pp. 15–23. Sources differ as to whether Flores Magón's father fought in the Mexican War, but agree that he fought in Mexico's struggles in the fifties and sixties.
3 R. F. M. to an unnamed woman, July 8, 1922, in *Ricardo Flores Magón, vida y obra,* ed. Grupo Cultural "Ricardo Flores Magón" (9 vols.; Mexico City, 1923), VI, 44–45.
4 Anaya Ibarra, *Precursores de la revolución,* pp. 19–21; Florencio Barrera Fuentes, *Historia de la revolución mexicana: la etapa precursora* (Mexico City, 1955), pp. 27–28. Amézcua *(Flores Magón,* pp. 19–20) treats Flores Magón's life in the years following this early political activity; other authors, for want of information, skip these years altogether.
5 Diego Abad de Santillán, *Ricardo Flores Magón, el apóstol de la revolución social mexicana* (Mexico City, 1925), pp. 5–7, 9–11; Barrera Fuentes, *Historia de la revolución,* pp. 28–112.
6 Abad de Santillán, *Ricardo Flores Magón,* pp. 11–12, 13,

16, 43; Barrera Fuentes, *Historia de la revolución,* pp. 147–60, 194.

7 Barrera Fuentes, *Historia de la revolución,* pp. 159–60; Abad de Santillán, *Ricardo Flores Magón,* pp. 14–16.

8 Abad de Santillán, *Ricardo Flores Magón,* p. 14; Agustín Cué Cánovas, *Ricardo Flores Magón, la Baja California y los Estados Unidos* (Mexico City, 1957), pp. 19–20; Barrera Fuentes, *Historia de la revolución,* pp. 195–97; Howard F. Cline, *The United States and Mexico* (Cambridge, Mass., 1953), p. 116.

9 Barrera Fuentes, *Historia de la revolución,* pp. 166–93; Cué Cánovas, *Ricardo Flores Magón, la Baja California y los Estados Unidos,* pp. 20–22.

10 Cué Cánovas, *Ricardo Flores Magón, la Baja California y los Estados Unidos,* p. 20; Cline, *The United States and Mexico,* pp. 117, 169.

11 Abad de Santillán, *Ricardo Flores Magón,* pp. 20, 36, 55–58; Barrera Fuentes, *Historia de la revolución,* pp. 204–6, 261–66.

12 Barrera Fuentes, *Historia de la revolución,* pp. 164, 213–14; Abad de Santillán, *Ricardo Flores Magón,* pp. 16–17.

13 Barrera Fuentes, *Historia de la revolución,* pp. 158–60, 194–95, 205–6, 245–48; Medina Amor, *No fué filibusterismo,* p. 63; Abad de Santillán, *Ricardo Flores Magón,* pp. 20–21, 28, 40–41.

14 The defense contended that the only major government witness committed perjury. See testimony before the House of Representatives Rules Committee in *Alleged Persecution of Mexican Citizens by the Government of Mexico,* 61 Cong., 2 sess. (Washington, 1910), 15–17, 43.

15 R. F. M. to his attorney, Harry Weinberger, May 9, 1921, in *R. F. M., vida y odra,* VI, 70–73; Barrera Fuentes, *Historia de la revolución,* p. 297.

16 The full story may be found in *Alleged Persecution of Mexican Citizens, passim.*

17 Good appraisals of Flores Magón's role prior to 1910 are to be found in Charles C. Cumberland, "Precursors of the Mexican Revolution of 1910," *Hispanic American Historical Review,* XXII (May, 1942), 344–56; Cline, *The United States and Mexico,* pp. 116–17; Cué Cánovas, *Ricardo Flores Magón, la Baja California y los Estados Unidos,* pp. 22–24.

18 Amézcua, *Flores Magón,* p. 31.

19 Barrera Fuentes, *Historia de la revolución*, p. 116.
20 *Ibid.*, p. 166; Abad de Santillán, *Ricardo Flores Magón*, pp. 8, 19, 44–45.
21 There are many good studies of anarchism. A brief, useful recent analysis may be found in G. D. H. Cole, *Socialist Thought: Marxism and Anarchism, 1850–1890* (London, 1954), pp. 213–37, 315–61.
22 R. F. M. to Nicholás Bernal, June 2, 1921, in *R. F. M., vida y obra*, VI, 9.
23 Code letters by R. F. M. to unknown parties, June 13, 15, 17, 1908 (Gen. Recs., Dept. of Just., Rec. Gp. 74, NA). The Justice Department's translation was a very poor one, and the above is slightly paraphrased, with the thought transcribed intact. An important controversial problem of Flores Magón historiography is the authenticity of documents. The genuineness of the above letters seems almost incontestable, as they are consistent with passages in a letter of Enrique Flores Magón to Praxedis Guerrero, June 9, 1908, quoted in Abad de Santillán, *Ricardo Flores Magón*, pp. 45, 46, and that author's comment on p. 44.
24 Edward H. Carr, *Michael Bakunin* (London, 1937), pp. 379–80.
25 See below, Chapter VI, *passim*.
26 Cline, *The United States and Mexico*, pp. 115–16; Charles C. Cumberland, *The Mexican Revolution: Genesis under Madero* (Austin, Texas, 1952), pp. 47–122; Stanley R. Ross, *Francisco I. Madero: Apostle of Mexican Democracy* (New York, 1955) , pp. 46–117.
27 *People's Paper*, August 13, 1910; *LR*, September 10, 1910.
28 *LR*, September 3, 1910. See also the issues of September 17, October 1, and November 12, 1910.
29 *Ibid.*, especially September 10, October 1, 8, 1910.
30 Ross, *Madero*, pp. 42–43.
31 *Ibid.*, pp. 124–35; Cumberland, *Mexican Revolution, Genesis*, pp. 124–29.
32 Enrique Flores Magón to Praxedis Guerrero, June 9, 1908, in Abad de Santillán, *Ricardo Flores Magón*, pp. 45–46.
33 Abad de Santillán, *Ricardo Flores Magón*, p. 59.
34 *LR*, December 10, 17, 24, 1910.
35 Circular reprinted in Abad de Santillán, *Ricardo Flores Magón*, pp. 65–66.
36 See issues of October 22, November 5, December 10, 17, 1910.

37   Documents enclosed in a letter from A. I. McCormick, U.S. Distr. Atty. for the So. Distr. of Calif., to U.S. Atty. Gen. George Wickersham, May 20, 1911 (Gen. Recs., Dept. of Just., Rec. Gp. 74, NA). The meaning of the word "troops" in regard to pay in the Federal army remained unspecific as to rank.

38   R. F. M. to Camilo Jiménez, December 20, 1911, in Medina Amor, *No fué filibusterismo,* p. 76.

39   *Investigation of Mexican Affairs,* Sen. Exec. Doc. No. 285, 66 Cong., 2 sess. (2 vols.; Washington, 1919–1920), II, 2514, quotes Flores Magón's own statement.

40   He did so without the Junta's authorization.—Amézcua, *Flores Magón,* p. 41.

41   *Praxedis G. Guerrero,* ed. Grupo Cultural "Ricardo Flores Magón" (Mexico City, 1924), p. 8; Abad de Santillán, *Ricardo Flores Magón,* pp. 68, 69.

42   R. F. M. to Enrique Flores Magón, June 7, 1908, in Abad de Santillán, *Ricardo Flores Magón,* p. 52.

CHAPTER II

1   Among the works that treat of the development of this area are H. H. Bancroft, *The Works of Hubert Howe Bancroft* (39 vols.; San Francisco, 1882–90), XV, 140–44, XVI, 712–19; Robert G. Cleland, *History of California: The American Period* (New York, 1922); and Paul N. Garber, *The Gadsden Treaty* (Philadelphia, 1923). Two good Mexican histories are Ulises Irigoyen, *Carretera transpeninsular de la Baja California* (2 vols.; Mexico City, 1943 and 1945) and especially Pablo L. Martínez, *Historia de Baja California* (Mexico City, 1956).

2   For Burr's plans, see Thomas Perkins Abernethy, *The Burr Conspiracy* (New York, 1954); for details of Texas filibustering, see Harris G. Warren, *The Sword Was Their Passport* (Baton Rouge, La., 1943).

3   R. R. Stenberg, "Polk and Frémont, 1845–1846," *Pacific Historical Review,* VII (September, 1938), 211–27.

4   William O. Scroggs, *Filibusters and Financiers* (New York, 1916), pp. 1–48.

5   *Ibid.,* pp. 34–48; R. K. Wyllys, *The French in Sonora (1850–1854)* (Berkeley, 1932); Horacio Sobarzo, *Crónica de la aventura de Raousset-Boulbon en Sonora* (Mexico City, 1954); Robert H. Forbes, *Crabb's Filibustering Expedition into Sonora, 1857* (Tucson, Ariz., 1952).

6 Andrew F. Rolle, "Futile Filibustering in California, 1888–1890," *Pacific Historical Review,* XX (May, 1951), 159–66.

7 Bancroft, *Works,* XVI, 195.

8 Robert G. Cleland, *California in Our Time, 1900–1940* (New York, 1947), pp. 109–10; *San Diego Union,* January 19, 1911.

9 Los Angeles newspapers, 1910–1911, *passim.*

10 Cleland, *California in Our Time,* pp. 28, 42–43.

11 *Los Angeles Express,* February 13, 1911; *San Diego Union,* January 22, 1911.

12 *Los Angeles Express,* June 21, 1911.

13 Ira B. Cross, *A History of the Labor Movement in California* (Berkeley, 1935), pp. 268–69, 281–84; Grace H. Stimson, *Rise of the Labor Movement in Los Angeles* (Berkeley, 1955), pp. 237, 331, 341.

14 Stimson, *Rise of the Labor Movement,* pp. 366–406; Cleland, *California in Our Time,* pp. 73–87.

15 Paul F. Brissenden, *The I.W.W.: A Study of American Syndicalism* (New York, 1919), pp. 257, 261; Hyman Weintraub, "The I.W.W. in California, 1905–1931" (unpublished Master's thesis, University of California at Los Angeles, 1947), pp. 23, 37–38.

16 Cleland, *California in Our Time,* pp. 40–44.

17 Stimson, *Rise of the Labor Movement,* pp. 347, 398–99, 407–8.

18 Frank Waters, *The Colorado* (New York, 1946); Carey McWilliams, *California, the Great Exception* (New York, 1949), p. 303.

19 David O. Woodbury, *The Colorado Conquest* (New York, 1941), a good journalistic history of the region, pp. 30–32, 45–158; U.S. Bureau of Foreign and Domestic Commerce, *Mexican West Coast and Lower California: A Commercial and Industrial Survey,* Special Agents Series No. 220 (Washington, 1923), 281, 300; Martínez, *Historia de Baja California,* pp. 478–79.

20 Woodbury, *Colorado Conquest,* pp. 104–10, 113–36, 278.

21 Cleland, *California in Our Time,* pp. 172–74; *Mexican West Coast and Lower California,* 300–301, 306; Waters, *The Colorado,* p. 308.

22 For example, the *Imperial Valley Press,* February 18, April 15, 29, 1911, contains several typical diatribes against Otis and the *Los Angeles Times.*

23 For instance, see the *Los Angeles Times,* April 5, 1911.

24 *Imperial Valley Press,* February 4, 1911, has an amusing gibe at the Wobblies' idleness.

25 Martínez, *Historia de Baja California,* pp. 461–75; *Mexican West Coast and Lower California,* 283, 323; George F. Deasy and Peter Gerhard, "Settlement in Baja California, 1768–1930," *Geographic Review,* XXXIV (October, 1944), 574–86.

26 *Mexican West Coast and Lower California,* 293; Los Angeles and San Diego press, 1911, *passim.*

27 *Mexican West Coast and Lower California,* 327–28; San Diego newspapers, 1911, *passim.*

28 *Mexican West Coast and Lower California,* 300, 306, 327; Eugene K. Chamberlin, "Mexican Colonization versus American Interests in Lower California," *Pacific Historical Review,* XX (February, 1951), 43–55, especially 44.

29 Los Angeles newspapers, 1911, *passim.*

30 *San Diego Union,* January 2, 1911; *Mexican West Coast and Lower California,* 327.

31 Rolle, "Futile Filibustering in California," *Pacific Historical Review,* XX, 160–61; Martínez, *Historia de Baja California,* pp. 463, 470.

32 Martínez, *Historia de Baja California,* p. 480. Before 1911, neither Vega nor other governors were able to do much in encouraging Mexican enterprises, because of the extensive foreign holdings.

33 Estimate pieced together chiefly from accounts in the San Diego press, 1911, especially *San Diego Union,* February 21, 24, May 14, 18, 1911.

34 Statements by Simon Berthold in the *Los Angeles Record,* February 17, 1911, and in the *New York Times,* January 30, 1911; Ethel Duffy Turner, "The Revolution in Lower California" (unpublished MS, 1956), p. 3.

35 Issue of December 7, 1910.

36 E. D. Turner, "The Revolution in Lower California," pp. 3–4; statement of Fernando Palomárez, quoted in A. I. McCormick, U.S. Distr. Atty. for the So. Distr. of Calif., to U.S. Atty. Gen. George Wickersham, May 20, 1911 (Gen. Recs., Dept. of Just., Rec. Gp. 74, NA).

37 Palomárez' statement in McCormick to Wickersham, May 20, 1911 (Gen. Recs., Dept. of Just., Rec. Gp. 74, NA); *Los Angeles Times,* June 26, 1912; *Revolutions in Cuba and Mexico,* Report of a Subcommittee of the Senate Committee on Foreign Relations, 62 Cong., 2 sess. (Washington, 1913), 255.

38 Palomárez' statement in McCormick to Wickersham, May 20, 1911 (Gen. Recs., Dept. of Just., Rec. Gp. 74, NA); Berthold's statements, *Los Angeles Record,* February 17, 1911, and *New York Times,* January 30, 1911.

CHAPTER III

1 Issues of December 10, 24, 1910, January 21, February 11, April 8, 1911. On April 8, the paper carried a "Manifesto to the Workers of the World," proclaimed on April 3, which was widely reprinted in the radical press.

2 See, for example, *Freedom* (London), *Agitator* (Lakebay, Wash.), *Il Proletario* (New York), *L'Era Nuova* (Paterson, N.J.), the *New York Call, Appeal to Reason* (Girard, Kan.), *Solidarity* (Newcastle, Pa.), the *Vorwärts* (Milwaukee, Wis.), February to June, 1911; Abad de Santillán, *Ricardo Flores Magón,* p. 75.

3 The IWW weekly, the *Industrial Worker* (Spokane, Wash.), reported regularly on Magonista action, and urged IWW's to join comrades who had already gone to Lower California. See especially issues of March 16, 30, April 20, 27, 1911; also, Hyman Weintraub, "The I.W.W. in California, 1905–1931," pp. 49–50.

4 Paul F. Brissenden, *The I.W.W.: A Study of American Syndicalism,* pp. 151, 234, 278. Many Wobblies of socialist persuasion remained members after most of the leadership had become anarcho-syndicalist. Many regarded the difference between socialism and anarcho-syndicalism as unimportant.

5 *People's Paper,* February 10, 1911; *LR,* February 11, 1911.

6 E. D. Turner, "The Revolution in Lower California," pp. 23, 24.

7 For the full text, see the *People's Paper,* February 10, 1911.

8 For a good recent analysis of the novelist's political and social ideas, see Gordon Mills, "Jack London's Quest for Salvation," *American Quarterly,* VII (Spring, 1955), 3–15, especially 5–6.

9 The paper would go from one extreme to the other, frequently, by its laments on the workers' hardships and suffering in the service of the unbending, well-entrenched capitalistic order, contradicting its assertion that capitalism would soon disappear.

10 *Los Angeles Herald,* February 6, 1911; *LR,* October 5, 1912.

11 A classic example of the dangers inherent in the naïve as-

sumption that a desire to participate constituted a guarantee of good faith was the rapid collapse of Robert Owen's famous New Harmony, Indiana, utopia in the 1820's. For a discussion of this and similar instances, see Mark Holloway, *Heavens on Earth: Utopian Communities in America, 1680–1880* (London, 1951), pp. 106–11.

12 For example, the *People's Paper,* November 18, 1910, reported the arrest in San Diego of one C. Hopkins, an IWW. Six months later, he played an active part in the Magonista fighting, but his actions made it evident that he was much more a soldier of fortune than a social revolutionary.

13 For an illustration, see Flores Magón's editorial in *LR,* March 4, 1911.

14 See the statement made by Dudley Robinson, Asst. U.S. Distr. Atty. for the So. Distr. of Calif., who subsequently prosecuted the Junta for violation of the neutrality laws, *Investigation of Mexican Affairs,* II, 2509; *Los Angeles Examiner,* February 13, 1911; *San Diego Union,* June 20, 1911.

15 For example, Chauncey Thomas, Commander-in-Chief, Pacific Fleet, U.S.N., reported that one of his marines, 1st Sgt. Lott, was solicited for service by a Magonista agent in the Red Flag, a San Diego tavern. He was promised a monetary reward and 140 acres of land if the revolutionists succeeded.—Thomas to Navy Dept., February 17, 1911 (Naval Records Collections of the Office of Naval Records and Library, Rec. Gp. 45, NA).

16 Long afterwards, *LR,* October 5, 1912, denied that such promises were made.

17 For instructions given to the men, see *LR,* December 10, 1910; *Investigation of Mexican Affairs,* II, 2508. For accounts of the smuggling system, see A. I. McCormick, U.S. Distr. Atty. for the So. Distr. of Calif., to U.S. Atty. Gen. George Wickersham, May 20, 1911 (Gen. Recs., Dept. of Just., Rec. Gp. 74, NA) and the interesting descriptions given by a Magonista soldier in the *Los Angeles Times,* April 23, 1911.

18 Statement by William Owen, *Freedom* (December, 1922), quoted in Abad de Santillán, *Ricardo Flores Magón,* p. 75.

19 At a meeting in San Diego, February 26, for example, $125 was collected.—*San Diego Sun,* February 27, 1911.

20 *Investigation of Mexican Affairs,* II, 2510.

21 Owen in *Freedom* (December, 1922), quoted in Abad de

Santillán, *Ricardo Flores Magón,* p. 75. Often subscription funds sent from Mexico were confiscated by Mexican officials.—*LR,* January 28, 1911.

22 Guillermo Medina Amor, *No fué filibusterismo,* pp. 55–57.

23 John Kenneth Turner, *Barbarous Mexico* (Chicago: C. H. Kerr & Co., 1911).

24 McCormick to Wickersham, April 14, 1911 (Gen. Recs., Dept. of Just., Rec. Gp. 74, NA); Medina Amor, *No fué filibusterismo,* pp. 58–59; a San Francisco Socialist to J. K. Turner, March [n.d.], 1911, in *Investigation of Mexican Affairs,* II, 2502; *Los Angeles Times,* March 21, 1911.

25 *Appeal to Reason,* February 25, 1911; John Kenneth Turner, "The Mexican Revolution," *Pacific Monthly,* XXV (June, 1911), 609–25, especially 624–25; *LR,* December 3, 1910.

26 Berthold's account, *Los Angeles Record,* February 17, 1911.

27 *New York Times,* February 13, 1911; *San Diego Union,* February 8, 1911; *Industrial Worker,* March 30, 1911.

28 Medina Amor, *No fué filibusterismo,* p. 33; E. D. Turner, "The Revolution in Lower California," p. 7; *Los Angeles Times,* April 8, 1911.

29 Medina Amor, *No fué filibusterismo,* p. 41; *LR,* February 18, 1911; *Los Angeles Times,* January 30, 1911; *Los Angeles City Directory, 1910.*

30 *Los Angeles Times,* January 30, 1911.

31 *Calexico Chronicle,* January 29, 1911.

32 Berthold's statement, *Los Angeles Record,* February 17, 1911; *Imperial Valley Press,* February 18, 1911; *Brawley News,* February 17, 1911.

33 *New York Times,* January 30, 1911; *Los Angeles Times,* February 2, 1911.

34 *New York Times,* January 31, 1911; *Los Angeles Times,* June 18, 1911.

35 Berthold's statement, *Los Angeles Record,* February 17, 1911. Newspapers such as the *New York Times,* January 31, 1911, and the *Los Angeles Express,* January 29, 1911, reported the total as $2,000. Unverified rumors had it that the rebels captured Mexicali in expectation of seizing a $300,000 payroll for workers employed in improving the Mexicali-Imperial Valley canal system.—*Los Angeles Times,* January 30, 1911; *San Diego Union,* January 31, 1911.

36 *Los Angeles Herald,* January 31, 1911.

37 *Calexico Chronicle,* February 14, 1911.

38 Department of State, *Foreign Relations of the United States, 1911* (Washington, 1918), 405; *New York Times,* February 12, 14, 1911; *Los Angeles Times,* February 15, 1911.

39 *Calexico Chronicle,* February 14, 1911. If the *Los Angeles Herald,* February 15, 1911, is to be believed, Leyva declared that he had provisions stocked for four months. It took one month for the army to fall very short of supplies. —*Los Angeles Herald,* March 15, 1911.

40 *New York Times,* January 30, 1911.

41 *San Diego Union,* February 2, 3, 4, 7, 10, 1911.

42 *Ibid.,* February 6, 8, 9, 12, 1911; *New York Times,* February 9, 1911. Although a skirmish almost certainly took place, the Liberals contended they merely returned to Mexicali to fetch reinforcements and supplies.—Berthold's statement, *Los Angeles Record,* February 17, 1911; *Appeal to Reason,* March 11, 1911.

43 *Revolutions in Cuba and Mexico,* 254; *New York Times,* February 16, 1911; *New York Call,* February 17, 1911.

44 *Brawley News,* February 17, 21, 1911; *New York Call,* February 17, 1911. There was a report that Vega was so badly defeated because he had received a message from Leyva, with the name of a Federal official forged thereto, stating that the rebel force at Mexicali was microscopic.—Lt. Drake, U.S.A., to Commanding Officer, Fort Rosecrans, March 1, 1911 (Recs. of the U.S.A. Commands, Dept. of Calif. & Tex., Rec. Gp. 98, NA); Otis to Secretary of the Interior Richard A. Ballinger, February 23, 1911 (*ibid.*).

45 *Brawley News,* February 21, 1911, made reference to the missed opportunity.

CHAPTER IV

1 The complexities of American neutrality law up to the time are discussed in full in Roy E. Curtis, "The Law of Hostile Military Expeditions as Applied by the United States," *American Journal of International Law,* VIII (January, April, 1914), 1–38, 224–56.

2 Capt. C. S. Babcock to Brig. Gen. Tasker H. Bliss, February 14, 1911 (Recs. of the U.S.A. Commands, Dept. of Calif. & Tex., Rec. Gp. 98, NA); *New York Times,* January 31, February 4, 1911.

3 *Foreign Relations, 1911,* 529–47. Quotations are from pp. 545–47.

4   *Los Angeles Times,* February 1, 1911.
5   *Foreign Relations, 1911,* 555–57.
6   *New York Call,* February 14, 1911; *Los Angeles Times,* February 15, 1911.
7   *Foreign Relations, 1911,* 556–58.
8   For the reaction of the American public to the events of 1910–11, see Howard F. Cline, *The United States and Mexico* (Cambridge, Mass., 1953), p. 128. The response to John Kenneth Turner's articles, "Barbarous Mexico," is indicative of the climate of opinion; the *American Magazine,* LIX (Nov., 1909–April, 1910), 9–14, prints favorable commentary and editorial opinion from all sectors of the country. And in 1911, in a number of newspapers throughout the country, an early comic strip, "Mutt and Jeff," showed its heroes in Mexico among the rebels.—See the *San Diego Sun,* spring, 1911, *passim.* For a discussion of the California bourgeois press and the American radical press, see the Essay on Sources, pp. 250–51.
9   Rómulo Velasco Ceballos, *¿Se apoderará Estados Unidos de América de Baja California?* (Mexico City, 1920), *passim;* Enrique Aldrete, *Baja California heroica* (Mexico City, 1958), *passim; El Imparcial* (Tijuana, B.C.), June 22, 1952 (a commemorative issue of that paper).
10 E. D. Turner, "The Revolution in Lower California;" Martínez, *Historia de Baja California,* pp. 481–520.
11 For instance, Peter Gerhard, "The Socialist Invasion of Baja California, 1911," *Pacific Historical Review,* XV (September, 1946), 295–304; for contrast, see the *Industrial Worker* for the years 1910–11.
12 Issue of February 3, 1911.
13 Issue of February 4, 1911.
14 *San Diego Union,* February 21 to 25, 27 to 28, 1911.
15 Issue of February 4, 1911.
16 *New York Times,* February 9, 1911.
17 *San Diego Union,* February 24, 1911.
18 *El Imparcial* (Mexico City), February 21, 1911; *El País* (Mexico City), February 15, 1911.
19 *Foreign Relations, 1911,* 445.
20 *San Francisco Chronicle,* February 6, 1911.
21 Biographical sketch inserted by Ferris in *Who's Who in the Pacific Southwest* (Los Angeles, 1913), pp. 137–38; Ferris' testimony at a congressional hearing, *Revolutions in Cuba and Mexico,* 386.

22 *San Francisco Chronicle,* February 24, 1911; *San Diego Union,* February 13, 1911.

23 *San Diego Union,* February 13, 1911.

24 *Revolutions in Cuba and Mexico,* 373–74.

25 *Ibid.,* 374–77; *San Francisco Chronicle,* February 6 to 9, 1911.

26 *San Francisco Chronicle,* February 6 to 9, 1911.

27 *Revolutions in Cuba and Mexico,* 374.

28 *San Francisco Chronicle,* February 6, 1911.

29 *Ibid.*

30 *Ibid.,* February 7, 1911.

31 *Ibid.,* February 9, 1911.

32 *Ibid.,* February 16, 1911.

33 Issue of February 20, 1911.

34 Issues of February 20 and 25, 1911.

35 *San Francisco Chronicle,* February 16, 1911; *Revolutions in Cuba and Mexico,* 376.

36 *¿Se apoderará Estados Unidos de América de Baja California?, passim.*

37 *Porfirio Díaz, Dictator of Mexico* (Philadelphia, 1932), p. 428.

38 *Los Angeles Times* and *Los Angeles Examiner,* June 6, 1912; *Los Angeles Times,* April 5, 1911; E. D. Turner, "The Revolution in Lower California," pp. 16–17, 52–53.

39 Issue of February 25, 1911.

40 Bliss to War Dept., February 16, 1911 (Recs. of the U.S.A. Commands, Dept. of Calif. & Tex., Rec. Gp. 98, NA).

41 *Ibid.,* February 24, 1911.

42 *New York Times,* February 23, 1911; all California newspapers, February 22 and/or 23, 1911. A Magonista sympathizer, writing in the *Appeal to Reason,* March 11, 1911, expressed regret over the misleading announcement; on the other hand, the Socialist *Vorwärts* (Milwaukee, Wis.), April 2, 1911, expressed the opinion that the alleged interview was an anti-Socialist plot by the *Los Angeles Times* to precipitate United States intervention in Mexico.

43 The report appeared in the Mexico City newspapers almost as quickly as in the American press. See *El Heraldo Mexicano,* February 23, 1911, and *El Imparcial,* February 25, 1911.

44 Paul F. Brissenden, *The I.W.W.: A Study of American Syndicalism,* p. 291; *L'Era Nuova,* April 29, 1911.

CHAPTER V

1 *LR,* January 21, 1911; *Investigation of Mexican Affairs,* II, 2514.

2 *LR,* February 25, 1911.

3 *Ibid. El Diario* (Mexico City), March 2, 1911, contended that the Silva group committed acts of plunder at Zaragoza and Guadalupe.

4 *LR,* February 25, 1911. Whether a circular of the type described by Flores Magón ever appeared is doubtful. No reference to it is made in Stanley R. Ross's recent biography of Madero in English, *Francisco I. Madero: Apostle of Mexican Democracy* (New York, 1955), pp. 144–45.

5 Documents enclosed in A. I. McCormick, U.S. Distr. Atty. for the So. Distr. of Calif., to U.S. Atty. Gen. George Wickersham, May 20, 1911 (Gen. Recs., Dept. of Just., Rec. Gp. 74, NA).

6 Information concerning the Liberals' activities outside Baja California is very slim. The brief biographies or studies of Flores Magón cited in the notes to the first chapter of this work either omit mention of the Liberals' mainland efforts in 1911 or refer only to the February episode. Nor have recent Madero scholars found more. Charles C. Cumberland in *The Mexican Revolution: Genesis under Madero* (Austin, Texas, 1952) makes no reference to the Magonistas in 1911. Ross (*Madero,* pp. 144–45) alludes only to the February action. The Mexico City newspapers made few references to them. Files of the provincial press for the period often have not survived, or are meager. The fact is that the Liberals were able to accomplish comparatively little, for the reasons traced above.

7 See, for example, the issue of March 4, 1911, in which reference is made to Liberal activity in Chihuahua, Coahuila, Vera Cruz, Oaxaca, Morelos, Sonora, and Durango.

8 *LR,* February 25, March 25, April 15, 1911; E. D. Turner, "The Revolution in Lower California," pp. 25–26.

9 *New York Times,* February 23, 1911.

10 *Ibid.,* February 18, 1911; Capt. C. A. Babcock, U.S.A., Calexico, to the Adjutant Gen. for the Dept. of Calif. & Tex., February 26, 1911 (Recs. of the U.S.A. Commands, Dept. of Calif. & Tex., Rec. Gp. 98, NA). Capt. Babcock estimates that more than 50 per cent were Americans.

11 *Los Angeles Examiner,* March 10, 11, 1911; *Los Angeles Herald,* February 23, March 6, 1911.

12 *Los Angeles Herald,* April 9, 1911; *Los Angeles Times,* April 10, 1911, June 26, 1912; *New York Times,* April 23, 1911.

13 *Revolutions in Cuba and Mexico,* 253–54; *New York Times,* April 23, 1911; *Los Angeles Herald,* February 18, 1911.

14 Los Angeles press, February 22, 23, 1911; Velasco Ceballos, *¿Se apoderará Estados Unidos de Baja California?,* pp. 68–69.

15 *Los Angeles Times,* April 14, 1911.

16 *Mexican Herald* (Mexico City), March 9, 1911; *Calexico Chronicle,* March 6, 1911; *Los Angeles Express,* March 6, 1911.

17 *Los Angeles Express,* March 7, 1911; *Los Angeles Times,* March 7, 8, 9, 1911; E. D. Turner, "The Revolution in Lower California," pp. 27–28.

18 *Los Angeles Herald,* March 9, 1911.

19 E. D. Turner, "The Revolution in Lower California," p. 28; *Los Angeles Express,* March 8, 9, 14, 1911; *Los Angeles Examiner,* March 10, 11, 1911; *Los Angeles Times,* March 10, 12, 1911.

20 During the short interval in which the foreigners were eliminated, the American consul in Ensenada, it is interesting to note, reported that the "leaders there are now working in greater harmony with the leaders on the Mexican mainland. The project of founding an independent republic in Lower California seems to have given way to the general revolutionary movement. It is reported that practically all the so-called Independent [*sic*] Workers of the World have abandoned the undertaking, as they were more deeply interested in the first mentioned project."—George B. Schmucker to State Dept., March 13, 1911 (Recs. of the For. Serv. Posts, Rec. Gp. 84, NA).

21 *Calexico Chronicle,* March 13, 1911; *Los Angeles Examiner,* March 14, 1911; *Los Angeles Herald,* March 13, 14, 1911; R. F. M. to Leyva, March 15, 1911, in Pablo L. Martínez (ed.), *El Magonismo en Baja California (documentos)* (Mexico City, 1958), pp. 28–30.

22 *Los Angeles Herald,* March 13, 1911.

23 Velasco Ceballos, *¿Se apoderará Estados Unidos de Baja California?,* pp. 60, 73–74, 86–87; *Foreign Relations, 1911,* 561–62.

24 *San Diego Union,* March 12, 13, 1911; *LR,* March 18, 1911.

25 *Los Angeles Herald,* March 15, 16, 1911; *Los Angeles Express,* March 15, 1911.

26 *Los Angeles Herald,* March 27, 1911; *Los Angeles Express,* March 27, 1911; Velasco Ceballos, *¿Se apoderará Estados Unidos de Baja California?,* p. 78.

27 *Los Angeles Times,* March 18, 1911; *San Diego Union,* March 18, 1911.

28 *New York Times,* March 21, 26, 1911; *Los Angeles Herald,* March 20, 1911; *San Diego Union,* March 19–23, 27, 1911. Estimates of numbers vary considerably.

29 José María Leyva, "El llamado filibusterismo de la Baja California," *Revista de Revistas* (February 9, 1936), pp. 11–12 of an unpaginated reprint distributed by Gen. Leyva.

30 *Los Angeles Express,* March 28, 1911.

31 Leyva, "El llamado filibusterismo," *Revista de Revistas,* February 9, 1936, pp. 12–13 of the reprint; *Los Angeles Herald,* March 28, April 2, 4, 1911; *Los Angeles Express,* March 31, April 1, 1911; *Calexico Chronicle,* March 11, 30, 1911. After his withdrawal, Leyva mentioned that his opposition to the large number of Americans in his force had been a factor important to his dismissal.–*Los Angeles Herald,* April 4, 1911.

32 *Los Angeles Express,* March 22, 31, April 1, 4, 1911.

33 R. F. M. to Vásquez Salinas, March 28, 1911 (Gen. Recs., Dept. of Just., Rec. Gp. 74, NA). In spite of the reception of monies by the Junta, R. F. M. chose to dwell on one of his favorite topics, the Liberals' impecuniousness, in telling Vásquez Salinas that there was a lack of funds for military purposes.

34 *Los Angeles Herald,* April 2, 1911. At the very beginning, Vásquez Salinas had been under consideration as commander, but delayed in joining the movement until after Leyva had been appointed.–R. F. M. to Vásquez Salinas, February 22, 1911, in Martínez (ed.), *El Magonismo,* pp. 25–26.

35 *San Diego Union,* March 28, 1911.

36 Issue of April 1, 1911.

37 *Los Angeles Express,* April 4, 1911; *San Diego Union,* April 1, 1911; Velasco Ceballos, *¿Se apoderará Estados Unidos de Baja California?,* p. 84.

38 *Los Angeles Times,* April 10, 1911; *Brawley News,* April 14, 1911; Velasco Ceballos, *¿Se apoderará Estados Unidos de Baja California?,* p. 93; Mayol to Secretary of War and

Navy, April 8, 1911 (Archivo de la Secretaría de la Defensa Nacional).

39 Mayol to Secretary of War and Navy, April 8, 1911 (Archivo de la Secretaría de la Defensa Nacional).

40 *Foreign Relations, 1911,* 415; *Los Angeles Times,* March 8, 1911.

41 *Los Angeles Times,* March 28, 1911; *Los Angeles Herald,* March 17, 1911.

42 See above, note 33; see also *Los Angeles Times,* April 10, 1911; Velasco Ceballos, *¿Se apoderará Estados Unidos de Baja California?,* p. 100.

43 *Los Angeles Examiner,* April 8, 12, 1911.

44 Los Angeles press, April 9, 10, 1911; the *Los Angeles Examiner,* April 9, 11, 1911, seemingly well-informed on battle losses, estimated rebel dead as 12 to 18, with 10 deserters, and Federals at about the same. Mayol's official account made no estimate of losses on either side, but over-estimated rebel numerical strength two and one-half times. —Vega to Secretary of War and Navy, May 12, 1911 (Archivo de la Secretaría de la Defensa Nacional).

45 *Los Angeles Express,* March 31, and *San Diego Union,* April 8, 1911, quoted Mayol as desirous of battle. Afterwards, he emphasized that his orders were to go to the Colorado.—*Los Angeles Herald,* April 11, and *Los Angeles Times,* April 10, 1911.

46 *Los Angeles Times,* April 14, 1911; *Los Angeles Examiner,* April 14, 1911.

47 Issue of July 6, 1911.

48 *Los Angeles Herald,* April 9, 1911.

49 Henry Lane Wilson, *Diplomatic Episodes in Mexico, Belgium and Chile* (Garden City, N.Y., 1927), p. 207; Henry F. Pringle, *The Life and Times of William Howard Taft* (2 vols.; New York, 1939), II, 701; *Los Angeles Times,* March 8, 10, 1911. Wilson's opinions were alternately highly regarded and distrusted by Taft and the State Department. On this occasion Taft followed too literally Wilson's frenetic advice.

50 For a discussion of the possibilities underlying the action, see J. Fred Rippy, *The United States and Mexico* (New York, 1931), pp. 333–34; for an example of the view that the United States probably consciously desired Díaz's downfall, see Ross, *Madero,* pp. 136–41.

51 *Los Angeles Times,* April 5, 1911; *San Diego Union,* March 10, 14, April 8, 1911.

52 In Recs. of the U.S.A. Commands, Dept. of Calif. & Tex., Rec. Gp. 98, NA.

53 *Ibid.* Ballinger forwarded the message to the War Department.

54 Otis to State Dept., February 23, 1911 (Gen. Recs. of the Dept. of State, Rec. Gp. 59, NA).

55 *Foreign Relations, 1911,* 558–62.

56 *Ibid.,* 561–62.

57 *Ibid.,* 562–64.

58 Bliss to Otis, April 18, 1911 (Recs. of the U.S.A. Commands, Dept. of Calif. & Tex., Rec. Gp. 98, NA).

59 Cumberland (*Mexican Revolution, Genesis,* pp. 126–28) expresses the feeling that the American government was lax and dilatory in dealing with Madero's organizational efforts in the United States.

60 *Foreign Relations, 1911,* 377, 413–14.

61 *Ibid.,* 371, 397–98. Italics supplied by the State Department.

62 McCormick to Wickersham, May 20, 1911 (Gen. Recs., Dept. of Just., Rec. Gp. 74, NA); *Los Angeles Times,* June 26, 1912; *Los Angeles Examiner,* February 20, 1911; *San Diego Union,* April 6, 1911.

63 *Foreign Relations, 1911,* 407–8.

64 Herrington to S. W. Finch, Director, Bureau of Investigation, March 27, 1911 (Gen. Recs., Dept. of Just., Rec. Gp. 74, NA).

65 *Ibid.*

66 *Foreign Relations, 1911,* 444, 470.

67 Issue of March 13, 1911.

68 *San Diego Union,* March 6, 1911; *Los Angeles Herald,* March 13, 1911.

69 *San Diego Union,* March 13, 1911.

70 *Ibid.,* March 14, 1911; *Los Angeles Herald,* March 13, 15, June 3, 1911.

71 Issue of March 7, 1911.

72 *El País,* March 29, 1911, expressed the Mexico City view very well.

73 Issue of March 4, 1911.

74 Issues of April 15, 22, 1911.

75 *Imperial Valley Press,* February 25, 1911.

76 *Ibid.,* March 18, 1911.

CHAPTER VI

1 Stanley R. Ross, *Francisco I. Madero: Apostle of Mexican Democracy* (New York, 1955), pp. 146–47, 149, 151; Charles C. Cumberland, *The Mexican Revolution: Genesis under Madero* (Austin, Texas, 1952), pp. 132, 137–38.

2 *LR*, March 18, April 22, 1911.

3 Ross, *Madero*, pp. 155–60; Cumberland, *Mexican Revolution, Genesis*, pp. 131, 134, 139–40, 147.

4 For three among many examples, see *New York Call*, April 11, 1911; *Agitator*, March 15, 1911; *La Follette's Magazine* (Madison, Wis.), March 18, April 1, 1911.

5 R. F. M. to Enrique Flores Magón, June 7, 1908, in Abad de Santillán, *Ricardo Flores Magón*, pp. 50–55.

6 *LR*, March 11, 1911.

7 R. F. M. to Enrique Flores Magón, June 7, 1908, in Abad de Santillán, *Ricardo Flores Magón*, pp. 51–52.

8 *LR*, March 18, 1911.

9 *Ibid.*, March 18, 25; April 1, 8, 22, 1911.

10 Issue of April 12, 1911.

11 The *Appeal to Reason*, June 17, 1911, expounds this Socialist doctrine clearly; the *Vorwärts* (Milwaukee, Wis.), April 2, 1911, has a heavy-handed explanation of why anarchism would never work in Lower California, but why eventually socialism would. Reading this critique, one is hard put to decide which group, socialists or anarchists, was farther removed from the grim realities of Baja California's economy.

12 A Flores Magón analysis, entitled "After the Triumph" (*LR*, January 28, 1911), expounds the anarchist thesis. On April 3, 1911, the Junta circulated a "Manifesto to the Workers of the World," which was an anarcho-syndicalist appeal.

13 Frank Tannenbaum, *The Mexican Agrarian Revolution* (Washington, 1930), Chapter I, especially pp. 3–4.

14 *LR*, April 8, 1911.

15 *Ibid.*, April 22, 1911; *New York Call*, April 13, 1911.

16 *LR*, April 1, 1911; Tannenbaum, *Mexican Agrarian Revolution*, pp. 157–58.

17 Flores Magón mentioned that a group of Los Angeles Socialists called on him to demand that he specify whether he was a socialist or an anarchist.–*LR*, April 15, 1911.

18 *Ibid.*, July 15, 1911.

19 Abad de Santillán, *Ricardo Flores Magón*, p. 75, quoting

a statement made by William G. Owen in 1922.

20 *Investigation of Mexican Affairs,* II, 2497. One crank wrote J. K. Turner that he would make available his invention, namely, cheap, smokeless powder: "This is reliable information; no American humbug."—*Ibid.,* 2497, 2501.

21 For one among innumerable reports, see *L'Era Nuova,* April 15, 1911.

22 *Investigation of Mexican Affairs,* II, 2497.

23 *Los Angeles Times,* June 6, 1912. Estimates are very difficult. At the neutrality trial, one Peter Martin, a spy, testified that the total from this source sent to the Junta from Mexicali was $400 to $1,000 per month. The upper figure is probably too high, the lower plausible. There was testimony to the effect that later, at Tijuana, $300 to $500 per month were collected there through imposts.—*Revolutions in Cuba and Mexico,* 230.

24 Paul F. Brissenden, *The I.W.W.: A Study of American Syndicalism,* p. 291.

25 *Los Angeles Times,* June 15, 1911.

26 Velasco Ceballos, *¿Se apoderará Estados Unidos de Baja California?,* pp. 127–28; E. D. Turner, "The Revolution in Lower California," p. 35; *Los Angeles Express,* April 21, 1911.

27 A. I. McCormick, U.S. Distr. Atty. for the So. Distr. of Calif., to U.S. Atty. Gen. George Wickersham, May 20, 1911 (Gen. Recs., Dept. of Just., Rec. Gp. 74, NA).

28 *Los Angeles Times,* February 18, 1911; *Los Angeles Herald,* February 18, 1911.

29 Without specifying amounts, the *Los Angeles Times,* June 15, 1911, stated, "It is known that large amounts were realized by these methods." As a further example, near Tijuana in May, one Silvano Preciado was supposed to be held prisoner until a sum of $500 was paid to Junta member Antonio de Pío Araujo. However, upon payment of $100, he was released. One of his companions, Lorenzo Orena, held for the same amount, was released gratis.—Testimony at the Pryce extradition hearing (*San Diego Union,* September 28, 1911).

30 *Los Angeles Times,* quoting United States Bureau of Investigation agents, June 23, 25, 1912. Under the circumstances, some might regard the *Times* or the secret agents as unreliable on such a matter.

31 *Los Angeles Examiner,* April 12, 1911.

32 For biographical data on Pryce, see *San Diego Sun,* May 9, 1911; *Los Angeles Express,* June 5, September 26, 1911; *San Diego Union,* September 27, 1911.

33 Dudley Robinson, Asst. U.S. Distr. Atty. for the So. Distr. of Calif., testified that Mexicans were usually in the majority.—*Investigation of Mexican Affairs,* II, 2508. There is evidence that between April 20 and 30 they were slightly outnumbered. At or near Mexicali were 110 members of the Pryce group, almost all of whom were non-Mexicans; simultaneously, the Mexican force there numbered merely 75.—Brig. Gen. Tasker H. Bliss to War Dept., April 30, 1911 (Recs. of the U.S.A. Commands, Dept. of Calif. & Tex., Rec. Gp. 98, NA). To the south were 100 men at El Alamo, 60 of whom were non-Mexican.—Consul George B. Schmucker to State Dept., April 24, 1911 (Recs. of the For. Serv. Posts, Rec. Gp. 84, NA). At San Quintín were 30 more Mexicans. This would add up to approximately 145 Mexicans and 170 foreigners, most of whom were Americans. On the other hand, it is not true that the Mexicans were only a small minority, as Flores Magón's critics have contended. —Velasco Ceballos, *¿Se apoderará Estados Unidos de Baja California?, passim,* and Peter Gerhard, "The Socialist Invasion of Baja California, 1911," *Pacific Historical Review,* XV (September, 1946), 295–304. See especially p. 295.

34 "But the most absurd and unfounded of all their [the capitalists'] statements is that we are using the fight here merely as a mask to get men into Lower California for the purpose of taking the holdings of Scabby Otis and his crowd and establishing a socialistic republic."—*Industrial Worker,* May 16, 1912. On the other hand, an old Wobbly interviewed many years later declared that the object of their effort was to "take over Lower California and establish an industrial republic."—Hyman Weintraub, "The I.W.W. in California, 1905–1931," p. 273.

35 *Industrial Worker,* June 8, 1911.

36 Peter B. Kyne, "The Gringo as Insurrecto," *Sunset Magazine,* XXVII (September, 1911), 257–67, lists most of the leader's friends; also, *LR,* April 15, 1911, in its account of the April 8 battle, mentions most of the same individuals.

37 *Los Angeles Express,* March 27, 1911.

38 *Calexico Chronicle,* April 27, 1911; *Imperial Valley Press,* April 29, 1911.

39 *Los Angeles Examiner,* April 23, 1911.

40 Issues of April 25, 27, 1911.

41 *Calexico Chronicle,* May 1, 1911; *Imperial Valley Press,* April 29, 1911.

42 Kyne, "The Gringo as Insurrecto," *Sunset Magazine,* XXVII, 260–61.

43 Issue of April 24, 1911. The same report appeared in the *San Diego Union,* April 24, 1911.

44 *Los Angeles Examiner,* April 24, 25, 1911; *Los Angeles Times,* April 16, 1911.

45 *Los Angeles Examiner,* April 13, September 27, 28, 1911.

46 *Los Angeles Times,* April 23, 1911. During this period, the Mexican government showed extreme dissatisfaction with United States neutrality law enforcement: see an agent's report in Martínez (ed.), *El Magonismo,* pp. 18–20.

47 *Los Angeles Herald,* April 29, 1911.

48 *Ibid.,* April 30, 1911; *Calexico Chronicle,* April 28, 1911.

49 *Los Angeles Times,* April 30, 1911; *Los Angeles Herald,* April 30, May 1, 1911.

50 *Calexico Chronicle,* April 28, 1911. Flores Magón chose to mention Vásquez Salinas' replacement without specifying a reason.—*LR,* May 6, 1911.

51 *Los Angeles Times,* May 2, 1911; *San Diego Evening Tribune,* May 1, 1911; *Calexico Chronicle,* April 28, May 1, 5, 1911.

52 *Calexico Chronicle,* April 28, May 8, 1911; *Los Angeles Herald,* April 30, 1911.

53 *LR,* May 6, 1911.

54 Velasco Ceballos, *¿Se apoderará Estados Unidos de Baja California?,* p. 107.

55 *Los Angeles Express,* April 21, 1911; E. D. Turner, "The Revolution in Lower California," p. 35; Martínez, *Historia de Baja California,* pp. 513–15.

56 Velasco Ceballos, *¿Se apoderará Estados Unidos de Baja California?,* pp. 106–7.

57 *Los Angeles Examiner,* June 5, 1912. This particular witness was unreliable, but this phase of his testimony is probably correct, as it is borne out by extant circumstantial evidence.

58 Velasco Ceballos, *¿Se apoderará Estados Unidos de Baja California?,* p. 79.

59 *Ibid.,* p. 80; statement of John R. Mosby to F. D. Simmons, Special Agent, Bureau of Investigation, July 22, 1911 (Gen. Recs., Dept. of Just., Rec. Gp. 74, NA).

60 Mosby's statement to Simmons, July 22, 1911 (Gen. Recs., Dept. of Just., Rec. Gp. 74, NA); Velasco Ceballos (*¿Se apoderará Estados Unidos de Baja California?*, p. 81) gives a summary of the diary of Werner Johnson, a member of the party. This diary, kept for approximately a three-week period, contains interesting details on the soldiers' day-to-day life at El Alamo, and the dissentions among them.

61 Velasco Ceballos, *¿Se apoderará Estados Unidos de Baja California?*, pp. 84–85, Johnson's diary.

62 *Ibid.*, pp. 82–85. On one of their first days in El Alamo, Johnson hopefully referred to having found small pieces of ore in the streets, but subsequently made no further reference to the subject.

63 *Ibid.*, pp. 83–85.

64 *Ibid.*, pp. 85, 113–14; George B. Schmucker, U.S. Consul in Ensenada, to State Dept., April 13, 17, 24, 1911 (Recs. of the For. Serv. Posts, Rec. Gp. 84, NA).

65 Affidavits submitted by various residents of El Alamo to State Dept. (Recs. of the For. Serv. Posts, Rec. Gp. 84, NA); George Murphy, U.S. Consul Gen. at Large, to State Dept., November 4, 1911 (*ibid.*).

66 Murphy to State Dept., November 4, 1911 (*ibid.*); Schmucker to State Dept., April 7, 1911 (*ibid.*); *San Diego Union,* April 13, 1911.

67 Affidavits submitted by various residents of El Alamo to the State Dept. [no month, no day], 1911 (Recs. of the For. Serv. Posts, Rec. Gp. 84, NA).

68 Mosby's statement to Simmons, July 22, 1911 (Gen. Recs., Dept. of Just., Rec. Gp. 74, NA); *San Diego Union,* April 13, 1911.

69 Mosby's statement to Simmons, July 22, 1911 (Gen. Recs., Dept. of Just., Rec. Gp. 74, NA).

70 Schmucker to State Dept., April 24, 1911 (Recs. of the For. Serv. Posts, Rec. Gp. 84, NA); affidavits by various El Alamo residents presented to the State Dept. (*ibid.*).

71 Murphy to State Dept., November 4, 1911, quoting an American resident of Ensenada who had talked to Glennon (*ibid.*).

72 Schmucker to State Dept., April 24, 1911 (*ibid.*).

73 Affidavits presented to State Dept. by various American residents of El Alamo [no month, no day], 1911 (*ibid.*).

74 Schmucker to State Dept., March 8, April 7, 17, 22, 1911 (*ibid.*); Martínez (ed.), *El Magonismo,* pp. 13–15, a report

of an investigation into Vega's conduct; Velasco Ceballos, *¿Se apoderará Estados Unidos de Baja California?*, pp. 86–87.

75 *Los Angeles Times,* April 20, 1911; *LR,* April 22, 1911; *El Imparcial* (Mexico City), April 28, 1911.

76 *El Imparcial* (Mexico City), April 28, 1911; *San Diego Union,* May 16, 1911; *LR,* May 6, 1911; Mosby's statement to Simmons, July 22, 1911 (Gen. Recs., Dept. of Just., Rec. Gp. 74, NA).

77 Velasco Ceballos, *¿Se apoderará Estados Unidos de Baja California?*, pp. 84, 109; *Los Angeles Herald,* April 23, 1911.

78 *San Diego Union,* May 6, June 3, 24, 1911; *Industrial Worker,* July 6, 1911.

79 Schmucker to State Dept., April 24, 1911 (Recs. of the For. Serv. Posts, Rec. Gp. 84, NA), with Glennon as the consul's source for this.

80 Affidavits submitted to State Dept. by El Alamo residents (*ibid.*); Frederick Simpich, the U.S. consul who succeeded Schmucker in the Ensenada post, to State Dept., June 27, 1911 (*ibid.*); Murphy to State Dept., November 6, 1911 (*ibid*).

81 Velasco Ceballos, *¿Se apoderará Estados Unidos de Baja California?*, p. 109; *San Diego Evening Tribune,* May 1, 3, 1911.

82 Schmucker to State Dept., April 19, 20, 22, 1911 (Recs. of the For. Serv. Posts, Rec. Gp. 84, NA); *El Imparcial* (Mexico City), April 28, 1911; *San Diego Union,* April 22, 27, May 1, 1911; *San Diego Evening Tribune,* May 1, 1911.

83 Velasco Ceballos, *¿Se apoderará Estados Unidos de Baja California?*, pp. 117–18.

84 *San Diego Evening Tribune,* May 2, 3, 1911; *Los Angeles Examiner,* May 3, 4, 1911; Schmucker to State Dept., May 8, 1911 (Recs. of the For. Serv. Posts, Rec. Gp. 84, NA).

85 *San Diego Union,* May 4–7, 1911; *San Diego Evening Tribune,* May 3, 4, 1911; *San Diego Sun,* May 5, 1911.

86 McCormick to Wickersham, May 20, 1911 (Gen. Recs., Dept. of Just., Rec. Gp. 74, NA); *San Diego Evening Tribune,* May 3, 1911. The *Los Angeles Examiner,* May 5, 1911, reported that the widow of one of the victims had to walk with her several children 24 miles to find aid.

87 *San Diego Union,* May 5, 1911; *Los Angeles Examiner,* May 5, 1911.

88 Schmucker to U.S. Senator Duncan U. Fletcher (Dem., Fla.),

January 24, 1917 (Recs. of the For. Serv. Posts, Rec. Gp. 84, NA).

89   Schmucker to State Dept., February 2, 1911, and Secretary Knox's reply, February 8, 1911 (*ibid.*).

90   Schmucker to State Dept., March 8, 13, 17, April 11, 24, 1911 (*ibid.*); see also Chapter IV, p. 59.

91   Schmucker to State Dept., April 10, 1911 (Recs. of the For. Serv. Posts, Rec. Gp. 84, NA). The *San Diego Union,* April 11, 13, 1911, and the *San Diego Evening Tribune,* May 9, 1911, contain some typical examples of criticism of Schmucker's work.

92   Schmucker to State Dept., March 8, April 7, 11, 22, 1911 (Recs. of the For. Serv. Posts, Rec. Gp. 84, NA).

93   Schmucker to State Dept., April 24, 1911 (*ibid.*).

94   Schmucker to State Dept., April 27, 1911 (*ibid.*).

95   Bliss to Lt. Col. William A. Shunk, Calexico, April 29, 1911 (Recs. of the U.S.A. Commands, Dept. of Calif. & Tex., Rec. Gp. 98, NA); Bliss to Gen. Enoch H. Crowder, April 30, 1911 [marked "Private"] (Bliss Papers, Library of Congress).

96   Bliss to Otis, April 21, 1911 (Recs. of the U.S.A. Commands, Dept. of Calif. & Tex., Rec. Gp. 98, NA).

97   Bliss to War Dept., April 26, 1911 (*ibid.*).

98   Wood to Bliss, April 28, 1911 (*ibid.*).

99   Bliss to War Dept., April 30, 1911 (*ibid.*).

100 *Congressional Record,* 62 Cong., 1 sess., XLVII (April 20, 1911), 447–52.

101 The oft-cited *Revolutions in Cuba and Mexico.*

102 Henry F. Pringle, *The Life and Times of William Howard Taft* (2 vols.; New York, 1939), II, 703.

Chapter VII

1   *LR,* May 6, 1911; Velasco Ceballos, *¿Se apoderará Estados Unidos de Baja California?,* pp. 106–7, 109–11.

2   *Investigation of Mexican Affairs,* II, 2503.

3   Particularly, the letter referred to in Ch. VI, pp. 104–5.

4   R. F. M. to Eulalio Baeza and Joaquín A. Ramos, May 4, 1911, in Velasco Ceballos, *¿Se apoderará Estados Unidos de Baja California?,* pp. 109, 111. E. D. Turner, one of R. F. M.'s staunchest defenders, seeks to dispose of the likelihood of serious insubordination by pointing out that Pryce was in the desert and could not be reached.—"The

Revolution in Lower California," pp. 36–37. However, the military leader had ample opportunity to ascertain Flores Magón's wishes before beginning his march. As Valenzuela and Quijada were acquainted with his desires, Pryce and Mosby could not have been unaware of them. At San Diego, after the battle of Tijuana, a soldier stated in an interview that they marched on the town without orders.—*San Diego Evening Tribune* and *San Diego Union,* both May 12, 1911.

5   The *San Diego Evening Tribune,* May 5, 8, 1911, estimates 150 defenders; Velasco Ceballos (*¿Se apoderará Estados Unidos de Baja California?,* p. 127) lists the low figure of 70, which, minus 14 desertions, became 56; Vega to Secretary of War and Navy, May 4, 1911 (Archivo de la Secretaría de la Defensa Nacional), gives the figure as 77 men, a few volunteers, and 32 reinforcements on their way, which would amount to 110 to 115.

6   Here again, figures vary. Los Angeles and San Diego newspapers list totals between 200 and 280; Capt. F. A. Wilcox listed the figure at 200.—Wilcox to Adjutant of the Dept. of Calif. & Tex., May 17, 1911 (Recs. of the U.S.A. Commands, Dept. of Calif. & Tex., Rec. Gp. 98, NA).

7   *Investigation of Mexican Affairs,* II, 2503.

8   *San Diego Sun,* May 9, 1911.

9   *Ibid.,* May 8, 9, 1911; *San Diego Union,* May 16, 1911. By coincidence, this battle opened on the anniversary of the day that the filibuster William Walker abandoned his venture in Lower California in 1854.—William O. Scroggs, *Filibusters and Financiers* (New York, 1916), pp. 47–48.

10 Velasco Ceballos (*¿Se apoderará Estados Unidos de Baja California?,* pp. 128–29, 132–33) makes the preposterous assertion that Capt. Wilcox permitted some of his soldiers to join Pryce's army for the final assault.

11 So Pryce maintained subsequently.—*Los Angeles Express,* June 20, 1911.

12 *Los Angeles Examiner,* May 10, 1911; *San Diego Sun,* May 9, 1911. Several newspapers reported the use of dumdum bullets by the Federals.

13 This battle account is based on the stories in the Los Angeles and San Diego papers, May 8–15, 1911, and Wilcox' summary to the Adjutant, May 17, 1911 (Recs. of the U.S.A. Commands, Dept. of Calif. & Tex., Rec. Gp. 98, NA).

14 Issue of May 10, 1911; this figure appears substantiated by

Wilcox' report to the Adjutant, May 17, 1911 (Recs. of the U.S.A. Commands, Dept. of Calif. & Tex., Rec. Gp. 98, NA), which listed 50 to 60 killed and wounded.

15 *Los Angeles Examiner,* May 10, 1911; *San Diego Sun,* May 9, 1911.

16 Subsequently, Pryce mentioned that he was most bothered by his men's behavior and by his losses in this battle.— Peter B. Kyne, "The Gringo as Insurrecto," *Sunset Magazine,* XXVII (September, 1911), 257–67.

17 *San Diego Union,* May 11, 1911; *San Diego Sun,* May 10, 1911.

18 *Los Angeles Times,* May 11, 1911; *San Diego Sun,* May 10, 1911; *Los Angeles Herald,* September 19, 1911.

19 *Los Angeles Examiner,* May 10, 1911; *New York Times,* May 11, 1911.

20 *San Diego Union,* May 10, 1911; *Los Angeles Examiner,* May 11, 1911.

21 *San Diego Sun,* May 12, 1911; *San Diego Union,* May 12, 1911. The *Industrial Worker,* May 25, 1911, pointed out the hypocrisy of "respectable, church-going people" engaging in looting, and *Solidarity,* May 27, 1911, also ridiculed the plundering by the "Y.M.C.A. boys."

22 *San Diego Evening Tribune,* May 12, 1911; *San Diego Union,* May 13, 1911.

23 *Los Angeles Times,* May 10, 1911; *San Diego Union,* May 11, 1911; Wilcox to Adjutant, May 17, 1911 (Recs. of the U.S.A. Commands, Dept. of Calif. & Tex., Rec. Gp. 98, NA).

24 See contemporary San Diego and Los Angeles newspapers.

25 Kyne, "The Gringo as Insurrecto," *Sunset Magazine,* XXVII, 259, 261–62, describes some of the more interesting characters. See also *San Diego Sun,* May 11, 1911. A minor legend evolved about the giant Negro.

26 Issue of May 12, 1911.

27 *San Diego Union,* May 11, 1911; *San Diego Sun,* May 10, 1911. Pryce gave the highest estimate, 20 per cent; his adjutant, Hopkins, the lowest, 5 per cent.—*San Diego Union,* May 11, 12, 1911. In his report on the battle, Capt. Wilcox listed the names of all the rebels wounded and captured, numbering 15, and every one of them had an Anglo-Saxon name.—Wilcox to Adjutant, May 17, 1911 (Recs. of the U.S.A. Commands, Dept. of Calif. & Tex., Rec. Gp. 98, NA).

28 Owen, on the English page, offered this explanation (*LR,* December 2, 1911), as did R. F. M. (*ibid.,* July 1, 1911).

29 Teodoro Hernández, *La historia de la revolución debe hacerse* (Mexico City, 1950), p. 122; Cué Cánovas, *Ricardo Flores Magón, la Baja California y los Estados Unidos,* pp. 63–65.

30 Velasco Ceballos, as could be expected, emphasizes this (*¿Se apoderará Estados Unidos de Baja California?, passim*); see also, *El Imparcial* (Tijuana), June 22, 1952, a commemorative issue, entitled "Gloriosa defensa de Baja California," which, though of limited value, does stress this point throughout.

31 Velasco Ceballos (*¿Se apoderará Estados Unidos de Baja California?,* pp. 141–42) prints a congratulatory letter; *LR,* May 13, 1911, hails the victory; Hopkins to Dunn, June 1, 3, 1911, in *Investigation of Mexican Affairs,* II, 2503, shows Pryce's reaction to the congratulations.

32 *LR,* May 6, 13, 1911; Emma Goldman, *Living My Life* (Garden City, N.Y., 1931), pp. 478–80.

33 *Solidarity,* May 6, 1911; *San Diego Union,* May 9, 1911; Goldman, *Living My Life,* pp. 478–80.

34 *Solidarity,* April 1, May 6, 1911; *San Diego Sun,* May 25, 1911.

35 *LR,* May 20, 27, 1911.

36 Martínez (ed.), *El Magonismo,* pp. 20–21.

37 *San Diego Sun,* May 25, 1911; *San Diego Evening Tribune,* May 25, 1911.

38 Harry W. Laidler, *A History of Socialist Thought* (New York, 1927), pp. 60, 65–66, 73, 113–14.

39 M. M. Bober, *Karl Marx's Interpretation of History* (Cambridge, Mass., 1948), pp. 70–275.

40 He fought well in the British army in the Boer War, and in the Canadian and British armies in World War I.—Glenys Hembry, American Liaison Officer, Central Office of Information, H.M. War Department, London, to the author, January 15, 1953.

41 *San Diego Union,* May 10, 1911; *Los Angeles Express,* May 10, 1911.

42 *San Diego Union,* May 11, 1911.

43 *San Diego Sun,* May 11, 1911.

44 *Ibid.,* May 10, 1911.

45 Issue of May 13, 1911.

46 *San Diego Union,* May 14, 1911; an identical report appeared in the *Los Angeles Herald,* May 15, 1911.

47   *Los Angeles Examiner,* May 15, 1911; *San Diego Union,* May 15, 1911.

48   Great emphasis is placed on the flag incident, as indicative of a filibuster, by Velasco Ceballos (*¿Se apoderará Estados Unidos de Baja California?,* p. 138); Martínez (*Historia de Baja California,* p. 510) maintains that only the American property holders' desire for protection was involved. Nevertheless, there was some ulterior significance in it; see the anarchist *Era Nuova,* June 24, 1911.

49   *San Diego Sun,* May 16, 1911; *Los Angeles Herald,* May 20, 1911.

50   *LR,* May 20, 1911.

51   *Los Angeles Examiner,* May 18, 1911; *San Diego Union,* May 18, 1911.

52   *San Diego Sun,* May 25, 1911.

53   *Los Angeles Herald,* May 15, 1911; *San Diego Evening Tribune,* May 15, 1911.

54   *Los Angeles Times,* June 7, 1912.

55   *Ibid.,* June 7, 1912, May 16, 1911; *San Diego Union,* June 2, 1911; *Investigation of Mexican Affairs,* II, 2511; *Revolutions in Cuba and Mexico,* 233.

56   *San Diego Union,* March 6, June 26, 1911.

57   Ferris' testimony, *Revolutions in Cuba and Mexico,* 377–78.

58   *Ibid.,* 378.

59   The account of the San Diego events is based on the reports in the three local newspapers, May 17 to 29, 1911, especially on those in the *Union.* Where there are quotations or additional sources, the appropriate authorities are cited.

60   Chief of Staff, Gen. Leonard B. Wood, to Bliss's Adjutant, April 18, 1911 (Recs. of the U.S.A. Commands, Dept. of Calif. & Tex., Rec. Gp. 98, NA).

61   Hopkins to Dunn, June 1, 3, 1911, in *Investigation of Mexican Affairs,* II, 2503.

62   *Investigation of Mexican Affairs,* II, 2499; *Los Angeles Times,* May 19, 1911.

63   *San Diego Union,* May 20, 1911.

64   Reprinted in the *San Diego Union,* May 22, 1911.

65   U.S. Atty. Gen. George Wickersham to Asst. Sec. of War Robert Shaw Oliver, May 27, 1911 (Gen. Recs., Dept. of Just., Rec. Gp. 74, NA). The Mexican government just barely missed having Pryce detained on the filibuster charge because of a tangle between jurisdictions and a dispute over

legal technicalities among departments of the United States government.—Sec. of State Philander C. Knox to Wickersham, May 20, 1911 (*ibid.*).

66 *San Diego Union,* June 16, 1911.

67 *Ibid.,* May 21, 1911.

68 Issue of May 22, 1911.

69 *San Diego Union,* May 14, 18, 24, 1911.

70 *Los Angeles Times,* May 18, 20, 22, 1911; Velasco Ceballos, *¿Se apoderará Estados Unidos de Baja California?,* pp. 166–67.

71 Velasco Ceballos, *¿Se apoderará Estados Unidos de Baja California?,* pp. 145–46, 157–61.

72 *San Diego Union,* May 25, 1911; Martínez, *Historia de Baja California,* p. 516.

73 Elías to Mexican Foreign Minister, May 24, 1911, reprinted in Martínez (ed.), *El Magonismo,* pp. 21–22; Velasco Ceballos, *¿Se apoderará Estados Unidos de Baja California?,* pp. 157–60.

74 *San Diego Evening Tribune,* May 17, 22, 1911.

75 *Ibid.,* May 22, 1911.

76 *Ibid.,* May 23, 1911.

77 *Ibid.,* May 19, 1911.

78 See above, pp. 129–30.

79 Velasco Ceballos, *¿Se apoderará Estados Unidos de Baja California?,* pp. 152–54.

80 *San Diego Union,* May 26, 1911; *San Diego Evening Tribune,* May 26, 1911.

81 *Foreign Relations, 1911,* 494–95, 501–3; *San Diego Union,* June 1, 1911.

82 Velasco Ceballos, *¿Se apoderará Estados Unidos de Baja California?,* p. 177; Martínez (ed.), *El Magonismo,* p. 14. Interestingly, some of them probably were United States citizens of Mexican descent.—*San Diego Evening Tribune,* June 16, 1911.

83 Reprinted in Martínez (ed.), *El Magonismo,* pp. 13–15.

84 Charles C. Cumberland, *The Mexican Revolution: Genesis under Madero* (Austin, Texas, 1952), p. 148; Stanley R. Ross, *Francisco I. Madero: Apostle of Mexican Democracy* (New York, 1955), pp. 162–63.

85 Ross, *Madero,* pp. 163–72; Cumberland, *Mexican Revolution, Genesis,* pp. 148–50.

86 Ross, *Madero,* pp. 177–82.

87 *LR,* May 6, 13, 20, 1911.
88 *Ibid.,* May 27, 1911; *San Diego Union,* May 23, 1911; *San Diego Evening Tribune,* May 25, 1911.
89 *Investigation of Mexican Affairs,* II, 2515; E. D. Turner, "The Revolution in Lower California," p. 46.
90 Wallace Stegner, "Joe Hill: the Wobblies' Troubadour," *New Republic,* CXVIII (January 5, 1948), 20–24, especially 22 and 38; Ralph Chaplin, *Wobbly* (Chicago, 1948), p. 186; E. D. Turner, "The Revolution in Lower California," p. 75.
91 *San Diego Union,* May 29, June 2, 1911.
92 The IWW's and some Italian anarchist volunteers made this charge, with or without foundation; see the *Industrial Worker,* July 6, 1911, and *L'Era Nuova,* June 24, 1911.
93 The question of numbers and proportions of the different elements is a vexing one. The *San Diego Sun,* May 26, 1911, estimated 1,000 soldiers, probably too high. The *San Diego Union,* June 2, 1911, guessed 500, nearer to the correct figure, and the *San Diego Evening Tribune,* May 29, 1911, 325. Martínez states (*Historia de Baja California,* p. 494) that the Mexicans constituted 50 per cent, "more or less." That it was far less is clear: a rebel leader on June 1 asserted that there were 140 Mexicans, 500 others.—*San Diego Sun,* June 2, 1911. An Italian anarchist, who quit in disgust at about this time, listed 300 adventurers, 80 IWW's, and *10* Mexicans, whose influence, he reported, was "zero."—*L'Era Nuova,* June 17, 1911.
94 *San Diego Union,* May 16, 20, 22, June 4, 1911; *San Diego Sun,* May 22, 24, 1911.
95 *San Diego Union,* May 22, 1911; *San Diego Sun,* May 22, 1911.
96 *San Diego Union,* May 31, June 1, 1911; *San Diego Evening Tribune,* May 31, 1911; *Los Angeles Examiner,* June 1, 1911.
97 *San Diego Sun,* May 26, 1911; *San Diego Union,* May 26, 27, 1911.
98 *Los Angeles Herald,* May 23, 1911.
99 Hopkins to Dunn, June 1, 3, 1911, in *Investigation of Mexican Affairs,* II, 2503; *San Francisco Chronicle,* June 17, 1911.
100 *Investigation of Mexican Affairs,* II, 2503.
101 Issue of May 31, 1911.
102 Issue of June 1, 1911.
103 *Investigation of Mexican Affairs,* II, 2503; *San Diego Union,* June 1, 1911.

104 *San Diego Union,* June 1, 1911; *San Diego Evening Tribune,* May 31, 1911; *Los Angeles Examiner,* June 1, September 24, 1911. The same rumor had spread at the time of Pryce's arrest in San Diego.—*San Diego Union,* May 20, 1911.

105 *Investigation of Mexican Affairs,* II, 2503.

106 *San Diego Union,* September 27, 1911.

CHAPTER VIII

1 *San Diego Union,* June 1, 1911; *San Diego Evening Tribune,* June 2, 1911.

2 *San Francisco Chronicle,* June 17, 1911; Peter B. Kyne, "The Gringo as Insurrecto," *Sunset Magazine,* XXVII (September, 1911), 267.

3 Issue of June 1, 1911.

4 *San Diego Union,* June 2, 3, 1911. For one or two days, on June 1 and 2, recruitment was halted.—*Ibid.,* June 2, 1911.

5 *Ibid.,* June 3, 1911.

6 *Los Angeles Times,* June 7, 1912.

7 *San Francisco Chronicle,* June 17, 1911.

8 *Investigation of Mexican Affairs,* II, 2503–4.

9 *San Diego Sun,* June 1, 1911; *San Diego Evening Tribune,* June 1, 1911.

10 See all three San Diego newspapers for June 1 and 2, 1911, especially the *Union.*

11 *Revolutions in Cuba and Mexico,* 378.

12 *Ibid.*

13 *Ibid.*

14 *Ibid.*

15 *Ibid.* There was a report, dated May 27, that the rebels tried to force the captain of Spreckels' yacht to bring them ammunition.—*El País,* May 28, 1911.

16 *Revolutions in Cuba and Mexico,* 379.

17 *Ibid.*

18 *San Diego Evening Tribune,* June 2, 1911; *Los Angeles Herald,* June 3, 1911.

19 *San Diego Sun,* June 2, 1911; *San Diego Union,* June 3, 1911.

20 *San Diego Evening Tribune,* June 2, 1911; *Los Angeles Herald,* June 3, 1911.

21 *San Diego Union,* June 3, 1911.

22 *Ibid.; Los Angeles Examiner,* June 3, 1911.

23 *Revolutions in Cuba and Mexico,* 379. Some versions de-

scribe Ferris as present at his own election.—*San Diego Sun,*
June 3, 1911; *Los Angeles Herald,* June 3, 1911. However,
since Ferris himself did not claim this, it may be assumed
that he was not in Tijuana at the election. The *Los Angeles Examiner,* June 19, 1911, carried an interview with
Ferris in which his account of the election is virtually identical with the one given above.

24 *Revolutions in Cuba and Mexico,* 379.
25 *San Diego Union,* June 3, 1911.
26 *Los Angeles Examiner,* June 3, 1911.
27 *San Diego Union,* June 3, 1911.
28 *Ibid.; Industrial Worker,* July 6, 1911.
29 *San Diego Sun,* June 15, 1911.
30 *San Diego Evening Tribune,* June 2, 1911.
31 *Revolutions in Cuba and Mexico,* 379.
32 *San Diego Sun,* June 2, 3, 1911.
33 *San Diego Union,* June 4, 1911.
34 *San Diego Sun,* June 6, 1911.
35 Issues of June 4, 5, 6, 1911.
36 *San Diego Union,* June 6, 1911.
37 *Ibid.,* June 5, 6, 1911; *San Diego Sun,* June 3, 1911.
38 *Los Angeles Herald,* June 10, 1911; *Los Angeles Examiner,*
    June 14, 1911.
39 *San Diego Union,* June 4, 1911.
40 *Ibid.;* see also above, Chapter VII, p. 130.
41 *San Diego Union,* June 4, 1911.
42 *Revolutions in Cuba and Mexico,* 384.
43 *Ibid.,* 379.
44 *Los Angeles Herald,* June 4, 1911.
45 Issue of June 4, 1911.
46 *Revolutions in Cuba and Mexico,* 379.
47 *Ibid.,* 384.
48 *San Diego Evening Tribune,* June 5, 1911.
49 *Revolutions in Cuba and Mexico,* 379; *San Diego Union,*
    June 6, 1911.
50 *San Diego Union,* June 6, 1911; *San Diego Sun,* June 5,
    1911.
51 Issue of June 6, 1911.
52 *San Diego Union,* June 6, 1911.
53 *Ibid.*
54 *San Diego Sun,* June 6, 1911.
55 *Los Angeles Herald,* June 3, 1911; *San Diego Sun,* June 2,
    3, 1911; *Los Angeles Express,* June 5, 1911.

56 *Los Angeles Express,* June 5, 1911; *New York Times,* June 6, 1911; *Mexican Herald,* June 6, 1911. In an interview with the Mexican journalist and historian José Valadés, 20 years later, Ferris stated that Pryce wanted to obtain Lower California for Great Britain.—E. D. Turner, "The Revolution in Lower California," p. 65. The Monroe Doctrine most certainly precluded this, and, at the time, Pryce referred to the peninsula in connection with the United States; apparently Ferris' memory of details had slipped. In the same interview he said that Pryce wished to intimidate Spreckels into giving him a large sum of money, but from his evidence given in 1912, this would appear to have been James. Ferris' sworn testimony of 1912 must be accorded preference over his recollections of 1931.

57 Kyne, "The Gringo as Insurrecto," *Sunset Magazine,* XXVII, 267.

58 *San Francisco Chronicle,* June 17, 1911.

59 *San Diego Evening Tribune,* June 10, 1911.

60 Issue of June 5, 1911.

61 *San Diego Union,* June 3, 1911.

62 *Ibid.,* June 19, 1911.

63 Enrique Aldrete, *Baja California heroica* (Mexico City, 1958), pp. 28, 64.

64 Velasco Ceballos, *¿Se apoderará Estados Unidos de Baja California?,* pp. 172–74.

65 Published June 22, 1952.

66 *Revolutions in Cuba and Mexico,* 231–33, 383, 381, 377.

67 *Industrial Worker,* July 6, 1911.

68 *LR,* June 10, 1911.

69 E. D. Turner, "The Revolution in Lower California," pp. 52–53; Cué Cánovas, *Ricardo Flores Magón, la Baja California y los Estados Unidos,* p. 89. A well-known work by an American historian holds this same view, omitting Ferris, however: Carleton Beals, *Porfirio Díaz, Dictator of Mexico* (Philadelphia, 1932), p. 428.

70 Pablo L. Martínez, "El mito del filibusterismo de 1911 en Baja California" (mimeographed reprint of a paper given in Mexico City, September 6, 1957), pp. 6–7, 10–11; also, Cué Cánovas, *Ricardo Flores Magón, la Baja California y los Estados Unidos,* pp. 51–52.

71 Martínez, "El mito del filibusterismo," p. 11; Martínez, *Historia de Baja California,* pp. 497, 518. Almost the same assertion can be found in E. D. Turner, "The Revolution

in Lower California," p. 57.

72 *Los Angeles Herald,* March 19, 1911; *Mexican Herald,* March 19, 1911.

73 *L'Era Nuova,* June 24, 17, July 1, 1911.

74 *Revolutions in Cuba and Mexico,* 233, 382, 285, 231.

CHAPTER IX

1 Schmucker to State Dept., April 7, 10, 24, 1911 (Recs. of the For. Serv. Posts, Rec. Gp. 84, NA); Imperial Valley Co. to Schmucker, April 7, 12, 1911 (*ibid.*); Leroy Little to Schmucker, April 28, 1911 (*ibid.*).

2 Knox to U. S. Embassy in Mexico City, April 29, 1911 (Gen. Recs. of the Dept. of State, Rec. Gp. 59, NA).

3 Velasco Ceballos, *¿Se apoderará Estados Unidos de Baja California?,* pp. 168–70.

4 Schmucker's telegrams to State Dept., May 1, 2, 7, 12, 1911 (Recs. of the For. Serv. Posts, Rec. Gp. 84, NA).

5 Schmucker to State Dept., May 23, 1911 (*ibid.*).

6 Interoffice State Dept. memorandum from H. C. H. to Wilbur J. Carr, Head of the Consular Service, May 24, 1911 (*ibid.*).

7 Schmucker to State Dept., May 26, 1911 (*ibid.*).

8 Sawday to State Dept., May 26, 1911 (*ibid.*); Drs. C. H. Powers and L. Y. Ketcham to State Dept., May 26, 1911 (*ibid.*).

9 State Dept. memorandum by Carr, June 10, 1911, summarizing an account of the consul's troubles by Capt. Knowles, who was Schmucker's attendant (*ibid.*).

10 Consul General at Large George Murphy to State Dept., November 4, 1911 (*ibid.*).

11 U.S. Senator George C. Perkins (Rep., Calif.) to Knox [no month, no day], 1911 (*ibid.*).

12 *San Diego Evening Tribune,* June 3, 1911.

13 Murphy to State Dept., November 4, 1911 (Recs. of the For. Serv. Posts, Rec. Gp. 84, NA).

14 Affidavit, Henry Pinel to State Dept. [no month, no day], 1911 (*ibid.*).

15 Murphy to State Dept., November 4, 1911 (*ibid.*)

16 Vega to Secretary of War and Navy, June 13, 1911 (Archivo de la Secretaría de la Defensa Nacional).

17 Consul Frederick Simpich to State Dept., September 8, 1911 (Recs. of the For. Serv. Posts, Rec. Gp. 84, NA); *San Diego Evening Tribune,* June 27, 1911.

18 Affidavits, D. W. Church and Henry Pinel to State Dept. [no month, no day], 1911 (Recs. of the For. Serv. Posts, Rec. Gp. 84, NA).

19 Affidavits, J. F. Morgan and Andrew Tissier to State Dept. [no month, no day], 1911 (*ibid.*).

20 The second Pinel affidavit to the State Dept. [no month, no day], 1911 (*ibid.*).

21 Affidavits, Mrs. E. W. Foster and D. W. Church [no month, no day], 1911 (*ibid.*).

22 Vega's report to the Secretary of War and Navy, June 13, 1911 (Archivo de la Secretaría de la Defensa Nacional). *San Diego Union,* June 15, 1911, reported 11 Indians dead; González reported 9 dead, 2 seriously wounded. Whether they were actually armed and defending themselves is questionable in the light of what followed.

23 Affidavits, Mrs. E. W. Foster, D. W. Church, Henry Pinel to State Dept. [no month, no day], 1911 (Recs. of the For. Serv. Posts, Rec. Gp. 84, NA).

24 Affidavit, J. F. Morgan to State Dept. [no month, no day], 1911 (*ibid.*).

25 Affidavits, Mrs. E. W. Foster, Henry Pinel to State Dept. [no month, no day], 1911 (*ibid.*).

26 Affidavit, D. W. Church to State Dept. [no month, no day], 1911 (*ibid.*); *San Diego Sun,* June 23, 1911. It might be contended that possibly the Americans did not tell the truth, or exaggerated. That this did not happen, however, is indicated by the affidavits of Riviera, Moore, and even González, the latter unsigned, obtained by Consul General at Large Murphy. Their statements largely substantiate the above details.—Murphy to State Dept., November 4, 1911 (Recs. of the For. Serv. Posts, Rec. Gp. 84, NA).

27 Vega to Secretary of War and Navy, June 13, 1911 (Archivo de la Secretaría de la Defensa Nacional).

28 *Ibid.*

29 Affidavits, Henry Pinel, J. A. Johnstone to State Dept. [no month, no day], 1911 (Recs. of the For. Serv. Posts, Rec. Gp. 84, NA).

30 Abad de Santillán, *Ricardo Flores Magón,* p. 51.

31 B. H. Sprankle to State Dept., July 29, 1911, Mrs. Anna M. Foster to State Dept., June 26, August 7, 1911, and Mrs. Elizabeth W. Foster to State Dept., June 21, July 31, 1911 (Recs. of the For. Serv. Posts, Rec. Gp. 84, NA).

32   Velasco Ceballos, *¿Se apoderará Estados Unidos de Baja California?*, pp. 179–80. J. Reuben Clark, Solicitor for the State Dept., drew up an interesting memorandum, October 28, 1911, apropos a request by Mrs. Anna M. Foster for a $250,000 compensation from the Mexican government, saying that, in view of the United States' poor record in protecting the lives of foreign nationals, there was little hope for large compensations from Mexico for the El Alamo murders (Gen. Recs. of the Dept. of State, Rec. Gp. 59, NA).

33   *Foreign Relations, 1911,* 564–65.

34   *Imperial Valley Press,* May 6, 1911.

35   *Foreign Relations, 1911,* 490–91.

36   *Ibid.,* 498–99.

37   *Ibid.,* 500–503.

38   *Ibid.,* 500.

39   McCormick to Wickersham, May 20, 1911 (Gen. Recs., Dept. of Just., Rec. Gp. 74, NA).

40   Wickersham to Knox, May 27, 1911 (*ibid.*).

41   Special Agent W. H. Llewellyn to Wickersham, June 3, 1911 (*ibid.*).

42   *San Diego Union,* June 10, 1911.

43   *Los Angeles Examiner,* June 15, 16, 21, 1911; *San Francisco Chronicle,* June 17, 1911; *Los Angeles Herald,* June 20, October 28, 1911; *LR,* July 15, 1911.

44   *San Francisco Chronicle,* June 17, 1911; *Los Angeles Express,* June 20, 1911.

45   *San Diego Union,* June 16, 17, 1911; *San Diego Evening Tribune,* June 15, 1911.

46   *San Diego Union,* June 16, 1911.

47   *Ibid.*

48   *LR,* July 1, 1911.

49   *Los Angeles Herald,* June 20, 1911.

50   *San Diego Sun,* June 15, 1911.

51   *LR,* June 10, 1911.

52   *Los Angeles Times,* May 25, June 15, 1911; *New York Times,* June 15, 16, 1911.

53   *New York Call,* June 8, 1911; *LR,* July 22, August 12, 1911; *New York Times,* June 20, 1911.

54   *LR,* June 10, 1911; *Los Angeles Examiner,* May 28, June 6, 1911.

55   *Calexico Chronicle,* May 2, 1911.

56   *Ibid.,* May 15, 1911.

57   *Ibid.,* May 15, 17, 31, June 2, 1911.

58 *Ibid.,* May 16, 1911.
59 Issue of May 20, 1911.
60 *Los Angeles Times,* May 20, 21, 1911; *Los Angeles Herald,* May 21, 22, 1911.
61 *Los Angeles Examiner,* May 28, 1911; *Los Angeles Times,* May 28, 1911; *San Diego Union,* June 10, 1911; *Brawley News,* June 9, 1911.
62 *San Diego Sun,* June 8, 1911.
63 Chandler to Otis, May 30, June 1, 1911 (Gen. Recs. of the Dept. of State, Rec. Gp. 59, NA).
64 Taft to Knox, May 31, 1911 (*ibid.*).
65 *Los Angeles Examiner,* May 28, 1911; *Los Angeles Herald,* May 29, 1911; *San Diego Union,* June 10, 1911.
66 Stanley R. Ross, *Francisco I. Madero: Apostle of Mexican Democracy* (New York, 1955), p. 184. As Madero announced repeatedly that he would send troops—*San Diego Union,* May 23, 1911; *Los Angeles Times,* June 3, 1911; *Los Angeles Examiner,* June 6, 8, 1911—but long held back from doing so, it may be that he hoped to bluff the Magonistas into surrendering.
67 E. D. Turner, "The Revolution in Lower California," p. 49.
68 *Foreign Relations, 1911,* 499, 503.
69 The radical press argued that the United States violated her position of neutrality between combatants in granting permission.—*New York Call,* June 9, 1911; *LR,* July 1, 1911.
70 They occupied Mexicali on June 26, 1911.—Martínez, *Historia de Baja California,* p. 502.
71 *Ibid.,* pp. 500–501; Velasco Ceballos, *¿Se apoderará Estados Unidos de Baja California?,* pp. 182–84; *Los Angeles Times,* June 18, 19, 1911; *Los Angeles Examiner,* June 18, 1911. Figures as to the number who gave up vary between 30 and 60, with 60 cited most frequently.
72 *San Diego Union,* June 8, 11, 1911.
73 *Ibid.,* June 10, 15, 1911.
74 *San Diego Sun,* June 14, 1911.
75 *San Diego Union,* June 13, 1911.
76 *Ibid.,* June 9, 1911; *San Diego Sun,* June 8, 9, 1911.
77 *San Diego Union,* June 11, 12, 21, 1911.
78 *Ibid.,* June 14, 1911. The full text of the message was enclosed in a letter of Harry L. Titus, secretary of the Spreckels companies, to Gen. Bliss, June 17, 1911 (Recs. of the U.S.A. Commands, Dept. of Calif. & Tex., Rec. Gp. 98, NA).

79   *San Diego Union,* June 14, 1911.

80   *San Diego Sun,* June 14, 1911.

81   Spreckels to Perkins, June 15, 1911 (Recs. of the U.S.A. Commands, Dept. of Calif. & Tex., Rec. Gp. 98, NA).

82   Bliss to War Dept., June 16, 1911 (*ibid.*).

83   Capt. F. A. Wilcox to Bliss, June 15, 1911 (*ibid.*).

84   Titus to Bliss, June 17, 1911 (*ibid.*).

85   Bliss to Titus, June 19, 1911 (*ibid.*).

86   *San Diego Union,* June 18, 20, 1911.

87   *Ibid.,* June 19–21, 1911; *San Diego Sun,* June 19–21, 1911; *Industrial Worker,* July 6, 1911; José María Leyva, *Aportaciones a la historia de la revolución* (Mexico City, 1938), pp. 25–28.

88   Vega to Secretary of War and Navy, May 20, 1911 (Archivo de la Secretaría de la Defensa Nacional).

89   *San Diego Sun,* June 23, 1911; Velasco Ceballos, *¿Se apoderará Estados Unidos de Baja California?,* pp. 177, 184.

90   Wilcox to Bliss, June 23, 1911 (Recs. of the U.S.A. Commands, Dept. of Calif. & Tex., Rec. Gp. 98, NA).

91   *San Diego Sun,* June 22, 1911; *San Diego Union,* June 23, 1911. Estimates on the rebels' numbers varied. The *Los Angeles Herald,* June 23, 1911, estimated 155 foreigners, 75 Mexicans; the *San Diego Union,* June 22, 1911, listed 206 foreigners, 65 Mexicans.

92   *Los Angeles Times,* June 23, 1911; *San Diego Union,* June 24, 25, 26, 1911; *San Diego Sun,* June 23, 24, 26, 27, 1911.

93   *San Diego Union,* June 24, 1911; *San Diego Sun,* June 23, 1911.

94   *LR,* July 1, June 10, 1911.

95   *Ibid.,* July 8, 1911; Abad de Santillán, *Ricardo Flores Magón,* p. 84.

96   R. F. M. to Tirzo de la Toba, June 26, 1911, in *Investigation of Mexican Affairs,* II, 2516–17; *New York Call,* June 11, 1911.

97   *LR,* June 10, 16, 24, July 1, 29, 1911.

98   *New York Call,* August 2, 1911, slightly paraphrased from a poor translation.

99   *Social Democratic Herald* (Milwaukee, Wis.), June 24, 1911.

100 Issue of June 17, 1911.

101 Eugene Debs, "The Crisis in Mexico," *International Socialist Review,* XII (July, 1911), 22–24. On the point of economic backwardness, and the impracticability of a proletarian revolution in such an environment, there is agree-

ment by the Italo-American Wobblies. See *Il Proletario,* June 23, 1911.

102 Issue of July 8, 1911.

103 *L'Era Nuova,* July 15, 1911.

104 *Industrial Worker,* August 10, 1911. For a further hint of suspicions concerning financial matters, see the Hopkins to Dunn letter, Chapter VIII, pp. 144–45.

105 *LR,* December 2, 1911.

106 *Industrial Worker,* January 8, 1912, by-line: "Covington Hall." The capitals in the text were double size, and the italics were supplied in the original.

107 Abad de Santillán, *Ricardo Flores Magón,* p. 75; *LR,* October 7, 1911.

108 Abad de Santillán, *Ricardo Flores Magón,* pp. 87, 90–94.

109 *LR,* July 1, June 24, September 30, July 22, July 1, 1911.

CHAPTER X

1 Stimson, *Rise of the Labor Movement,* pp. 400–407; Ira B. Cross, *A History of the Labor Movement in California* (Berkeley, 1935), p. 287.

2 Hyman Weintraub, "The I.W.W. in California, 1905–1931," pp. 37–38; Emma Goldman, *Living My Life* (Garden City, New York, 1931), pp. 494–500.

3 Los Angeles press, September 13–29, 1911; Bryce to Knox, July 31, August 26, 1911 (Gen. Recs., Dept. of Just., Rec. Gp. 74, NA); Hattie Biggs to Taft, July 28, 1911 (*ibid.*); State Dept. to Hattie Biggs, August 23, 1911 (*ibid.*).

4 *Los Angeles Herald,* October 28, 1911.

5 Edmund L. Smith, Clerk, U.S. Distr. Court for the So. Distr. of Calif., to the author, April 24, 1952. A thorough search in the Justice Department records in the National Archives and in public repositories in California has not uncovered a transcript. However, there are indications it may exist in private hands.

6 Frank Roney to Congressman John P. Nolan (Dem., Calif.), June [no day], 1913, with attached affidavits (Wilson Papers, Library of Congress); E. D. Turner, "The Revolution in Lower California," pp. 76, 81–85.

7 James A. Finch, Pardon Atty., U.S. Dept. of Justice, to U.S. Atty. Gen. James C. McReynolds, June 30, 1913 (Wilson Papers).

8 *Ibid.,* E. D. Turner, "The Revolution in Lower California," pp. 84–88.

9 Affidavits attached to the letter of Frank Roney to Congressman Nolan, June [no day], 1913 (Wilson Papers); E. D. Turner, "The Revolution in Lower California," p. 86.

10 *Investigation of Mexican Affairs,* II, 2518; *Los Angeles Examiner,* June 6, 1912; *Los Angeles Express,* June 6, 1912.

11 *Los Angeles Examiner,* June 26, 1912; *Los Angeles Express,* June 25, 1912.

12 Wilson to Nolan, July 22, 1913 (Wilson Papers).

13 Enrique Aldrete, *Baja California heroica* (Mexico City, 1958), *passim.* On the southeastern outskirts of Tijuana there now stands a monument commemorating the defeat of the filibusters of 1911.

14 Madero terminated his relations with the Liberals in 1906. —Stanley R. Ross, *Francisco I. Madero, Apostle of Mexican Democracy* (New York, 1955), p. 43. Pío Araujo broke with them finally in 1914.—Abad de Santillán, *Ricardo Flores Magón,* p. 71. The others did so in 1911.

15 *LR,* February 25, June 24, July 8, August 5, September 2, 1911.

16 R. F. M. to Tirzo de la Toba, June 26, 1911, in *Investigation of Mexican Affairs,* II, 2516–17.

17 *LR,* June 10, July 1, 1911.

18 *Ibid.,* August 5, 19, 26, September 2, 16, October 7, 1911.

19 José María Leyva, *Aportaciones a la historia de la revolución, passim.*

20 Manuel Bonilla, Jr., *El régimen maderista* (Mexico City, 1922), p. 65.

21 Schmucker to U.S. Senator Duncan U. Fletcher (Dem., Fla.), January 24, 1917, and Secretary of State Robert Lansing to Fletcher, February 8, 1917 (Recs. of the For. Serv. Posts, Rec. Gp. 84, NA).

22 E. D. Turner, "The Revolution in Lower California," p. 83; Medina Amor, *No fué filibusterismo,* p. 44.

23 *San Diego Union,* May 21, June 26, 1911; *San Diego Sun,* June 30, 1911.

24 A. I. McCormick, U.S. Distr. Atty. for the So. Distr. of Calif., to Wickersham, April 4, 1912 (Gen. Recs., Dept. of Just., Rec. Gp. 74, NA).

25 *San Diego Union,* December 9, 1913; *Los Angeles Herald,* June 19, 1911.

26 *San Diego Union,* December 9, 1913, August 24, 1927; *Los Angeles Times,* March 6, 1926, August 23, 1927, December 5, 1930, March 13, 1933.

27 *Los Angeles Herald,* June 3, 1912.
28 Edmund L. Smith, clerk, U.S. Distr. Court for the So. Distr. of Calif., to the author, March 13, 1952.
29 Glenys Hembry, American Liaison Officer, Central Office of Information, H.M. War Department, London, to the author, January 15, 1953.
30 *R. F. M., vida y obra,* VI, 74.
31 Abad de Santillán, *Ricardo Flores Magón,* p. 102; *Congressional Record,* 67 Cong., 4 sess., LXIV (December 19, 1922), 682.
32 *Congressional Record,* 67 Cong., 4 sess., LXIV (December 19, 1922), 690–91; Abad de Santillán, *Ricardo Flores Magón,* pp. 109–12.
33 *Congressional Record,* 67 Cong., 4 sess., LXIV (December 19, 1922), 682–87.
34 *Ibid.* (December 11, 1922), 298.
35 *Ibid.* (December 14, 1922), 486–88. A debate in the House of Representatives, following R. F. M.'s death, between Representatives George Huddlestone (Dem., Ala.), and Walter F. Lineberger (Rep., Calif.), well summarized the differing points of view.—*Ibid.* (December 11, 14, 19, 1922), 298–300, 485–90, 682–97.
36 R. F. M., respectively, to Gus Treltsch and T. Brothers, April 4, 1922; Helen White, June 28, 1921; and Nicolás Bernal, December 6, 1920, in *R. F. M., vida y obra,* VI, 16, 23–24.
37 *Ibid.,* II, 30.
38 Rafael Carillo, *Ricardo Flores Magón* (Mexico City, 1945), p. 47.
39 *R. F. M., vida y obra,* II, 23–24.
40 Abad de Santillán, *Ricardo Flores Magón,* p. 128.
41 *R. F. M., vida y obra,* III, 83.
42 Ralph Chaplin, *Wobbly* (Chicago, 1948), p. 310.
43 Abad de Santillán, *Ricardo Flores Magón,* p. 128.
44 Carillo, *Ricardo Flores Magón,* p. 53.
45 *Ibid.*
46 Teodoro Hernández, *La historia de la revolución debe hacerse* (Mexico City, 1950), pp. 123–24.

ESSAY ON SOURCES

It is not the purpose of this essay to present an exhaustive evaluation of all sources used in the preparation of this work. Rather, this is an attempt to assess the significance of those sources that were most specifically concerned with the Flores Magón episode in Baja California. Several important works dealing with the period or the Mexican nation in a more general fashion will not be discussed here; they are mentioned in the notes in the appropriate places.

Archival Materials and Manuscripts

From the time of his arrival in the United States, Flores Magón was under the surveillance of the American authorities. In consequence, the National Archives house a quantity of material concerning him and the Liberal Party. Signally significant among these are the General Records of the Department of Justice, Record Group 74, especially for the year 1911, but also for long before and after that date. This material includes correspondence between the Attorney General's office and the United States District Attorneys, and, quite frequently, the reports of the agents of the Bureau of Investigation. The State Department deposits are nearly as valuable as those of the Department of Justice. The General Records of the Department of State, Record Group 59, present the diplomatic correspondence relating to the Flores Magón movement in Mexico, including Lower California, while the Records of the Foreign Service Posts, Record Group 84, contain the messages to and from Consul George B. Schmucker and his successors in Ensenada. As the United States Army maintained a very close observation of the military, and, to some extent, the political, events across the border in Lower California, the Records of the United States Army Commands, Department of California and Texas, Record Group 98, were of importance. This is especially true of those reports written by the observant Brigadier General Tasker H. Bliss. The future chief of staff's sound judgment lends importance also to the material found in his private papers, in the Library of Congress. The Woodrow Wilson Papers, likewise in the Library of Congress, are of lesser importance to the matter at hand.

As for the Mexican Archives, the reports sent by the Díaz government officials stationed in Baja California to the Ministry of War and Navy tend to confirm, and infrequently to add new details to, the information available in the National Archives of the United States. At the time the writer visited Mexico City, the materials in Foreign Relations were not available for scholarly examination.

Printed Government Documents

Three United States government documents stand out. The Department of State, *Foreign Relations of the United States, 1911* (Washington: Government Printing Office, 1918) gives the diplomatic correspondence relating to the construction of dikes in the Imperial Valley and estimates the over-all political import of Magonism, as well as its manifestations along the California border. Moreover, it yields information, complementary to that found in the Justice Department's archival deposits, relating to the intricacies of the neutrality laws. As events in Mexico aroused strong feelings in the United States for a decade, two investigations were made under the sponsorship of the United States Senate Committee on Foreign Relations. In 1919–20, that committee released a two-volume compendium of hearings, *Investigation of Mexican Affairs,* Senate Executive Document No. 285, 66 Congress, 2 session (2 vols., Washington: Government Printing Office, 1919–20), concerning events in Mexico for the past decade. Some of the material in Volume II concerns the happenings of 1911. Part of this, in turn, is actually reprinted from an earlier report, *Revolutions in Cuba and Mexico,* Report of a Subcommittee of the Senate Committee on Foreign Relations, 62 Congress, 2 session (Washington: Government Printing Office, 1913). Unlike *Investigation of Mexican Affairs, Revolutions in Cuba and Mexico* is not easy to obtain. The latter has an abundance of material not to be found elsewhere, such as the direct testimony of Dick Ferris. Of some use regarding the periods prior to and subsequent to 1911 are two more Congressional documents. *Alleged Persecutions of Mexican Citizens by the Government of*

Mexico, 61 Congress, 2 session, Report of a Special Committee set up under H.J. Res. 201 (Washington: Government Printing Office, 1910) has the information gleaned by United States Representatives concerning the Liberals' difficulties in the United States between 1904 and 1910, and the *Congressional Record,* Volume LXIV, 67 Congress, 4 session, covers a debate on the floor of the House of Representatives, in December, 1922, that sheds some light on the last few years spent by Flores Magón in American prisons.

Newspapers and Periodicals, Radical and Conventional

As the Liberal movement was steeped in controversy, the examination of news materials, whatever their orientation, had to be undertaken with great care. Not only did such perusal provide great help in gathering the usual odds and ends not otherwise available, but it also permitted, in this case, the cautious drawing of conclusions in the many instances in which there existed conflicting versions of debatable events, the estimation of the accuracy of the coverage of a radical movement in the mass-circulation press, and, similarly, the worth, or lack of it, of the reportage in the radical press. These sources were essential in providing data concerning the financial support furnished the Magonistas by radical groups in the United States.

It goes without saying that Flores Magón's *La Regeneración* (Los Angeles) for 1911, and certain numbers for 1910 and 1912, was indispensable. The weekly conveys the flavor of the Junta's anarchism and contains much factual information, many editorials illustrating the leader's basic tenets, hints as to various plans, and the natural history of various disputes. As for other radical journals, the anarchist or anarcho-syndicalist ones included the *Industrial Worker* (Spokane, Wash.), the *Agitator* (Lakebay, Wash.), *Solidarity* (Newcastle, Pa.), Emma Goldman's *Mother Earth* (New York), and the Italian-language weeklies, *Il Proletario* (New York) and *L'Era Nuova* (Paterson, N.J.). Of these, the *Industrial Worker,* whose following participated extensively in events, was the most vociferous, and *L'Era Nuova* the most informative. The Socialist publications, the *Appeal to Reason* (Girard, Kan.), the *New York Call,* the *People's Paper* of Los Angeles, the *Chicago Daily Socialist,* and the *International Socialist Review* (Chicago), among others, made numerous, and frequently useful, comments. Of the radical papers that were neither anarchist nor socialist, the Single Tax weekly, the *Public* of Chicago, occasionally printed items friendly to the Liberals. Almost alone in complete opposition to the Magonista movement was the *Weekly People* (Detroit), edited by Daniel DeLeon, who repudiated anti-statist radicalism.

The West Coast mass-circulation newspapers were of great help. The Imperial Valley had one daily, the *Calexico Chronicle,* and two weeklies, the *Brawley News* and the *Imperial Valley Press.* In San Diego, there were the potent Spreckels-owned *San Diego Union,* and its sister, the *San Diego Evening Tribune,* as well as E. W. Scripps's *San Diego Sun.* Los Angeles had five dailies. First in influence ranked the *Los Angeles Times* and Harrison Gray Otis. The general also controlled, but did not consistently dominate, the *Los Angeles Herald,* an evening daily given to sensationalizing. Next was the Hearst-owned *Los Angeles Examiner,* which, like its brethren across the country, usually dwelt on the melodramatic side of the news. The most factual and accurate paper in the city was the moderately liberal evening *Los Angeles Express.* Finally, there was the small-circulation, semiradical, semisensationalist *Record,* copies of which for the year of 1911 are hard to find. Among the above newspapers, the *San Diego Sun* and the *Los Angeles Express* were at times favorably disposed toward the Liberals. In addition, because the Imperial Valley correspondent of the *Los Angeles Examiner* was Otis B. Tout, the editor of the *Calexico Chronicle,* who often favored the Liberals, this Hearst paper sometimes had friendly accounts. The papers controlled by Otis and Spreckels were, as could be expected, consistently unfriendly to the Magonistas. This was particularly true of the *Los Angeles Times,* which the *Imperial Valley Press,* in its February 18, 1911, issue, accused of being the worst "offender against truth and decency" in its border reports. The *New York Times* provided ample coverage of the California situation.

The Mexico City newspapers, *El Heraldo Mexicano,* the *Mexican Herald, El Imparcial, El Diario,* and *El País,* which were controlled at least indirectly by the Díaz government, were chiefly useful in reflecting the old regime's reaction to the manifestation of extreme radicalism on the northwestern frontier. Their straight news stories came largely from the Associated Press.

Books, Pamphlets, Theses

Among the books published in Mexico on the Magonista phase of the Revolution of 1911, by far the most important are Pablo L. Martínez, *Historia de Baja California* (Mexico City: Libros Mexicanos, 1956), which is now available in a 1960 English translation by Mrs. Ethel Duffy Turner, and Rómulo Velasco Ceballos, *¿Se apoderará Estados Unidos de América de Baja California?* (Mexico City: Imprenta nacional S.A., 1920). The first is a solid study of the whole span of peninsular history, and for the 1911 period provides a quite detailed account, very friendly to the Magonistas, though with several inaccuracies, a few of them significant. The second is violently and distortedly anti-Magonist, but has some essential documents. In addition there are a number of comparatively rare, and sometimes very useful, Mexican sources that Dr. Francisco Dueñas Montes of Mexicali made available to the writer. Among these are the reminiscences of John Kenneth Turner's widow, Ethel Duffy Turner, "The Revolution in Lower California," a typescript written in 1956; José María Leyva, *Aportaciones a la historia de la revolución* (Mexico City: privately printed, 1938); *El Magonismo en Baja California (documentos)*, edited by Pablo L. Martínez (Mexico City: Editorial "Baja California," 1958); and Martínez' "El mito del filibusterismo de 1911 en Baja California," a paper read in Mexico City, September 6, 1957; Guillermo Medina Amor, *No fué filibusterismo la revolución magonista en la Baja California* (Mexicali: Ediciones "Amor," 1946); and Jenaro Amézcua, *¿Quién es Flores Magón y cuál su obra?* (Mexico City: Editorial Avance, 1943). More readily available and also very important are Florencio Barrera Fuentes, *Historia de la revolución mexicana: la etapa precursora* (Mexico City: Biblioteca del Instituto Nacional de Estudios Históricos de la Revolución Mexicana, 1955), the best work on the Liberals and Flores Magón before 1911; and Agustín Cué Cánovas, *Ricardo Flores Magón, la Baja California y los Estados Unidos* (Mexico City: Libro Mex Editores, 1957).

Mrs. Turner's recollections, greatly expanded, are now available as a near-biography, *Ricardo Flores Magón y el Partido Liberal Mexicano* (Morelia, Michoacán: Editorial "Erandi," 1960). Next best is the Anarchist Diego Abad de Santillán's older biography, *Ricardo Flores Magón, el apóstol de la revolución social mexicana* (Mexico City: Grupo Cultural "Ricardo Flores Magón," 1925). The nine-volume paperback edited and published by the Grupo Cultural "Richaro Flores Magón," *Ricardo Flores Magón, vida y obra* (Mexico City, 1923), consists largely of Flores Magón's letters and editorials. All of these books leave much about 1911 unexplained.

Three among many secondary works were of especial value. These were Paul F. Brissenden, *The I.W.W.: A Study in American Syndicalism* (New York: Columbia University Press, 1919);

Grace H. Stimson, *Rise of the Labor Movement in Los Angeles* (Berkeley: University of California Press, 1955); and Hyman Weintraub, "The I.W.W. in California, 1905–1931" (unpublished Master's thesis, University of California at Los Angeles, 1947).

Articles

Several articles had more than average worth. These were Eugene K. Chamberlin, "Mexican Colonization versus American Interests in Lower California," *Pacific Historical Review*, XX (February, 1951), 43–55; Roy E. Curtis, "The Law of Hostile Military Expeditions as Applied by the United States," *American Journal of International Law*, VIII (January, April, 1914), 1–38, 224–56, the best study of the American neutrality law covering the period up to 1914; Peter Gerhard, "The Socialist Invasion of Baja California, 1911," *Pacific Historical Review*, XV (September, 1946), 295–304, which is unfriendly to the Magonistas; José María Leyva, "El llamado filibusterismo de la Baja California," *Revista de Revistas* (February 9, 1936); and John Kenneth Turner, "The Mexican Revolution," *Pacific Monthly*, XXV (June, 1911), 609–25. The last two were written by individuals closely involved in Magonista matters.

Interviews

Personal interviews were helpful chiefly in providing background and atmosphere. The writer's frequent visits and exchange of correspondence with Dr. Francisco Dueñas Montes over the last decade aided immeasurably. Other valuable conversations were held with Enrique Flores Magón's two sons and his daughter in Mexico City, 1955; General José María Leyva, also in the capital city and during the same summer; and the late Carlos Mendoza, a member of the "Defenders of National Integrity" Committee, in Agua Caliente, B.C., in 1951. There were talks also with Willedd Andrews, defense attorney for Flores Magón in 1912, in Los Angeles, 1952; Dudley Robinson, the prosecuting attorney in the same trial, Los Angeles, 1954; Carlos Pfeiffer, a spectator of the 1911 events along Baja California's West Coast, in Ensenada, 1951; David Zárate, a citizen of Ensenada prominent in 1911, in Ensenada, 1951; and Enrique Aldrete, once Colonel Vega's private secretary, in Tijuana, 1951.

INDEX

255